GAY SPIRIT

GAY

SPIRIT:

MYTH

AND

MEANING

MARK

THOMPSON

ST. MARTIN'S PRESS
NEW YORK

Portions of the following articles by the editor have appeared in *The Advocate* and are used here by kind permission of Liberation Publications, Inc.: "Double Reflections: Isherwood and Bachardy on Art, Love and Faith"; "Children of Paradise: A Brief History of Queens"; "Harry Hay: A Voice From the Past, A Vision For the Future"; "In the Shadow of the Red Rock: The Radical Fairies Convene"; "The Evolution of a Fairie: Notes Toward a New Definition of Gay"; "In the Service of Ecstasy: An Interview with James Broughton." In addition, grateful acknowledgement is made to the following for permission to reprint previously copyrighted material: James Broughton for "Hermes—Bringer of Heats," excerpted from *Ecstasies*, copyright © 1983 Syzygy Press and James Broughton; Farrar, Straus & Giroux, Inc., for excerpts from *My Guru and His Disciple* by Christopher Isherwood, copyright © 1980 by Christopher Isherwood, and *Christopher and His Kind* by Christopher Isherwood, copyright © 1976 by Christopher Isherwood; Michael Bronski and South End Press for excerpts from *Culture Clash*, copyright © 1984 by Michael Bronski; the *New York Native* 69 (August 1–14, 1983) for "We, the Fairy Headhunters," copyright © 1987 by Tobias Schneebaum; Geoff Mains and Gay Sunshine Press for excerpts from *Urban Aboriginals: A Celebration of Leathersexuality*, copyright © 1986 by Geoff Mains; *Frontiers* (June 1983) for "A Separate People Whose Time Has Come," copyright © 1987 by Harry Hay; Mitch Walker and Treeroots Press for excerpts from *Visionary Love*, copyright © 1980 by Mitch Walker; *ONE* magazine 2, no. 6, for "What Is Religion?" by D. B. Vest, copyright © 1954 by *ONE*, Inc., and *ONE* 3, no. 3 for "A Future for the Isophyl" by

Permissions continued on page 311

Design by John Fontana

Library of Congress Cataloging in Publication Data

Thompson, Mark, 1952-
    Gay Spirit

    1. Homosexuals.   2. Homosexuality.   I. Title.
HQ76.25.T49   1987   306.7'66   87-4452
ISBN 0-312-00600-4

First Edition

10 9 8 7 6 5 4 3 2 1

to Patricia Schupbach,
spirit giver,
and to James Broughton,
mentor and friend

CONTENTS

PART III

A World of Our Making: Myth and Meaning

A selection of photographs follows pages 117 and 254.

ACKNOWLEDGMENTS

Inspiration for this book has come from the numerous gay artists, poets, writers and photographers whom I have been privileged to know during the course of my decade-long tenure as journalist and cultural editor for *The Advocate*, the national gay news magazine. It is their illuminating work that has defined and given substance to gay culture. I wish to particularly thank my editor-in-chief, Robert I. McQueen, whose friendship and generous support has enabled me to explore avenues of personal expression not otherwise available during these years.

In addition, the insight and information provided by the following individuals has been of assistance in compiling this book: Adrian Brooks, for an angel's memory; Brent Harris and Richard Hall, for literary encouragement; Peter Hartman, for astute cultural analysis; Harry Hay, Jim Kepner and Harold Norse, for historical notes; Frank Logandice, for insight into matters of gender; Olaf Odegaard, for notes on *RFD;* Cathy Toldi, for sharing the inner journey; and, of course, all the contributors to this volume.

I am especially appreciative of the encouragement and blessings of family and friends. I am indebted to M. R. Ritley, who prepared the manuscript on an electronic composing system—the book would not have been possible without her efforts—and to Loren MacGregor, who typed some of the chapters.

Finally, I want to acknowledge the innovative work and guidance of Mitch Walker, as well as the extraordinary contributions to gay culture made by Don Kilhefner over the years—he, more than any one individual, has made this book possible. Every idea has a genesis, however, and in this case a seed was planted by Malcolm Boyd. His nurturance and generosity of spirit are a testament of faith, and of the heart.

PREFACE

In a book with far-ranging ideas, such as this, it is important to define certain terms and purpose. To begin, the word *gay* should not be confused with *homosexual,* as by definition they mean quite different things. *Gay* implies a social identity and consciousness actively chosen, while *homosexual* refers to a specific form of sexuality. A person may be homosexual, but that does not necessarily imply that he or she would be gay.

This book is primarily intended for gay men. Lesbians and feminist women have already created a considerable body of work examining spiritual issues. Gay men have only recently begun to explore issues of spirit and faith to any degree, an interest no doubt stimulated by the serious matters of life and death posed by the health crisis now besieging our community. But it is hoped that men and women of all sexual persuasions will find enlightening material contained here.

Another reason for compiling this book was to see where a certain strain of gay male expression and thought was currently at; to document it and, ideally, to preserve it for future use. There has been relatively little writing about gay men, spirit and religion in a mainstream, traditional sense (John Boswell's *Christianity, Social Tolerance, and Homosexuality* notwithstanding), and even less from a non-Western and visionary perspective. This book is very much about the other side of the picture usually presented in gay studies, one that is often highly political and reflects an East Coast bias. Much of the writing collected here has come from the gay experience as lived on the West Coast. In terms of gay life, this anthology of articles concentrates on the spirit of the thing, rather than its outer manifestations.

INTRODUCTION

In a time of so much dying, the creation of a consciousness born out of love is a miraculous act. We stand at the edge of time and watch old technologies wither, familiar gods laid to rest, indigenous lifeforms eradicated from the earth, the annihilation of the planet itself be made a possibility, and a horrible blight extinguish those in our midst. The compliant face of death points in all directions in this, our age: to the outer world of substance and form, to the inner world of myth and meaning. Chaos, terror and uncertainty seem the only true human inheritance in this, our age.

In a world so used up, where even hope has been betrayed as a disposable commodity, there stands a vision of the future as magnificent and shimmering as the silver sword plunged into stone. The sword is known by many names. For some people its name is *gay*, and it has released them from a long buried past. Sustained by a sexuality as old as humankind but mired in the depths of Western consciousness, which has tried either to colonize or to destroy them (as it has so many others), these gay people finally stand at the edge of our time, resilient and resourceful, tending to the new life necessary for the future.

This is parable, of course, but told in the manner best known to such storytelling: out of a compelling need. It is for this same reason that this book exists.

Gay spirit, the psychic and creative energies generated by people we now call *gay,* has always existed on the outer shores of our culture's collective consciousness. Paradoxically, it has also been at the very center of its fascination and capacity for cruel repression. The dual status of this spirit force has been used by Western culture, perhaps unknowingly, to its advantage; as if a body, struggling in continuous inner conflict, has managed to propel itself forward on some quirky course. But the body, unable to exorcise its own being, has come undone, releasing this suppressed spirit. That spirit lives among us now, inquisitive and newborn. This book is a collection of stories, ideas and myths about the possibilities of that spirit—suggesting ways in which gay people might find a place and purpose in human culture that is unique to themselves.

This is a relatively new idea. In the distant past, gay people were labeled heretics, demons and perversions of nature, thus providing justification for the genocidal campaigns unleashed against them. In more recent times, gay people have been categorized pseudoscientifically, placed in the false and arbitrary ghetto of homosexuality, forced into a social role that has no social purpose, similar to the way native peoples around the world have been contained and rendered impotent. Gay people have had to live on the edge of the global village or to work within its mainstream in denial or disguise. As a result, emotional wounds run deep and are long remembered. It is here, at this wounded place, that our lives find shared ground, our spirits a common tongue. This myth about our sexuality had been devised by those who could not possibly understand us yet who knew enough to benefit from our oppression.

The quest for authentic inner experience, the awakening to other forms of reality, are experiences common to shamans all over the world, throughout recorded history.* A shaman will seek out that inner wounded place, ritually enter it, descend to the underworld of instinct and emotion, undergo great tests of faith, and then ascend aboveworld to a new consciousness, bearing insight and wisdom for use in the mid-

---

*Shaman is being used here primarily to suggest an archetypal image or concept of transformation, rather than to describe a person or mystical practice specific to a particular time or place. As Mircea Eliade explains in his classic study, *Shamanism: Archaic Techniques of Ecstasy* (New Jersey: Princeton University Press, 1964), "Shamanism in the strict sense is preeminently a religious phenomenon of Siberia and Central Asia." However, as he further states, shamanistic techniques and practices can be found in most "primitive" cultures around the world. And while shamanism can generally coexist with other forms of magic or religion, it is best defined specifically as the *technique of ecstasy*. According to Eliade, shamanic initiation usually comes from profound experience of "sickness, dreams and ecstasies," turning certain individuals within a given society into "technicians of the sacred"—an initiatory process involving suffering, death and resurrection; a symbolic ascent to the sky or descent to the underworld. Shamans assume a specialized role—usually as guides or agents of transformation—within the soul-life of their community. (The shamanic role, it should be noted, is different from the role played by the berdache, which is one primarily of *mediation*. Both roles are discussed in this book in terms of the potential social/spiritual capacities they suggest for gay people today.) Shamans, explains Eliade, are "separated from the rest of the community by the intensity of their own religious experience. . . . We frequently find the shamanic (that is, ecstatic) experience attempting to express itself through an ideology that is not always favorable to it. . . . The shaman begins his new, his true life by a 'separation'—by a spiritual crisis that is not lacking in tragic greatness and in beauty."

dleworld of our daily reality. This symbolic cycle of death and rebirth is intuitively understood by any gay person who has gone through the "coming-out" process—claiming and creating an identity from the shadow realms of a false self—and it can be applied on a planetary scale as gay people come out in numbers not previously imagined. What gifts might they bring from a consciousness now appraised and named? And why and how has this happened? There is a relatively untapped potential to the gay experience, one rich in promise for humanity in its wholeness—in fact, necessary for the very preservation of that wholeness—as humankind struggles for acceptance of itself.

To mythologize an act is to give it meaning, and the following writers give new meaning to the coming-out experience. Together they create a new myth about its mysteries.

The path of the shaman, the inner journey of death and rebirth, is a particularly useful idea to evoke at this time. For many gay men death is not a metaphor but a painful reality, as a generation succumbs to the effects of a deadly virus. How to make sense from such horror? How to suggest that in the center of such destruction lies the seed for future awakening? The media assaults us with images of the dying, we ache from the personal awareness of death in our midst, collectively we take that trip to the underworld. Most of us will return and live with a *knowing* unique to our culture. And it is for this reason, too, that this book exists.

In creating new myths for themselves, gay people need to return to the questions asked by the founding members of the Mattachine Society nearly forty years ago: Who are we? Where have we come from? What are we here for? The self-definition sought by members of America's first gay political organization is also to be found in the writings of such gay visionaries as Walt Whitman, Edward Carpenter, Gerald Heard and others who are included here. In an attempt to answer these questions, gay studies today have been polarized, stymied by the absolutes implied in the nature versus nurture discourse currently employed. To simplify: An *essentialist* view holds that gay people have existed throughout recorded human history, an errant offspring of nature; a *constructivist* view says that our notion of gay people has been formulated by the values of contemporary society and that it would be impossible to draw an analogy between homosexuality as practiced in ancient Greece and, for an example, as it is defined today in America's extensive gay subculture. Both concepts are largely irreconcilable; one trying to link feelings and behavior across vast stretches of time and variant cultures, the other destructuring modern perceptions of homosexuality as medical and psychological conceits.

The quest for a gay identity cannot be contained within a dialogue of opposites, a rational either/or approach. Perhaps answers lie somewhere in between, waiting to be forged from a synthesis of biological and social factors—that is, a situation of *both/and*. Yet, an essential problem remains.

Both ideas sit at opposite ends of a spectrum that still uses sexuality as its determining gauge. Should gay people be defined by an act of desire or by a way of being? Perhaps we could be considered in terms of certain cultural roles we enact, by the work we seem to do best. I would define gay people as possessing a *luminous* quality of being, a differentness that accentuates the gifts of compassion, empathy, healing, interpretation and enabling. I see gay people as the *in-between ones*; those who can entertain irreconcilable differences, who are capable of uniting opposing forces as one; bridge builders who intuit the light and dark in all things. These people who seem to spring from between the cracks, these androgynous alchemists, have a certain and necessary function for life on this planet. For me, gay people represent the archetype of innocence, a shaman's tool that allows access to a more primal world, one where his/her work is done.

By *innocence*, I mean a wide-eyed sense of wonder about the world and its possibilities. Gay-centered eros, which illuminates life with its own peculiar light, frees gay people from certain tasks and obligations (which seem assigned at birth to others), allowing them to expand on life in different ways. This freedom usually lasts only until weary defensiveness, self-hatred and cynicism encroach, turning magical potential into the bitterness of failed expectation. How to keep this innocence alive in a time that has lost all heart, center and balance? Where are the new directions? For gay men there have been precious few beyond the notion of a liberated sexuality.

While the world of our inheritance founders, many strands of divergent cultural, sexual and spiritual experience are coming together to form a New Idea—a numinous image of the future glimpsed through ancient windows—of which the gay movement is one thread. (Although few have spoken about the essential role their movement has to play in this burgeoning New Age.)

This vision has been informed by many of the writers in this book and also by my life experience of growing up gay in a small town on the West Coast. I spent long afternoons sitting on the cliffs of Big Sur, looking out over the Pacific, aware of Asia on the distant shore and the mysteries promised there. East met West in the gaze of a lonely California boy. The configuration of ocean and continent's end produced a deep respect for the earth's power—a spirituality, if you will. This experience was later combined with the political awakenings provoked by my gayness. It was a potent synthesis that has nurtured the deeper questions I now ask of myself and others.

This book is a reflection of my own personal evolution, a spiral path from the outer world to an inner one. It begins by examining "our place in the world"—specifically, the culture and identity gay people have begun to construct for themselves. Is what we now term *gay culture* just a further isolation from our function as culture makers at large? Or is it essential business in the task of creating a unique identity? What is the role of gay people in the arts, in the institutions of religion and in the exploration of human sexuality? What gifts do we bring to the understanding of these? And then, what is "the world within ourselves"? If we play a crucial role in defining society, how has society defined us, and on what terms can we claim that definition as a truth? The book looks at that most personal possession of all, our dreams, and concludes by examining "a world of our making"—one informed by dreams and the power that is contained deep within them.

Elsewhere, I say that it is time for gay people simply to do their work. By this I mean, I'm doing mine here, as an interpreter and recorder of these times. It is a moment to affirm our past and, in the process, make a history—to reimagine, reinvent and retell our lives; to reconnect at the deepest level of our dreams; to make our own myths.

I have no answers to the questions asked here, only this collection of voices and visions that suggests possibilities. They begin by claiming spirit in defiance of the military state; celebrate, by telling the stories of a buried people who argue for life.

—Los Angeles, Vernal Equinox, 1986

GAY SPIRIT

PART

1

Our Place in the World: Culture and Identity

JUDY GRAHN

FLAMING WITHOUT BURNING: SOME OF THE ROLES OF GAY PEOPLE IN SOCIETY

The attempt to define a gay sensibility, and then determine if it has any effect on the larger culture, is an elusive one. Sensibility, *in this case, has been variously described as possessing a humorous irony known as* camp, *as existing as an aesthetic force on society's cutting edge, or as totally lacking any moral good. Is ours a sensibility that arises from some innate quality or out of a particular minority experience? However it is defined, gay sensibility does seem to have an enormous impact on many cultural forms.*

In the following chapter, noted lesbian poet Judy Grahn says that gay people are closely watched to see "what constitutes the limit of a thing—too far out, too much, too low, too bad . . . too sexual. People watch their reflection in our behavior in order to judge their own. . . . We are essential to them knowing who they are." This is a traditional gay role, explains Grahn, and one she explores in depth throughout history and myth in her book, Another Mother Tongue: Gay Words, Gay Worlds.

Gay people, then, provide mirror images for others, and vitally necessary ones. But to extend the poet's metaphor even further and examine its underside: Since most people are comfortable only with what they want to see in a mirror, the relationship between the subject and its reflection—its reverse image—will remain perplexed, subconsciously troubled, perhaps even unacknowledged. By its very nature, a gay sensibility must disturb all those who cannot see past its surface illusions and perceive the shadowy twin image of themselves it presents.

I feel that the sensibility in question is a crucial factor within the larger cultural *need to regenerate, grow and change. It is a transformative force, created from numerous gay lives, past and present—what W. H. Auden called "the Homintern"*—that mercurial sphere of influence spun by artists, bards and wise queens with sophisticated tastes everywhere. Gay sensibility could be defined through certain acts and artifacts arising from a particular type of cultural experience—that is, engagement with the consciousness of difference.*

As for myself, awareness of difference began at an early age. Disinterest in belligerent competition and the expectations of traditional male roles was obvious. Why did the solitude of long country walks seem more appealing than the jingoism of homecoming games? How could the story of a small girl in Oz come to hold so much meaning? The story, and others like it, seemed to read me, as I lay curled up in the window seat of the local library for countless hours. Years later, I would attempt to make stories of my own by holding thin strips of motion picture film up to a bare light bulb, cutting and rearranging bits of celluloid reality into a picture that would somehow encompass my own life; that of a stranger in an even more peculiar land. Sensitivity to qualities of parody, artifice, style and fantasy were all accentuated. And later still, I would come to understand these things as traits collectively shared by so many other gay men and revealed in their creative work time and time again. But how did I know I was different? I simply felt that I was. There are reasons for that difference that I now claim, which will be discussed later in this book.

During a time when gay rage and moral indignation is palpable, it is important that gay consciousness—whatever the reason for existence—and its cultural value be fully investigated. What are its elements, what is its intrinsic worth? As Judy Grahn does here, the writers who follow in this section begin that task—one perhaps not so elusive after all—by illustrating some of the cultural roles gay consciousness inhabits, and the twists and turns in the human story it spawns.

While it has been remarkable enough for me to realize, during the lengthy process of writing *Another Mother Tongue*, that gay people have a history—continual, interwoven, and worldwide—what is more remarkable and will probably preoccupy

---

*Poet Harold Norse actually coined the word *Homintern* in 1939; a takeoff on Comintern, or Communist International, it was meant to suggest a global homosexual network. Norse conveyed the phrase to Auden in a conversation, who used it a few years later in an article written for *Partisan Review*.

me for the rest of my life is the understanding that gay people have social purpose.

This idea, implicit in the information I have gathered about *Winktes, Mahus,* bulldykes, flaming faggots, and other ceremonial gay figures from tribal, village, and modern urban times, is staggering. That is, it is staggering out in front of my vision like a madman while my rational mind tries to catch up.

My irrational mind has known all my life, being gay *is* being special. I do *not* just happen to love someone of the same gender, and if only society understood what a nice person I am, patriarchal men would stop beating me away from "their" women and I would get equal wages for equal work and become willing to wear a dress.

The fact is, of all the people in my assimilated Swedish family who could wear a bright gold tooth in the front of their mouths for decoration, I am the one who does. And if I did not have a gold tooth, I would certainly get a tattoo. When I quit smoking in 1979 and began to gain weight, I looked on the doctors' charts for appropriate weights for men and for women and picked for myself the weight for men. On purpose. Because I am closely watched. I have always been closely watched by people around me and by strangers, and this is because I am a dyke.

Society uses me. Society uses all gay people who participate in gay culture, for special purposes. We are closely watched to see what constitutes the limit of a thing—too far out, too much, too low, too bad, too outrageous, too soft, too dangerous, too rough, too cultured, too aggressive, too sexual. One of the strongest measures heterosexual culture has is how close each of its members comes to being "like a faggot" or "like a dyke." We are essential to them knowing who they are.

We are, at times, an "opposite pole" located, or locating ourselves in front of, or behind, or off to the side of, the society around us. This is a pole with mirrors. People watch their own reflections in our behavior in order to judge their own. Society does this whether or not we consciously acknowledge to ourselves that it is happening. We are mirrors for "masculine" and "feminine" strength and beauty—at least.

Sometimes we are mirrors for "good" and "evil," horror and tenderness. Most important, at the very heart of our culture, where the imagemakers live, we continually reveal to society the content and changeability of its imagery, the variety of possibilities, and finally (when we are really cooking) we may even venture forth with the idea that all imagery is an illusion.

This use of poles (or fairy wands) causes alarm. It even causes alarm in *me,* and I am often doing it.

The question of how to make the modern world safe enough for us to function as gay people is important, of course. Sometimes the cushion of acceptance is the difference between life and sublife. But safety has always been upstaged in my own heart by another question: What, as a gay person, am I doing here? What is the purpose of my life and all my hard-won, special characteristics, experiences and insights? Where can I get the courage to act from my own inner core?

Writing *Another Mother Tongue* has led me to expand this question geometrically. What are we gay people, as a group, doing here?

The Navajo people have traditionally acknowledged the particular role of the cross-dressing shamanic priesthood of gay people: the *nadle,* meaning "changers." These people are accorded high status among the Navajo, a status that was eroded only by the pressures of antigay white colonialism.

Gay has equaled *changer* in function in contemporary U.S. society as well. The most visible mass example of this is probably lesbianism/ feminism. Less obviously, though just as dramatically, the hippie counterculture movement drew much of its nourishment from the heavily gay neighborhood of Haight-Ashbury in San Francisco.

In contemplating our purposes as gay people in an American landscape I am not, now, thinking of the leadership and excellence displayed by gay (whether recognized or not) persons, of the individual who excels with daring deeds in his or her field. There are plenty of examples of these. And there are plenty of gay people who are complete schlocks at every job they take on. Nor am I thinking of leadership in terms of elected office or public figurehead.

I am thinking of a different kind of leadership and influence, of the complex exertion of gay characteristics learned in a gay setting from gay cultural figures such as dykes and fairies, leather queens and lesbian baseball players. I am not, now, thinking of myself as a lesbian poet, gay writer and speaker, founder and supporter of a number of lesbian institutions. I am thinking of myself as a neighborhood dyke, standing out on my primarily white, working-class street in a jacket with a thousand zippers and Levis and a Greek fisherman's cap, short hair and some things that definitely resemble sideburns.

What does it mean, to impact on society as a gay person—historically, politically, at the level of image—and personally?

Personally, knowing my own presence as a visible lesbian might alter my white, working-class neighborhood in meaningful ways helps calm my terrors of waking with a cross burning out front.

You may be wondering what impact my mere presence could possibly have. Firstly, by my clothes and bearing I model a certain freedom for women. Secondly, as two women living together, my lover and I strengthen the position of every married woman on the block, whether she knows and appreciates it or not. (Her husband probably does.) Thirdly, by parenting a child we present an obvious example of alternate family structure.

All of this puts ideas (some of them wonderful, some completely hideous) into people's minds, freeing them from the hidebound serfdom any one-dimensional thought system engenders. (And I consider that an all-gay ghetto quickly becomes a one-dimensional thought system as well.)

Here in my suburban neighborhood where I am a rather obvious dyke, by my appearance and my being itself, I am an alternative thought structure. This would be equally true if I were a flaming faggot, though the nature of my impact would be different.

There are certainly gay roles played out in society. I know this because I am a person who plays one. I have been a public lesbian since 1963 when I picketed the White House for gay rights with the Mattachine Society, though a more appropriate dating is probably the "costume day," during my sixteenth year in sex role–bound 1956, when I wore a Julius Caesar outfit to school. I knew the statement I was making and so did everyone else, for they avoided me. The statement was "Girls can be God," and also "Surely the emperor-general has no clothes after all, given that a simple peasant maiden is wearing them."

In medieval times the word for *heresy* and the word for *homosexual* were synonymous in several languages. What *heresy* means literally is "choice" (from *herite*). Politically—and historically—*gay* represents choice, a range of lifestyles, sexual behaviors, attitudes and approaches to life. Suppression of choice begins with and accompanies the suppression of gay people. We are inextricably bound, historically and politically, with ideas of pluralism, tolerance, multiculturality, sexual expression and free choice.

Is there a gay sensibility? No. There is not a gay anything; we are much more diverse than that. There are gay countercultures, undergrounds, circles, cliques, ghettos, histories and sensibilities. How do I know when a sensibility is gay? Because gay people gather around it and sense it and project it and act it out. Some of these sensibilities stem from our history and particular psychic values, some from our suppression and the special positions we hold within the various ethnic, racial, gender, et cetera, spheres of our society.

I am sister to the faggots who love Dorothy's red shoes and the whole story of *The Wizard of Oz*. What a gay story it is, of a seeker who discovers that dreams are real and reality, dream . . . of a seeker who along with her companions learns that the qualities we need to fulfill our life paths are within us and reveal themselves as we use them. Of a seeker who learns that the people we need to help us in our understandings will appear when we are ready for them and that authority, especially patriarchal authority, is a sham—it *does not even exist* except as our beliefs and our fears give it credence, form and power over us.

Quentin Crisp said it another way, when asked if the homosexual's lifestyle as a survivor has anything to teach other people: "Oh, yes. They will have the burden and the enjoyment of being survivors, of being outside and of being aware that every day they live is a kind of triumph. And this they should cling on to. They should make no effort to try and join society. They should stay right where they are and give their name and serial number and wait for society to form itself around them. Because it certainly will."

We hold leadership positions—unofficially, even wildly—whether we're aware of doing this or not. This happens to the extent that a gay person speaks from his or her *inner being* of knowing, as the dykes and faggots at the core of our culture usually do. They know that to lead means to locate your own pole—your faggot's or witch's wand— and stick it in the ground. See what kinds of fires are kindled around it, in the minds of men and women.

We need laws, rights and protections so we can go about flaming without burning. But let's not forget that flaming is sometimes one of the things we do. As for our safety, maybe it's like what Vine Deloria, Jr., said about leadership among American Indian people— that you can never know whether the crowd is following you or chasing you.

Maybe they're doing both.

MICHAEL BRONSKI

REFORM OR REVOLUTION? THE CHALLENGE OF CREATING A GAY SENSIBILITY

As journalist Michael Bronski notes in the following chapter—an excerpt from his book Culture Clash: The Making of Gay Sensibility *(South End Press, 1984) —gay people have long played a central role in society as creators of the arts, presenting by way of their very natures "images of beauty to a culture that has demanded only the most utilitarian necessities." This being the case, how does society's fear and abuse of gay people reflect on its relationship to the creative process? As too often revealed, it seems conditioned to react by distrusting the world of the imagination. By not honoring the qualities of originality, of* otherness, *so inherent within the consciousness of gay people, society cuts itself off from these avatars of its own transformation.*

In addition to being one of the most important forces shaping Western culture, the gay sensibility has also been one of the most progressive, liberating and visionary. The association of homosexuality with the sexual and the cry of "sex obsession" has been used to attack homosexuals and anything connected with them. But it is precisely this quality, this "obsession with sex," that is the basis of the liberation offered by the gay sensibility. Gay men have constantly argued in favor of an open sexual imagination, sought to present images of beauty to a culture that has demanded only the most utilitarian necessities and portrayed alternative worlds as a release from oppressive reality. Because gay men are producers, consumers and promoters of culture, their influence has, in certain historical periods, been noticed and usually condemned. Yet the influence they have exercised upon culture was in the interest of all people and was often gratefully accepted and absorbed. Freeing sexuality and eroticism is an impulse everyone feels on some level, no matter how much they consciously support the existing system. Whenever the threat of that impulse seemed too great, repression occurred.

Victorians were perfectly happy to accept Oscar Wilde until his message became too clear. From the very beginnings of modern gay sensibility, people suspected that promoting "art for art's sake" was really a high-toned coverup for promoting sexual pleasure. When Wilde wrote to Douglas, "It is a marvel that those red rose-leaf lips of yours should have been made no less for the music of song than for the madness of kissing," he tried explaining it to the court in artistic and literary terms. Although it fit conveniently into his aesthetic theories, everyone understood the passage's sexual intent. After the second World War, there was a backlash in America against homosexuals and the gay sensibility. The country was attempting to restabilize itself and to reestablish the rigidity of economic, sexual, and gender roles that the war had thrown askew. The sexualizing and nongender-defined influence of homosexuals was considered very threatening.

In Victorian England or the contemporary United States, homosexuality and the gay sensibility are viewed as examples of decadence and nonproductive desire and experience. Pleasure has never ultimately been appreciated or integrated by Western culture; rather than being seen as a legitimate end in itself, it was always yoked with punishment or duty. Unrestrained sexual passion, culturally connected to the arts (a passion of a different sort), was in conflict with the existing power structure. Defending homosexuality and gay culture is thought by many to be a defense of unadulterated pleasure. From the writings of the Greek philosophers through the Middle Ages and the present, there has been little philosophical interest in pleasure as an end unto itself. The repressed social majority, viewing homosexuality and anything connected with it as unrestrainable pleasure, called it a sin, a crime or a disease.

For over a hundred years, gay people have been creating and promoting culture that has been assimilated into the mainstream. This was a way for gay men to achieve some form of upward mobility within the existing social structure. It was also a way for mainstream culture to diffuse the threat of gay culture. There was an advantage to both sides in this process that was tacitly recognized, but rarely discussed openly. Mainstream culture borrowed from the gay sensibility but never acknowledged the source.

The post-Stonewall gay liberation movement insisted upon the relevance of gay culture to the political aims of the movement and began to spell out explicitly the covert influence of gay sensibility over the years. The movement's combination of politics and culture was something really new on the American political and social scene. Taking their cue from earlier liberation movements—especially black liberation and the second wave of feminism—gay activists began the work of understanding gay oppression. They denied and rejected the religious, legal and medical stigmas that had plagued homosexuals for centuries. Like other oppressed groups, they insisted upon being completely accepted by society.

As gay liberation grew, different strategies and factions emerged. Some women and men focused upon the civil rights aspects of the struggle, working to reform laws and to secure legal rights for lesbians and gay men. Their impact upon society was limited, not only by the existing social standards under which they were trying to operate but also by the rigidity of legal and governmental systems themselves. Others believed that securing rights under the existing system would never change the system itself, nor even question the precepts upon which it is based.

Another branch of the lesbian and gay movement remained closer in spirit to the political philosophies of the first post-Stonewall gay liberation groups. Eschewing a simple stand on civil liberties, these men and women named heterosexism an oppression, connected in the-

ory and practice to the oppression of other peoples. Taking their cues from the sexual political analysis of feminism and the cultural analysis of the black liberation movement, they attempted a synthesis that understood homosexuals as a distinct social and cultural group whose oppression stemmed from the same hierarchical, patriarchal and antisexual precepts that ruled the rest of the world.

Focusing primarily upon sexuality and gender definitions, gay liberationists called for the elimination of prohibitions against different forms of sexual behavior that challenged gender roles. They were less concerned with passing antidiscrimination laws than with creating a society and culture that would celebrate sexual expression. While gay rights activists worked in the sphere of legal reform, gay liberationists intended to effect profound social change.

The dichotomy between reform and revolution has been present in all progressive movements. While the benefits of progressive reforms are tangible and have the potential to change people's lives and consciousness, I believe there are reasons, theoretical and historical, why reformism is shortsighted and quite possibly doomed to failure. Erotophobia is such a tenacious strain of Western culture that it affects every aspect of our lives. It informs our attitudes toward women, children, race, class and toward sexuality in general. It has perpetuated strict sexual and gender roles, which in turn support and reinforce the erotophobia that fostered them. Homosexuality, with its blatant disregard for sexual assignments, flies in the face of this system. Homosexuality represents an antithesis of Western cultural teaching about sex and gender and is by definition the rejection of erotophobic values. Because the fear and hatred of sex is so intrinsic to Western culture, it would be almost impossible for homosexuality to attain any real acceptance within that culture. What may happen, and what has happened in the past, is that society bends the rules a bit, tolerating *some* people. The idea is containment and regulation.

In the long run, gay liberation's most lasting and effective changes will come through cultural rather than electoral or legal channels. Although all homosexuals are disfranchised from the mainstream, the legislative approach to gay liberation runs the risk of giving social power only to those homosexuals deemed "acceptable"—that is, straight-

looking and straight-behaving. Cultural change, in contrast, has the potential to radicalize and transform basic social structures, consequently attacking the very foundations of all systems of oppression.

Historically, profound social change has occurred along with cultural change. Gay men, since they have been a major cultural force during the past hundred years, are in a good position to enact social change. Until the Stonewall riots, gay men influenced culture covertly. For some, this became an act of social mobility, gaining them a certain amount of acceptance and credibility. For homosexuals as a group, it made the world a more tolerable place; their subculture was beginning to surface in the majority culture, reducing gay isolation and negation. But all the cultural change wrought by these people—and in the past hundred years, there has been an enormous amount—did not have as strong an effect as it might have because it was not always recognized as overtly homosexual. To be overtly homosexual, in a culture that denigrates and hates homosexuality, is to be political.

The Stonewall riots provided the opportunity for a broad-based movement for gay liberation. This movement, and the sensibility that grew with it, was a product of the experiences and politics of both gay men and lesbians. In a male-dominated society, much of gay culture has been defined and shaped by men. Feminism has shown that women can and have created and influenced culture. A movement dedicated to gay *and* lesbian liberation meant that women and men could form a new culture that would bear the unique imprint of a nonsexist gay sensibility.

The gay movement today is split between the reformist and the cultural/sexual liberationist positions. The reformists feel that the liberationists are unwilling to make concessions to mainstream society in the interests of acceptability. They criticize gay activists who flaunt their separateness, maintain a distinct sexual identity, and refuse to adhere to usual sexual or gender arrangements, claiming that they ruin gay people's chance for acceptance within the system. Most gay people fall between these two positions: They want legal reforms but also need the cultural affirmation for their lives offered by gay liberation.

The gay liberation movement has set up a complex network of organizations, publications, support systems and cultural outreach that

has established an autonomous, strong and positively gay-identified culture that is taken seriously within gay communities and by mainstream society. Creating this culture has been an overt and political action.

The impact this has had and will have upon mainstream culture cannot be underestimated.

DENNIS ALTMAN

WHAT PRICE GAY

NATIONALISM?

Cautionary words about gay nationalism *are offered in the following chapter. As Dennis Altman, an Australian writer and academic, points out, there is a danger in too narrowly circumscribing the gay experience, in too rigidly fixing it on sexuality's fluid course. Isolating difference for its own sake, or solely in terms of a prescribed "lifestyle," would betray it. Altman here contributes the probing voice of informed dissent: "The price we have paid for the creation of a gay community may be a culture that is too inward-looking, too ready to accept unnecessarily limited ambitions."*

Just as we use the term *sex* to mean both sexuality and gender, so the term *culture* has both anthropological and aesthetic meanings. If we speak, for example, of gays and film we may have in mind both how a gay perspective informs the films of Fassbinder and Pasolini *and* a sociological explanation of why gay men are so attracted to the films of Judy Garland and Barbra Streisand.

There is clearly a gay culture in the anthropological sense. More accurately, there are a number of overlapping cultures divided not only by gender—with lesbians and gay men sharing certain, but only certain, aspects of it—but also by class, race and geography. I am thinking here of what is often referred to as "gay lifestyle"—that whole set of values, assumptions, symbols and styles of behavior, from keyrings to camp humor, that allow us to believe we have more in common with someone else once we know he or she is gay.

Even this version of culture is limited to certain times and places; for all the interest in Sapphic Greece or medieval homoeroticism, it is unlikely that many of us would recognize ourselves in these worlds if some time machine were capable of plunging us backward into history. (I am less convinced than Judy Grahn of the continuing and seamless history of gay people, though I think she spins wonderful myths that become, in turn, part of our present culture—in both senses of the word.) Even in today's world the social construction of *gayness* becomes very different once we move outside the Western world.

Once we think of culture in its *aesthetic* sense—that is, once we argue that there is a certain *sensibility* in artistic production that stems from the homosexuality of the artist—we are in real trouble. Even if we take two of our nineteenth-century icons, Oscar Wilde and Walt Whitman, it seems clear that Wilde's style is more akin to that of W. S. Gilbert—who was not gay—than to Whitman's. Another example: Mae West's writing is much "gayer" than May Sarton's, even though Sarton is one of our leading gay writers.

In talking about the gay sensibility of art we are usually dealing with at least two variables: the sexuality of the artist and the subject matter of the art. Today these often coincide, as in lesbian coming-out novels and gay male photographs of leather bars. But they need not; homosexuality is not a theme reserved to homosexual artists— nor should it be.

I wonder if there mightn't be a case for abandoning the search for a gay sensibility altogether, and with it the sort of reductionism that makes us assume that the homosexuality of writers, artists and film-makers is the most important thing about them. Such writers as James Baldwin and Gore Vidal have strenuously resisted these categories for the very good reason that they lead us to overlook the breadth of the author's work, to concentrate on *Giovanni's Room* and *Myra Breckinridge* and ignore *Go Tell It on the Mountain* and *Lincoln*.

Resistance to being classified as a gay artist comes largely from an older generation (one thinks also of Marguerite Yourcenar and Patrick White); it becomes easy for the postliberation generation to dismiss resistance as residual self-hate. But there is a sense, too, in which the cult of asserting gayness through art has become a dead end, a refusal to recognize the extent to which sexuality is only one aspect of any human's identity; there is an oppressiveness to emphasizing it to the exclusion of all else as much as there is to ignoring it. Gay liberation implies both that we recognize the importance of our sexuality—and that we transcend sexuality as a category used to divide people.

Much of contemporary gay culture is political in that it stems from a desire to describe and to assert the sense of identity that many of us have come to associate with homosexuality. As part of this we have produced, over the past decade and a half, a quite remarkable set of cultural institutions—publications, bookstores, choruses, theater groups, et cetera—and for large numbers of people this provides the basis for a genuine sense of community. The problem comes when this sense of community, which is the anthropological form of culture, is confused with the aesthetic; and we start imposing demands on writers, artists and filmmakers to show the world not as they see it but as we want them to see it. (Gay films, for example, are too often judged in terms of whether they depict us in a way that is politically useful, not whether they are good films.)

Ultimately, the idea of gay culture may turn out to be a reactionary idea, leading us to accept too easily that what we are and do is of relevance only to ourselves, rather than being part of the broad panorama of human behavior. A gay cultural perspective should be one that never denies or hides homosexuality but that uses the experience of homosexuality to illuminate larger questions of the human condition (this is *not* a plea for the "after all, we're all sexual" line).

In an ideal world there would be no conflict between universality and community. In reality there is a precarious balance between developing a culture for ourselves and winning recognition as relevant within the broader world. Too often the latter seems to involve "selling out"; the Harvey Fierstein of *Torch Song Trilogy* is a much more radical figure than the Fierstein of *La Cage aux Folles*, which owes much of its success to the fact that it provides nongay audiences with the comforting illusion that homosexuality is an exotic costume party that has nothing to do with them. The largest challenge now facing gay artists is to find ways of reaching a larger audience without in any way compromising their particular gay experience.

The past decade and a half has seen the creation of a gay and lesbian "nation," much as nineteenth-century Europe saw the creation of Czech and Romanian "nations." To be gay has taken on meanings that go far beyond sexual and affectional preference, binding us through a whole set of communal, religious, political and social activities with other gays. (This is the anthropological sense of gay culture.) But nationalism has its price.

The problem is that we can become too obsessed with the internal life of one community to remember that the best art is that which transcends boundaries, reaching people outside the world from which it comes. We have argued in the past—correctly—that nongay society offers us no space in which to develop any expression of our own. Our very success in carving out such space has meant that we too easily accept our books only being reviewed in gay publications and sold in gay stores or, perhaps, in the "gay section" of liberal bookshops. As the gay world expands, it becomes relatively easy to live in a cultural and intellectual ghetto, to see only plays and films, read only books and magazines that proclaim themselves gay or lesbian. (And often these terms become further barriers, so that gay women and men find nothing of interest in each other's works.)

Let me end where I began. The films of Fassbinder and Pasolini are interesting precisely because they were made by men whose homosexuality infuses their work, and yet they are by no means confined to homosexual themes. (Both filmmakers died tragically, though in different ways, as victims of the death by violence and accident that remains too often a theme of gay life.) It may be significant that neither was American, and that in America there is both more space for gay culture than anywhere else and more difficulty in moving easily between a gay and a wider cultural world. The price we have paid for the creation of a gay community may be a culture that is too inward-looking, too ready to accept unnecessarily limited ambitions.

WILLIAM S. BURROUGHS

THOUGHTS ON

A GAY STATE

While many gay men were organizing themselves politically on the West Coast of the United States during the 1950s, there were others who pursued a different kind of vision. Theirs was more an artistic quest, an exploration of inner reality, a world as much in need of liberation as the body politic. It was a time when traditional ideas about art and literature were being confronted and stretched, and a generation was rapidly coming to terms with the absurd and dangerous illusions of a tranquilized society. It was a generation—which in the lexicon of Allen Ginsberg—was ready to Howl. ("I saw the best minds of my generation destroyed by madness . . .")

Not surprisingly, gay people were at the very center of this cultural investigation, as indeed, they had played similar pivotal roles in other ground-breaking eras for the arts: the Bloomsbury circle in London before World War I; Berlin between the wars; and the cultural renaissance of the 1960s springing from Paris, New York and San Francisco, to name just a few recent examples.

One of the more influential figures to emerge from this time was William S. Burroughs, a man then struggling with a powerful addiction to drugs, who went to the very edge of accepted reality—of personal limit—and returned as a writer bearing new and visionary information about his craft. Burroughs, and the experimental writers of the day—Jack Kerouac, Harold Norse, Brion Gysin, Ginsberg and many others—created a stylistic revolution in literature, a fresh way to view the juxtaposition of words themselves. Startlingly simple, but radical in its potential, their technique disrupted syntax and linear structures of thought to create new context and form. By destabilizing the traditional use of words, they sought to disrupt social and religious prejudices and to cut words from their persuasive power over beliefs and actions. Burroughs has since referred to his writing as "an inoculation, a talisman against the nodded-out flirtations with death, and against the things itself."

Burroughs and his contemporaries serve as powerful examples—those on society's edge, with little invested at its core, subverting the status quo in their own search for meaning. This is the role of the artist, of course, whether homosexual or not. But like shamans drawing with sticks in the sand, these artists made their ritual magic—and merrily so. As a result, they refreshed and rejuvenated the international culture around them.

Since Naked Lunch, *the first of his many novels that brought this "cut-up" technique to wide public attention, William S. Burroughs has written intensely about the diverse forms that human culture can take. In the following brief chapter, he outlines a few thoughts about the form that a specifically gay culture might take. His vision of a gay state is more a state of mind than a state of being, an approach that protects difference but is still inclusive of others.*

In the past, I have used the analogy of the State of Israel when advocating a gay state. Such a state would necessitate a geographic location. On careful second thought I realize that the complications involved in setting up a sovereign gay state might well prove insurmountable and the advantages doubtful. We should rather look toward an organization within the existing state that can be set up anywhere; the closest model I can can think of is to be found in Chinese Tongs.

Tongs provide very definite and valuable services to Tong members: physical protection against violence, robbery and extortion; legal aid in the event of criminal or civil action against Tong members, or legal aid in instigating criminal or civil charges; medical aid, gratis or at reduced prices; job and housing aid and advice; a meeting place where Tong members can make business and social contacts; and recreational facilities in a protected context. These services are provided by Tong members, doctors, lawyers, accountants—who contribute their services, volunteer patrols, and contribute dues levied according to the individual's ability to pay. Tongs are powerful organizations. They can invoke a boycott against bars, restaurants and other businesses or individuals who discriminate against or cheat Tong members.

Consider the Tong in action . . . Here is Wong Lee. He arrives in a strange town without a job or a place to stay. He goes immediately to his Tong and presents letters of introduction. The Tong will find him a place to stay. They will find him a job and protect him from violence, robbery and extortion. It is axiomatic in criminal circles that you can't rip off a Chinaman. He will fight to the death before he gives up his money. And other Chinese will rush to his defense, perhaps, in this case, with baseball bats and meat cleavers. So robbers leave Chinese alone. If Wong Lee gets sick, the Tong provides medical aid and takes care of his family. He can meet like-minded people in the Tong—playing fan-tan, or whatever, in a protected (Chinese only) environment.

Now, apply this model to gay Tongs. (No reason why there can't be more than one.) Greg arrives in a strange town and goes to his Tong. He is immediately eligible for all the services provided by a Chinese Tong. He can be directed to a gay rooming house or hotel or one sympathetic to gays. He can get a job, medical and legal aid. He will be protected against violence by patrols operating around the clock. In the event of a blackmail attempt he can take his complaint to the protection department for legal advice. (No doubt the Tongs will build up contacts in the police department with gay or sympathetic officers.) The Tongs will be powerful organizations that can bring down boycotts on any restaurants, bars or hotels that refuse to serve gays. The Tongs will be a voting block that can influence legislation directly; they can put up gay candidates for public office. In return, of course, members will contribute according to their abilities. Greg, let us say, is into martial arts—he will serve on protection patrols. He may be a doctor or lawyer—he will contribute his services to the appropriate department. Public relations is an important area for gay writers, magazines, TV and radio performers. It may be argued that the gay ghetto already performs these services. Some do, to be sure. However, as far as I know, there is no organized national defense program to stop violence against gays.

Setting up and operating gay Tongs will involve discipline and hard work. This presents a real challenge to the gay community. Can gays protect themselves from violence and keep their heads at the same time? Can they function effectively in an organized context? Can they establish units that will operate over a period of time? Can they extend the services of the gay Tongs to any area of America?

The demonstrations against the infamous Dan White verdict were salutary but sporadic. What is needed is disciplined, unrelenting pressure and *organization*. Only if the gay Tongs are organized so they can function nationwide as a unit can they begin to exert power as a voting block. Gays are estimated as 10 percent of the population—if such a block can exert unified pressure, that pressure will make itself felt nationwide.

A French writer, whose name escapes me, spoke of "l'affreuse frivolité" of homosexuals: the "frightful frivolity" of homosexuals. Some homosexuals, to be sure, could never get together on anything! Any group, in order to exert power and protect its interests, must transcend its obvious weaknesses.

Consider the Gay Protection patrols: GP. Their function is to protect gays against street violence. I'll extemporize from an actual case: Three gays were walking down Christopher Street in New York City, arm in arm. A gang of youths charged them, screaming, "We are sick of you gays on *our* streets!" One of the gays suffered a broken jaw. The police arrived an hour later. But suppose one of the victims had called the Tong protection number. Five GPs arrive in ten minutes, while the attackers are still there. They can show the boys that they don't own the streets. They can force the youths into a confrontational situation. If the youths attack, they will have to be dealt with in physical terms. If not, they can be forced into ignominious retreat.

It is obvious that such a fracas can involve legal complications. The attackers can claim they were attacked without provocation and bring criminal and civil action. That is where the legal department goes into action, as well as the public relations department. It's all in a day's work. If gays don't fight back, they will continue to be victimized. *Remember Stonewall!*

The gays are not alone in this fight. Street violence is a national problem, and the answer is simple. The Guardian Angels have shown us the way. They are doing what all citizens should be doing: patrolling the streets and subways and stopping violent crime—by force, if necessary. Suppose every able-bodied man between eighteen and eighty, after a period of training, was enrolled in a volunteer street patrol. He could give eight hours of his time once every two weeks to volunteer work. Such patrols could wipe crime off the streets of America, since they would outnumber the muggers, rapists and queer-bashers twenty to one. So gays join an all-out nationwide effort to eliminate street violence, no matter who the target of violence may be. It's good public relations and good sense.

BOB GALLAGHER AND ALEXANDER WILSON

SEX AND THE POLITICS OF IDENTITY: AN INTERVIEW WITH MICHEL FOUCAULT

"We have to not only affirm ourselves as an identity, but as a creative force," says Michel Foucault, one of France's best-known contemporary philosophers. Foucault's declaration reflects an important question: Should gay people embrace a social identity that was largely created from the sexual mores of the late nineteenth century, or pursue "relationships of differentiation, of creation, of innovation . . . an identity to our unique selves"?

Although his many publications have been translated into sixteen languages, Foucault is most widely known for his three-volume History of Sexuality. *His daring system of analytic thought, known as structuralism, made him a cult figure to students and intellectuals around the world, and created a theoretical platform for the pioneering work of such gay historians as Jeffrey Weeks, Jonathan Katz, John D'Emilio and Allan Berube. Foucault, who died in June 1984 at the age of fifty-seven, was also known for his outspoken opinions on gay rights, making no secret of his own sexual orientation. His death, from a reported "illness of the nervous system," came only a few months after the following interview was conducted.*

Foucault argues that history must not be regarded from an essentialist perspective

—that is, using a generalized conceit such as "patriarchy" or "class struggle"—but by directly examining how people actually construct and express their daily lives. If gay people are truly to know themselves, suggests Foucault, they must examine and rely on their own potential—in short, create themselves—rather than insist on conforming to the socially constructed role of the "homosexual," a consciousness that has primarily been defined by others. In the past, progressive movements have demanded the liberation of desire, says Foucault. Instead, "We have to create new pleasure. And then maybe desire will follow."

Foucault challenges us with a crucial distinction—a choice lived, if not considered, by many individuals discussed in this book who have empowered themselves with an identity at least partially of their own invention, whether it be as leather man, drag queen, radical fairie or poet shaman. As Michel Foucault states here, "To be the same is really boring."

Michel Foucault was a historian, philosopher, critic and social theorist. He was professor of the history of systems of thought at the College de France in Paris and also taught in the United States, at Berkeley. Foucault's work has been the center of much attention and controversy in Europe since the early 1960s. Along with his formidable colleagues Claude Levi-Strauss, Jacques Lacan, Louis Althusser and Roland Barthes, Foucault revolutionized contemporary thought about culture and society. His work has lent considerable energy to French social movements from May 1968 to the present day, yet it is only rather recently that it has disrupted Anglo-American thinking and become something of a pop phenomenon in our own culture.

Perhaps Foucault's most disruptive work is the *History of Sexuality*, the first volume of which was translated in 1978. The book fundamentally challenges the accepted Freudian explanations of sexuality. For Foucault, sexuality is not an instinctual drive that is either successfully or unsuccessfully repressed. The Victorian era, for example, contrary to conventional wisdom, should not be understood as a period of sexual denial and silence. Rather, just the opposite was happening: There was an explosion of curiosity and discourse about sex.

Most importantly, Foucault argues, this explosion of the discourse on sex is the actual *creation* of the category of "sexuality." We have come to understand sexuality as a distinct area of human behavior, whose nature and laws of development are to be scientifically uncovered. Foucault, however, sees sexuality as a category that has been carved out, isolated, given meaning and made secret. Thus, it becomes a way of organizing and making sense of a variety of activities and potentials within human society. Sexuality is not so much the expression of "the essence of our being" as it is the creation of our history and understanding of the world.

What does all this have to do with sexual politics or homosexuality? In this interview, as elsewhere, Foucault argues that our sexuality is *something we make* in our everyday experimentation with sex and pleasure. Hence, homosexuality is a historical creation developed out of the nineteenth century through the complex interplay between individuals' erotic practices and sexual regulation, control, "scientific" knowledge and labeling (via medical, religious and legal institutions). For homosexuals, this translates into an understanding of gayness not as a psychological or biological predisposition (a mere playing out of sexual impulses and preprogrammed gender roles) but as our relationship to our sexual practices and forms of pleasure. This means we can't take much for granted about a gay identity, a gay community or a unified gay politics. Questions of sexual freedom and politics no longer find easy answers based on allowing those psychological or biological types to express their "natural" (or should we say "unnatural") orientations. Foucault's thinking challenges an entire political strategy already in place within the gay movement; it has profound—and perhaps unsettling—implications for our understanding of ourselves as homosexuals.

Foucault's notion of sexuality, some people say, denies us a history that allows us to name Plato, Michelangelo and Sappho as our ancestors. Furthermore, his ideas undermine our ability to defend our lives by claiming to be a minority in need of protection, for our minority status is based on our assertion that we have a sexual *orientation*. But if gay sexuality is not based on some kind of orientation, then that whole politics becomes questionable.

This is a welcome and healthy controversy. For some time now, there has been a pressing need to reexamine the theoretical underpinning of a sexual politics. Foucault doesn't begin with "human nature" (as a traditional gay or feminist politics does) but with our everyday experiences of pleasure and sex. And in so doing, Foucault challenges all of us. We must define who we are, who we can become, what our community consists of and how we're going to change the world so it will accommodate us. This challenge—and invitation—doesn't come from a naïve or idealistic individualism but from an understanding that we are shaped by our sexual identity, and that it is in turn shaped by us. It is not a simple matter of accepting or denying our sexual identity; we must continually construct it. Let us hope that it will be an identity strong enough to protect us, and flexible enough to liberate us.

GALLAGHER/WILSON: *You suggest in your work that sexual liberation is not so much the uncovering of secret truths about one's self or one's desire as it is a part of a process of defining and constructing desire. What are the practical implications of this distinction?*

FOUCAULT: What I meant was that I think what the gay movement needs now is much more the art of life than a science or scientific knowledge (or pseudoscientific knowledge) of what sexuality is. Sexuality is a part of our behavior. It's a part of our world freedom. Sexuality is something that we ourselves create —it is our own creation, and much more than the discovery of a secret side of our desire. We have to understand that with our desires, through our desires, go new forms of relationships, new forms of love, new forms of creation. Sex is not a fatality; it is a possibility for creative life.

That's basically what you're getting at when you suggest that we should try to become gay—not just to reassert ourselves as gay.

Yes, that's it. We don't have to discover that we are homosexuals.

Or what the meaning of that is?

Exactly. Rather, we have to create a gay life. To *become.*

And this is something without limits?

Yes, sure. I think when you look at the different ways people have experienced their own sexual freedoms—the way that they have created their works of art—you would have to say that sexuality, as we now know it, has become one of the most creative sources of our society and our being. My view is that we should understand it in the reverse way: The world [regards] sexuality as the secret of the creative cultural life; it is rather a process of our having to create a new cultural life underneath the ground of our sexual choices.

Practically speaking, one of the effects of trying to uncover that secret has meant that the gay movement has remained at the level of demanding civil or human rights around sexuality. That is, sexual liberation has remained at the level of demanding sexual tolerance.

Yes, but this aspect must be supported. It is important, first, to have the possibility—and the right—to choose your own sexuality. Human rights regarding sexuality are important and are still not respected in many places. We shouldn't consider that such problems are solved now. It's quite true that there was a real liberation process in the early 1970s. This process was very good, both in terms of the situation and in terms of opinions, but the situation has not fully stabilized. Still, I think we have to go a step further. I think that one of the factors of this stabilization will be the creation of new forms of life, relationships, friendships in society, art, culture and so on, through our sexual, ethical and political choices. Not only do we have to defend ourselves, but we have to affirm ourselves; not only affirm ourselves as an identity but as a creative force.

A lot of that sounds like what, for instance, the women's movement has done, trying to establish their own language and their own culture.

Well, I'm not sure that we have to create our *own* culture. We have to *create* culture. We have to realize cultural creations. But in doing so, we come up against the problem of identity. I don't know what we would do to form these creations, and I don't know what forms these creations would take. For instance, I am not at all sure that the best form of literary creation by gay people is gay novels.

In fact, we would not even want to say that. That would be based on an essentialism we need to avoid.

True. What do we mean, for instance, by "gay painting"? Yet, I am sure that from the point of departure of our sexual choices, from the point of departure of our ethical choices, we can create something that will have a certain relationship to gayness. But it must not be a translation of gayness in the field of music or painting or what have you, for I do not think this can happen.

How do you view the enormous proliferation in the last ten to fifteen years of male homosexual practices: the sensualization, if you like, of neglected parts of the body and the articulation of new pleasures? I am thinking, obviously, of the salient aspects of what we call the ghetto— porn movies, clubs for S/M or fistfucking, and so forth. Is this merely an extension of another sphere of the general proliferation of sexual discourses since the nineteenth century, or do you see other kinds of developments that are peculiar to this present historical context?

Well, I think what we want to speak about is precisely the *innovations* that those practices imply. For instance, look at the S/M subculture, as our good friend Gayle Rubin would insist. I don't think that this movement of sexual practices has anything to do with the disclosure or the uncovering of S/M tendencies deep within our unconscious, and so on. I think that S/M is much more than that; it's the real creation of new possibilities of pleasure, which people had no idea about previously. The idea that S/M is related to a deep violence, that S/M practice is a way of liberating this violence, this aggression, is stupid. We know very well what all those people are doing is not aggressive; they are inventing new possibilities of pleasure with strange parts of their body—through the eroticization of the body. I think it's a kind of creation, a creative enterprise, which has as one of its main features what I call the desexualization of pleasure. The idea that bodily pleasure should always come from sexual pleasure, and the idea that sexual pleasure is the root of *all* our possible pleasure —I think *that's* something quite wrong. These practices are insisting that we can produce pleasure with very odd things, very strange parts of our bodies, in very unusual situations, and so on.

So the conflation of pleasure and sex is being broken down.

That's it precisely. The possibility of using our bodies as a possible source of very numerous pleasures is something that is very important. For instance, if you look at the traditional construction of pleasure, you see that bodily pleasure, or pleasures of the flesh, are always drinking, eating and fucking. And that seems to be the limit of the understanding of our bodies, our pleasures.

The point is to experiment with pleasure and its possibilities.

Yes. Pleasure also must be a part of our culture. It is very interesting to note, for instance, that for centuries people generally, as well as doctors, psychiatrists and even liberation movements, have always spoken about desire, and never about pleasure. "We have to liberate our desire," they say. No! We have to create new pleasure. And then maybe desire will follow.

Is it significant that there are, to a large degree, identities forming around new sexual practices, like S/M? These identities help in exploring such practices and defending the right to engage in them. But are they also limiting in regard to the possibilities of individuals?

Well, if identity is only a game, if it is only a procedure to have relations, social and sexual-pleasure relationships that create new friendships, it is useful. But if identity becomes *the* problem of sexual existence and if people think that they have to "uncover" their "own identity," and that their own identity has to become the law, the principle, the code of their existence; if the perennial question they ask is, "Does this thing conform to my identity?" then, I think, they will turn back to a kind of ethics very close to the old heterosexual virility. If we are asked to relate to the question of identity, it has to be an identity to our unique selves. But the relationships we have to have with ourselves are not ones of identity, rather they must be relationships of differentiation, of creation, of innovation. To be the same is really boring. We must not exclude identity if people find their pleasure through this identity, but we must not think of this identity as an ethical universal rule.

But up to this point, sexual identity has been politically very useful.

Yes, it has been *very* useful, but it limits us and I think we have (and can have) a right to be free.

We want some of our sexual practices to be ones of resistance in a political and social sense. Yet, how is this possible, given that control can be exercised by the stimulation of pleasure? Can we be sure that these new pleasures won't be exploited in the way advertising used the stimulation of pleasure as a means of social control?

We can never be sure. In fact, we can always be sure *it will happen* and that everything that has been created or acquired, any ground that has been gained, will, at a certain moment, be used in such a way. That's the way we live, that's the way we struggle, that's the way of human history. And I don't think that is an objection to all those movements or all those situations. But you are quite right in underlining that we always have to be quite careful and to be aware of the fact that we have to move on to something else, that we have other needs as well. The S/M ghetto in San Francisco is a good example of a community that has experimented with, and formed an identity around, pleasure. This ghettoization, this identification, this procedure of exclusion and so on—all of these have as well produced their countereffects. I dare not use the word *dialectics*—but this comes rather close to it.

You once mentioned that what upsets people most about gay relations is not so much sexual acts per se but the potential for affectional relationships that are carried on outside the normative patterns. These friendships and networks are unforeseen. Do you think what frightens people is the unknown potential of gay relations, or would you suggest that these relations are seen as posing a direct threat to social institutions?

One thing that interests me now is the problem of friendship. For centuries after antiquity, friendship was a very important kind of social relation: a social relation within which people had a certain freedom, a certain kind of choice (limited of course), as well as very intense emotional relations. There were also economic and social implications to these relationships—they were obliged to help their friends, and so on. I think that in the sixteenth and seventeenth centuries we see these kinds of friendships disappearing, at least in the male society. And friendship begins to become something other than that. You can find, from the sixteenth century on, texts that explicitly criticize friendship as something dangerous.

The army, bureaucracy, administration, universities, schools, et cetera—in the modern senses of these words—cannot function with such intense friendships. I think there can be seen a very strong attempt in all these institutions to diminish, or minimize, the affectional relations. I think this is particularly important in schools. When they started grade schools with hundreds of young boys, one of the problems was how to prevent them not only from having sex, of course, but also from developing friendships. For instance, you could study the strategy of Jesuit institutions about this theme of friendship, since the Jesuits knew very well that it was impossible for them to suppress this. Rather, they tried to use the role of sex, of love, of friendship, and at the same time to limit it. I think now, after studying the history of sex, we should try to understand the history of friendship, or friendships. That history is very, very important.

And one of my hypotheses, which I am sure would be borne out if we did this, is that homosexuality became a problem—that is, sex between men became a problem—in the eighteenth century. We see the rise of it as a problem with the police, within the justice system, and so on. I think the reason it appears as a problem, as a social issue, at this time is that friendship had disappeared. As long as friendship was something important, was socially accepted, nobody realized men had sex together. You couldn't say that men *didn't have sex* together—it just didn't matter. It had no social implication, it was culturally accepted. Whether they fucked together or kissed had no importance. Once friendship disappeared as a culturally accepted relation, the issue arose, "What is going on between men?" And that's when the problem appears. And if men fuck together, or have sex together, that now appears as a problem. Well, I'm sure I'm right, that the disappearance of friendship as a social relation and the declaration of homosexuality as a social/political/medical problem are the same process.

If the important thing now is to explore anew the possibilities of friendship, we should note that, to a large degree, all the social institutions are designed for heterosexual friendships and structures and for the denial of homosexual ones. Isn't the real task to set up new social relations, new value structures, familial structures, and so on? One of the things gay people don't have is easy access to all the structures and institutions that go along with monogamy and the nuclear family. What kinds of institutions do we need to begin to establish, in order not only to defend ourselves but also to create new social forms that are really going to be alternative?

Institutions. I have no precise idea. I think, of course, that to use the model of family life, or the institution of the family, for this purpose and this kind of friendship would be quite contradictory. But it is quite true that since some of the relationships in society are protected forms of family life, an effect of this is that the variations that are not protected are, at the same time, often much richer, more interesting and creative than the others. But of course, they are much more fragile and vulnerable. The question of what kinds of institutions we need to create is an important and crucial issue, but one that I cannot give an answer to. I think that we have to try to build a solution.

To what degree do we want, or need, the project of gay liberation today to be one that refuses to chart a course and, instead, insists on opening up new avenues? In other words, does your approach to sexual politics deny the need for a program and insist on experimentation with new kinds of relations?

I think that one of the great experiences we've had since the last war is that all those social and political programs have been a great failure. We have come to realize that things never happen as we expect from a political program; and that a political program has always, or nearly always, led to abuse or political domination from a bloc, be it from technicians or bureaucrats or other people. But one of the developments of the 1960s and 1970s that I think has been a good thing is that certain institutional models have been experimented with without a program. Without a program does not mean blindness—to be blind to thought. In my opinion, being without a program can be very useful and very original and creative, if it does not mean without proper reflection about what is going on or without very careful attention to what's possible.

Since the nineteenth century great political institutions and great political parties have confiscated the process of political creation; that is, they have tried to give to political creation the form of a political program in order to take over power. I think what happened in the 1960s and early 1970s is something to be preserved; that there has been political innovation, political creation and political experimentation outside the great political parties, and outside the normal or ordinary program. It's a fact that people's everyday lives have changed from the early 1960s to now, and certainly within my own life. And surely, that is not due to political parties but is the result of many movements. These social movements have really changed our whole lives, our mentality, our attitudes, *and* the attitudes and mentality of other people—people who do not belong to these movements. And that is something very important and positive. I repeat, it is not the normal and old traditional political organizations that have led to this examination.

MARK THOMPSON

DOUBLE REFLECTIONS: ISHERWOOD AND BACHARDY ON ART, LOVE AND FAITH

Christopher Isherwood often said that gay men constituted a type of "tribe"—and a queer one at that, a term he much preferred to the word gay. If collectively asked, this extended and subterranean network would probably acknowledge Isherwood as a distant but approachable spiritual father. Primarily through his writings, Isherwood helped to provide a moral center for many gay men. "Many of my brothers have suffered a terrible guilt because of their nature," he once said. But as the writer makes clear in Kathleen and Frank, *a book about his parents, "Despite the humiliations of living under a heterosexual dictatorship and the fury he has often felt against it, Christopher has never regretted being as he is."*

In the following interview, conducted two years before his death on January 4, 1986, Isherwood talks about his impressions of the gay subculture, his visionary friend Gerald Heard, his spiritual beliefs, and what it has been like to live openly in a homosexual relationship with a man much younger than himself. Over three decades had passed since the time when forty-eight-year-old Isherwood met, and fell in love with, eighteen-year-old Don Bachardy. For many, their relationship was a point of honor—a powerful symbol of the possibilities gay men have for nurturing one another.

Don Bachardy stands in the middle of his sun-drenched, all-white studio, one foot scuffing the bright spots of blue, red, yellow and orange paint that surround him like an iridescent pool. The colorful splashes on the floor are the center point of an otherwise tidy room; vivid, larger-than-life portraits of friends and acquaintances—"those people who fascinate me"—hang neatly on the walls. "They reveal more about themselves than they think they do," he says, as if to explain the faces.

Bachardy, whom one art critic called "California's most distinguished portraitist," has painted or drawn hundreds of people—the famous and the unknown—over the past twenty years. But he can't remember the number of times he's captured the image of his lover, mentor and friend, Christopher Isherwood. "Countless times," he smiles. It is these images—in moods ranging from fiery to innocent—some of which adorn the covers of Isherwood's many novels and biographies, that attest to the complex and enduring nature of their relationship.

In *October*, a collaborative book of writing and drawings documenting a month of their lives in 1979, Isherwood playfully talks about one evening's sitting: "Don often describes his work as a confrontation. He himself, with a pen gripped in his mouth ready for use when it is needed instead of a brush, reminds me of a pirate carrying a dagger between his teeth while boarding the enemy. He seems to be attacking the sitter. So now I counterattack. Summoning up all my latent hostility, I glared at him unwaveringly, with accusing eyes. While he was working, he didn't seem to be noticing this. Yet he recorded it. The finished drawing is scary; my old face is horrible with ill-will. Most satisfactory."

When we met in February 1984, the two men were celebrating thirty-one years together, which is about the same amount of time that separates them in age. In *Christopher and His Kind*, the autobiography that ends with Isherwood's emigration to America from England in 1939, the author foretells his remarkable union with Bachardy. Standing at the rail of the ship in the New York harbor, looking hopefully at the land where he will spend more than half his life,

Isherwood asks himself if he "will find the person you came here to look for—the ideal companion to whom you can reveal yourself totally and yet be loved for what you are, not what you pretend to be." Isherwood will have to wait a long time until that discovery. However, "[Bachardy] is already living in the city where you will settle. He will be near you for many years without your meeting. But it would be no good if you did meet him now. At present, he is only four years old."

Bachardy, now a handsome forty-nine years old, has matured as an artist with his own particular vision. Underlying all of his work is a boldness of line and a clarity of focus. Faces, broadly painted in startlingly bright colors, are shaped by a few incisive strokes. In the drawings, all unnecessary material is eliminated; the image is pared down to the central, penetrating gaze of the sitter.

It is this quality of seeing that distinguishes Isherwood's prose style as well. His clarity of vision—Isherwood's emblematic "I am a camera" at its most refined—may be most evident in *A Single Man*, the 1964 novel that critics and author alike regard as his finest work. Widely regarded as the best British novelist of his generation, Isherwood has a seemingly artless style: spare yet lucid, resonant with subtle wit and irony, generated from deep compassion and relentless self-observation.

For the fortunate, such insight can develop after years of pursuing their craft, but for Isherwood and Bachardy, the ability to focus on the essential nature of a subject has undoubtedly been informed by their daily spiritual practice, a form of Hindu philosophy known as Vedantism. In the Vedantic teachings, all reality is considered as a single whole; it is the believer's goal to transcend the limitations of self-identity and realize unity with that wholeness.

Isherwood was first introduced to Vedantic teachings and to Swami Prabhavananda (the Hindu monk who was to become Isherwood's spiritual mentor until his death in 1976), by British writer and philosopher Gerald Heard. The two men had known one another in London and renewed their friendship when Isherwood arrived in Southern California in the spring of 1939, two years after Heard's own immigration west. Heard had greatly changed during those intervening years, and at first Isherwood was suspicious of his friend's newfound religion.

In *My Guru and His Disciple*, Isherwood explains his initial reticence: "My interpretation of the word *God* had been taken quite simple-mindedly from left-wing antireligious propaganda. God had no existence except as a symbol of the capitalist superboss. He has been deified by the capitalist so that he can rule from on high in the sky over the working-class masses, doping them with the opium of the people, which is religion, and thus making them content with their long hours and starvation wages.

"I soon had to admit, however, that Gerald's 'this thing'—leaving aside the question of its existence or nonexistence—was the very opposite of my 'God.' True, it was by definition everywhere, and therefore also up in the sky, but it was to be looked for first inside yourself. It wasn't to be thought of as a boss to be obeyed but as a nature to be known—an extension of your own nature, with which you could become consciously united. The Sanskrit word *yoga*, ancestor of the English word *yoke*, means "union," and hence the process of achieving union with the eternal omnipresent nature, of which everybody and everything is a part."

Isherwood's introduction to Vedantism through Heard felt strange, yet mysteriously compelling, and soon the writer was won over. "I shall be grateful to him as long as I live," Isherwood would later record in his spiritual autobiography. "Indeed. I believed in [Heard] *because* he was theatrical, because he costumed himself as a ragged hobo, because his beard was Christlike but trimmed, because some of his lamentations over the human lot had a hint of glee in them and some of his scientific analogies a touch of poetic exaggeration. . . . What made his company so stimulating was that he seemed to be so intensely aware. Awareness was his watchword."

Isherwood and Bachardy have created a graceful, harmonious way of life for themselves in their Santa Monica, California, home, a lovely, stuccoed house that spills down the terraced edge of a scenic canyon, which empties into the Pacific. The afternoon of our visit found Bachardy between sittings and Isherwood resting from his current project, a book of annotated memoirs covering his further adventures in America. Both men were filled with warmth and humor.

THOMPSON: *Do you feel that your religious faith has helped you to see things in a different way?*

BACHARDY: I'm not conscious of it, but certainly, if it's of any value at all, it's bound to enter into every corner of one's life, everything one does. If it changes one's self, basically, in deep ways, then of course it must affect everything one does . . . I want to understand myself, and I want other people to understand me and my work. I don't want to create any mystery as an artist. I think one has to believe that what one's doing is clear. I like my things to be clear and simple. It's just my nature. There are perfectly good artists who practice the reverse of what I do—who revel in mystery and suggestion.

Many people are curious about the bright colors used in your portraits.

BACHARDY: I know it seems peculiar to people who look at my work, but it seems to me that I'm working—I'm using— I'm *reproducing* the colors I see. And then I look later at the paintings and think, "His face couldn't *possibly* have been that orange!" But I can only tell you that while I was doing it, it didn't seem to me outlandish at all!

Christopher, you've previously stated that "it is very dangerous to equate a homosexual relationship with heterosexual marriage. You drag in the whole bourgeois system of obligation and concepts of ownership." How do you avoid that in your relationship with Don?

ISHERWOOD: Well, I think there's no overall rule on how to avoid problems like that. I mean, you can only avoid it in any given relationship—it depends entirely on the two people. It's almost an unanswerable question.

BACHARDY: I do think it helps not being *legally* sanctioned in any way. Of course, when we started living together in the early 1950s, there was much less encouragement from the outside world to help us cement our relationship. We really did have to do it by ourselves. And so, it was something we really *wanted* to do, rather than something that we felt obligated to do in any way.

Where could you look for support for your relationship then?

BACHARDY: I think we—at least I—felt quite like a pioneer.

I didn't know anybody else who was having experiences anything like mine.

ISHERWOOD: Quite a lot of people were shocked, of course, at the difference in our ages. It would have been much more convenient if we'd been approximately the same age.

BACHARDY: You see, when we met I wasn't an artist. That didn't come until years later, and that made it all the more difficult. Once I managed to establish myself as an artist in my own right, then an awful lot of the pressure was reduced. And pressure, really, that I had put on myself. It was very important for me to be able to feel independent and be somebody in my own right. Because Chris was already a very well-known person when I met him, I achieved this, of course, with all kinds of support and encouragement from Chris.

ISHERWOOD: I think I did realize that, ideally, when there's a difference in age, the younger person should make an independent career, because that's exactly what's most likely to keep the relationship going.

So you encouraged this artistic interest in Don right from the start?

ISHERWOOD: I can't claim to be so farsighted. I had absolutely no idea that he had any artistic talent whatever; and anyway, I'm far too arrogant about my own opinion on writing to ever venture an opinion on any of the other arts. But it has been the most . . . absolutely delightful, marvelous thing—when you realize that the other person has a vocation just as strong as yours.

Have gay styles and taste—the way gay people interact with one another—really changed that much from the 1940s and 1950s?

BACHARDY: No. I don't see any difference, basically, in the people themselves. It's just the openness now that is the most profound difference. But in the behavior of gay people we know or know of, it's much the same.

ISHERWOOD: Of course, if one could have *seen* then what it would be like now, we'd probably say, "My God! We won! We're saved! It's the millennium! It's everything! Enjoy!" And people nowadays would say, "Are you kidding?" But it *is* much better now.

There's so much activity—on every social, political and artistic level—within the gay community right now. Is there any particular aspect of this that attracts you?

ISHERWOOD: I must say that I feel rather out of it, in the sense that—I don't know whether you'll agree with me, Don— I don't feel personally that I'm constantly a part of the gay community; rather a large majority of the people who come to this house happen to be gay. It's not quite the same thing. My conscience, in a way, says to me perhaps I ought to be more *in* the gay community—although I can understand people for whom activism is a whole, full-time life occupation. Just being gay really keeps you busy from morn until eve if you do it whole-heartedly rather than in an ideal manner, if you're constantly working for your gay brothers and sisters.

BACHARDY: I wouldn't say that the vast majority of people who come here are gay! It seems to me we see almost as many heterosexual people. For instance, the great majority of my friends in the art world are heterosexual. And in a way, I do feel a certain responsibility *not* to spend all of my time with my own kind, because I do feel that one should expose oneself to heterosexuals, for one's own benefit and for theirs. I think it's very important for us to carry our message! I think it helps the cause, to create a positive image in the heterosexual world.

How do you both feel about having your private selves revealed openly over the years?

BACHARDY: Oh, there's a lot of the private part of myself that hasn't been seen by anybody. I think there are even a few small areas that haven't been seen by Chris!

You've both been very open in discussing your relationship. What made you take this step toward openness, when so many other people of comparable stature in the literary and art worlds have chosen not to?

BACHARDY: We didn't have a choice! First of all, the big difference in our ages brought attention to us. And because Chris was already known when I met him, that kind of made it impossible for us to be in the closet, because it was just too . . .

remarkable. This older writer living with such a young person. In a way we didn't have a choice, it seems to me. There was never any kind of trying to hide or cover up the kind of relationship we had. We've always had many heterosexual friends who just took it for granted, even in the 1960s. There was never any question of keeping anybody in the dark about it.

ISHERWOOD: I'm very militant, you know, in a quiet way, about it. I wish I could say I was a gay activist. I can't feel that I am one, not according to real standards of activism, but I do feel a certain responsibility. I couldn't possibly turn heterosexual; that would be like cowardice in the face of the enemy . . . or something you could never live down. I'd have to go live on one of the remote islands of the South Pacific, it would be such a disgrace. I'm being facetious, but that really is what it amounts to. I do feel that anybody who belongs to one of the many minorities feels this. We don't want to give other people a reason to panic. And let me say this: It was very much easier for us because we were in the arts. We were never employed by anybody who demanded any kind of concealment, and we were largely on our own—not pleasing any boss, as it were, except ourselves, and that made it easier.

What are your feelings about the gay movement at this point? Are there any new directions we should be looking at?

BACHARDY: I don't doubt it. But, on the other hand, I think the great thing is for us all to try to give each other courage. That's all that matters. And if some of us are timid, so much the more reason for others of us not to be.

You must be amazed at the rapid development of the gay subculture since 1969.

ISHERWOOD: I do find it astonishing. It shows that somehow it's absolutely in the development of mankind. A lot of people have put forth the theory, as you well know, that it is a kind of device on nature's part. If mankind won't stop overpopulating, then Mother Nature will intervene and start creating so many gays that the population declines! That's sort of farcical when one says it like that, but somewhere in there is a kind of inner truth. I do think the human race, with all its frightful mistakes and its feuds with itself, does intend to survive.

I'm very curious about your friendship with Gerald Heard, who first introduced you to the Vedanta Society. However, to begin, what does the word vedanta *mean?*

ISHERWOOD: The word *vedanta* really only means "that which is taught or written in the Vedas." And the Vedas are the basic Hindu scriptures. If there were such a word, the equivalent would be *Biblianto* in the Christian tradition. Something that is *about* what's in the sacred Hindu books; that's all.

I understand that Heard was very outspoken on the subject of gay rights in Los Angeles in the 1940s and 1950s.

BACHARDY: It's a great shame he didn't live to see this gay liberation movement. He would have adored it and certainly would have been one of the leaders, I'm sure.

ISHERWOOD: But there's something very interesting that very few people know about Heard: He felt that the homosexual temperament was potentially very, very, very important; way beyond the question of choosing a boy rather than a girl, rather than a camel. I don't just mean the mere difference in sexual choice, but there was a real kind of *potential* in homosexuals—or at least in some homosexuals. In other words, a kind of homosexual *genius*, in the sense that there's an Irish genius or a black genius. There is a kind of indwelling potentiality which might play a great role, and he did in fact write some material about this. He was a deeply visionary person, always fascinated by all kinds of possibilities, potentialities in people and groups.

Did he say what this potential was?

ISHERWOOD: Well, I suppose really you'd have to say that it was a type of sophistication. That's not saying very much, because that applies to practically anything. But it's the kind of sophistication where, if gays were to live up to their deeper intuitions and their . . . *flair* for dealing with other people, they could perhaps really make a tremendous social contribution to life—a sort of *sanity* that came out of refusing to play the heterosexual role in this society; that they had something else to offer. I'm sure that in Gerald's case—because he was very much a monastic, sex was not of overwhelming importance to him—I suppose his was really a state of semimonasticism. There was some kind of *disinterested* quality to it. And by *disinterested* I don't mean *uninterested*; I mean *disinterested* in the sense that you were rather above the ordinary motivation . . . Like almost everybody who is as remarkable as Gerald was, he was probably a bit of an elitist. He certainly believed in the castes, in the Hindu sense, in other words, that there are people who are just born with certain potentialities—and therefore, of course, duties.

BACHARDY: On the point of whether he was an elitist or whatever, don't you think that anyone who practices celibacy can't help but develop a certain sense of superiority?

How influential was Heard for you? Do you share his belief in this "potentiality"?

ISHERWOOD: Yes. I can't say that I feel quite as . . . convinced. I mean, obviously every group of any kind has a great deal to contribute—which it never does contribute [to the greater mass]. And *certainly* we have something to contribute; there's no question about *that* . . . Gerald was a rare creature altogether; he breathed another air, in a way.

I'm interested in hearing about the founding father of your spiritual order—Ramakrishna. He was a very eccentric guru who lived in India in the 1850s and cross-dressed, I believe.

ISHERWOOD: The cross-dressing thing is very peculiar. Well, Ramakrishna was—psychologically—a sort of religious genius in a way, because he went at it to the limit of everything; which is a real sign of genius, I guess. The reason for wearing women's clothes was twofold. He was a tremendous devotee of God in God's aspect of the Divine Mother. That is to say, the whole thing, be it the Virgin or any female images of God. And in this sense he would try to identify. It was really an attempt to intensify his meditation on the figure of the female God. Being like all geniuses an eccentric—I mean from the point of view of the world; he acted quite oddly in many circumstances—he really did these things, I think, to startle his disciples. It's in exactly the same sense as St. Francis of Assisi, who was also very unconventional. He was nuts because he preached to birds! . . . There's a kind of innocence, an openness there—the result so breathtaking. It was like being a queen, in a way; it had that marvelous purity you sometimes find in the very best kind of homosexual who is sort of a bit silly, but you feel he's absolutely . . . in the truth.

And you have felt this way about Ramakrishna and your immediate teachers?

ISHERWOOD: Oh, yes. I've felt that. You have to feel that way about religious teachers or else they're not much good. That sort of simplicity is very remarkable . . . *Truth* is always the operating word. There are lies, and there's truth, and the truth that you must tell is not somebody else's truth—I mean, when it comes to something that you're in a position to tell the truth about. That's all it's all about.

You must feel closely identified with Ramakrishna?

ISHERWOOD: Our teacher had been the disciple of a man who'd known Ramakrishna. And not only known him, but was one of his *closest* disciples. So we had an awfully short line. I mean, if you compare that with having some connection with one of the apostles of Jesus of Nazareth, you begin to see it has a certain power. This was an incredible connection! You really couldn't help feeling that if there's anything in this stuff at all, you are getting it from the horse's mouth.

Elsewhere in your book My Guru and His Disciple *you describe how difficult it has been to maintain a concentrated spiritual life. What keeps you to that discipline?*

ISHERWOOD: I don't see it as very remarkable. If you have that kind of contact and it's meant anything, what it amounts to is that you do little acts of what the Catholics call recollection, a phrase I always like, find very helpful and descriptive. You remind yourself every day that it's no joke: It really is true what it means to you, personally, in your life.

In other words, it's maintaining a sense of clarity and purpose about your life.

ISHERWOOD: Yes, just reminding yourself. But as I say, I like the Catholic phrase, recollection.

You had been friends with W. H. Auden since childhood, Christopher. Did he understand your interest in Hinduism?

ISHERWOOD: To some extent—but he was very Christian. He was very much under the influence of his mother, which sort of sounds odd because Auden was such an individualist—but he really was. She was a deep Christian, and to him that was the way. At that time I didn't think I had any religion at all. But the minute I met a Hindu who happened to be my kind of guy then, of course, exactly the same thing happened, except I turned into a Hindu instead of turning into a Christian. That's the only difference. It couldn't matter less. True religion is all essentially one.

This was not an issue in your friendship?

ISHERWOOD: Oh, no! Auden was a very *sophisticated* kind of Christian! He understood the object of worship doesn't have to be A rather than B; that's not at all what it's all about.

He didn't think, for instance, that Christopher had gone off to California and gotten entangled in some sort of cult.

ISHERWOOD: Well, he used to talk like that, in a kind of pitying way. He would spout this sort of heathen mumbo jumbo. But he was a very downright sort of person. He had opinions and thought that the Christian faith was the only one that really had any sort of validity. But he knew in his heart that it wasn't the only one, although he felt, too, that one had to be true to one's roots.

You felt that you had no religion?

ISHERWOOD: I was Anglican, which usually means you turn into an atheist for at least a few years and then recover from it and either go on to become a real Christian or else . . . But you know, God help anyone who was a Hindu or Buddhist or anything else.

What was it about Hinduism that attracted you?

ISHERWOOD: It was this man, this particular man I met through Heard. You must start with an individual. You can't just read a book, for example, and say, "All right. Now I'm a Buddhist." It just doesn't work like that. There *has* to be somebody; there had to be some kind of human spark.

Do you mind being asked about your spiritual life?

ISHERWOOD: What I feel about all of this stuff . . . The Hindus have a marvelous thing that they say: If you've had any real spiritual experience, *hide it*, as you would hide from other people the fact that your mother was a whore! Strong words! In other words, for God's sake, shut up about it! And I'm mindful of that, unless, of course, I'm speaking with people who are seriously interested. I do think one has to be reticent. But that's another matter altogether. You probably realize that we've been completely frank with you because we were being asked serious questions.

MARK THOMPSON
CHILDREN OF
PARADISE:
A BRIEF HISTORY
OF QUEENS

In contemporary Western society, few figures are held in greater contempt, or considered more useless or perverse, than the drag queen. But in many non-Christian and preindustrialized cultures, those who bridged the genders were placed in a position of honor and ritual purpose. As Judy Grahn points out in Another Mother Tongue: Gay Words, Gay Worlds *(Beacon Press, 1984): "In tribal/pagan realms cross-dressing often meant entering a magical state involving taking on a persona or spirit of a god being for public ceremonial purposes." Cross-dressed men and women assumed a variety of roles: healers and mediators of spiritual life, as well as daily life within their community.*

The magical role of the gay shaman has been recorded in many cultures around the world: Among the Ambo people of South West Africa they were known as the omasenge; *in Polynesia they were called the* mahu; *in Central and North American Indian tribes they were referred to as the* berdache, *a term European colonizers used to generalize the many names the native tribes had for their sacred transvestites. The Oglala called their gay magic men* winkte. *The Crow Indians of Montana used* bote, *meaning "not-man, not-woman." Among the Zuni of New Mexico, men of the tribe who pursued the skills and activities of the opposite sex—for example, those who became potters or weavers—were called* Lhamana. *And the Navajo named their gay shamans* nadle. *A Navajo elder once said, "I believe when all the* nadle *have passed away, it will be the end of the Navajo culture."*

In the Americas, as in the pre-Christian and indigenous cultures of Europe, an uninhibited expression of homosexuality was often applied to sacred ritual, an understanding about sex and spirit that has long since been obliterated through centuries of genocide and cruel repression of pagan sensibilities.

Today, the religious role of those who bridge gender has been reduced to a tragic and trivialized cipher, a faint echo of the symbolic importance it once had in human culture. Yet, in many societies around the world, some gay men continue to cross-dress. But unlike the many heterosexual men who do so largely with guilt and shame, gay transvestites wear their adornment as public celebration. By doing so they release the feminine energy that's usually kept locked within the male psyche and set free laughter that can empower hearts and minds more than any rigid devotion to the protocol of gender. As Holly Woodlawn once said, "Man or woman? What difference does it make as long as you look fabulous!"

For gay men, drag is still theater, a form of public ritual. And while seemingly divorced from any spiritual or social context, it is still possible to scrape away layers of cultivated Christian dogma and glimpse a small example of the useful ways in which cross-dressing can serve a community. We'll begin with one summer night in San Francisco, not too many years ago.

The word is out at the corner of Powell and Columbus. It's midnight, and a large theater marquee spelling PALACE illuminates the milling crowd below in gaudy neon hues. There are men in rouge and green eyeshadow and women wearing black leather jackets and bowler hats. Inside, the theater is packed to capacity, and cheap wine and joints are freely passed from row to row.

Backstage, confusion is equally rife. Performers stand in front of mirrors and tug on costumes pieced together from moulting boas, old satin dresses and papier-mâché hats. Nearby, a naked man dusts his body with silver glitter, while a woman, some months pregnant, rehearses the words to "I Want a Little Sugar in My Bowl." Curtain time has come and gone and the audience roars its good-natured impatience. The lights suddenly dim and a voice booms through the dark, "Ladies and gentlemen! The all-new, all-singing, all-electric, all cardboard Cockettes!" The troupe enters to cheers, a spectacle of rouged nipples, dimestore jewelry and lamé codpieces. Goldie Glitters, playing a fiendish gossip columnist, Vedda Viper, steps forward and screeches, "All the dirt, all the stars, no matter whose life I fuck up!"

Later, while a bearded torch singer croons "Can't Help Loving That Man of Mine," a backdrop of cardboard calla lilies in bloom begins to collapse. Cast, crew, and even a few audience members rush on stage to rescue the sagging set piece. But the balance is lost, and the lilies exit in a cloud of dust. Someone on stage stamps his foot. "I'm tired of this. Let's do something else."

And they did.

"The lobby of the Palace Theater was a beautiful place to be gay," one observer of the times said. "It was crowded with the extraordinary, the bizarre decadents who created an underground renaissance." It was 1970, and radical drag—"gender fuck"—was in vogue. The first angry howls of gay revolt were still reverberating across the land, and the national tragedies and creative liberation of the previous decade were finding perspective. That a small band of gay men on the West Coast had taken to wearing dresses and beards at the same time seemed, to some people, a needless confusion of the issues at hand. A few critics dismissed the glittery phenomenon as a quaint last gasp of the hippie counterculture, and others thought it made some sort of polymorphous perverse political statement about the future. The men in question couldn't have cared less. Almost no one perceived the sensation for what it really was—a form of gay consciousness asserting itself.

"We were exploding the myth of romance and glamour, the myth of success," I would be told years later by Martin Worman, who had gone on from the troupe to direct theater in New York. "Of course, it was political, but no one among us verbalized it. We had no need of rhetoric. We were madcap chefs cooking up a storm and the ingredients were magic and tribal anarchy."

The Cockettes were symptomatic of an entire generation flipping out from a lifetime of popular culture—a gut-wrenching angst combined, in this case, with a budding gay sensibility. Conceived on the back seat of a 1953 pink Cadillac parked at the intersection of Hollywood Boulevard and Madison Avenue, weaned on the junky excrement of television, they saw American culture in full circle. And, recognizing themselves, they let out a cry of chaos and rage.

"Among the other myths, we were also exploding nostalgia," said Worman. "We never took the poses and ambiance of another decade seriously; we were pointing up the absurdities. But in our wake, old clothes and old songs became ends in themselves. Nostalgia became an insidious tool used by mass marketeers to cover up the shortages of spirit, imagination and raw materials in the post-Vietnam and post-Watergate bankruptcy." The Cockettes *were* outrageous because their theater was a pastiche of every used-up myth, fable and lie they had ever watched, read or been taught. And their audience laughed, as if looking into a crazy-house mirror.

Poet Allen Ginsberg, who fondly remembers the Cockettes, told me that the notoriety of the group "affected the entire suburban culture" that was to follow. "Kids who wanted some way to express difference from the homogenized television culture adopted the plumage of these [radical tranvestites]. The Cockettes were part of a large-scale spiritual liberation movement and reclamation of self from the homogenization of the military state. They were expressing themselves as actual people with their own natures and tendencies, rather than being ashamed— and doing it with humor."

The role of the fool, the trickster, the *contrary one* capable of turning a situation inside out, is one of the most enduring of all archetypes. Often cross-dressed or adorned with both masculine and feminine symbols, these merry pranksters chase through history, holding up a looking glass to human folly. Confidants to kings and commoners, teller of truths, and cloaked in many disguises, these queer figures seem to spring from the shadow realm that lies between the worlds of above and below. It is a role that seems particularly suited to gay men, and in San Francisco it is possible to trace a succession of such men playing the role with glee.

On the more tolerant West Coast, men dressed as women have always been a recognized part of the social landscape. Men cross-dressed in the rough-hewn frontier of the mid-nineteenth century, before most women would make the long and dangerous trip from the East. And drag performers in Barbary Coast music halls were not uncommon later, echoing other cultures' use of men in feminine roles, as in Greece, England and Japan. During the 1950s, Jose Sarria reigned as San Francisco's most celebrated drag queen. Ensconced at the Black Cat, a bohemian bar in North Beach not too many blocks from the venerable Palace Theater, Sarria would enact madcap, one-man parodies of such classic operas as *Carmen* to packed houses.

"I decided that if I was going to be labeled a queen, I would be the biggest, best queen there was," he would say to me twenty-five years later. There was a method to his mayhem, and raising gay self-esteem during a time of near-unanimous moral and legal sanctions against homosexuality was a conscious act on Sarria's part. The husky chanteuse would conclude each performance at the famous bar with a brief talk on gay rights, and then lead the entire audience in a rousing version of "God Bless Us Nellie Queens." In 1961, Sarria was the first person to run for public office in the United States as an openly gay candidate. His tally of nearly six thousand votes—for a seat on the city's governing board—sent shock waves through San Francisco's political establishment. The election also necessitated Sarria's first suit of men's clothing.

"Our humor is our key. If we lose that we're dead," he said. "The cross-dressing was part of our humor. Yes, it was our camp. I dressed at the Black Cat to show some of the absurdities expected of women. I poked fun to make gay people laugh, but when they started to laugh too hard I turned the joke around on them. I played one against the other. I wanted the queens to see how ridiculous they were, too."

During those early days there "were maybe twenty-five who dressed like me" in San Francisco, said Sarria, but those uninhibited individuals seemed to give permission for many others to follow. Thirty years later, an extensive network of cross-dressed "Royal Courts"—with Sarria crowned its first empress—had developed throughout the western United States, involving hundreds of gay men in dozens of cities, from Seattle to San Diego, Denver to Monterey. However, among other gay organizations, "We continue to be the most controversial, the most misunderstood and the most disliked," said one prominent member of the drag community. "One can compare the gay court system to the Shriners, Elks or other similar social community-service organizations. No one personally receives monetary gain from the tens of thousands of dollars raised at our functions every year. The money goes directly back into the community."

Bold drag queens have always been the revolutionaries of the gay movement: disfranchised, near the bottom of any community's pecking order (including their own), but empowered with lessons of nonattachment and the realization that they stand with those who have the least to lose in their fight against social injustice. Over the last several decades the confrontational, campy words and images created by public drag personas such as Sarria at the Black Cat, Michelle at the Village Club, Charles Pierce at the Gilded Cage ("Drag is dirty work, but someone has to do it!"), and Doris Fish all over town have inspired their audiences. That's not to mention the vertiginous effect made within their community by a virtual constellation of drag title holders—duchesses and dukes, empresses and emperors, and dowager queens—and the hundreds of other cross-dressed men who have filled San Francisco streets with Gay Pride celebration in June and on other occasions throughout the year; each man standing—politically, at least—center stage.

"In the early days [the 1950s] we really had to stick together," recalled Sarria, "and we'd often meet to talk about police harassment and how to cope with it. When police officers came in you'd telephone the next bar down the line and say, 'Watch out—he's wearing a trenchcoat and a pair of green slacks—and headed your way.'

"That bar would then be alerted. Tell a queen and you tell the world! The law said that an officer had to make himself known. Well, by the time he got to the Black Cat we'd play the national anthem for him and all stand up. He'd always leave just furious."

The Black Cat was internationally known before it was forced to close its doors on Halloween of 1963, when its liquor license was revoked. "There was nobody who came to San Francisco who did not go there," said Sarria. "And I always told them that being homosexual was nothing to be ashamed of and how important it was to be proud and united." As with the clichés of gender role, it was men in dresses who took society's other warped expectations to absurd extremes; making these impositions on the primacy of self transparent for all to see —and thus easier, ultimately, to shed.

It was the so-called effeminate men—those who cross-dressed—who were among the first to fill the front ranks of San Francisco's gay civil rights movement. Such was the case in New York City as well, most notably during the Stonewall riots in late June 1969 that, more than any event, have come to symbolize the modern-day struggle for homosexual equality. One reporter of the three-day riots, which were ignited by routine police harassment of a Village gay bar called the Stonewall Inn, observed that "those usually put down as 'sissies' and 'swishes' showed the most courage and sense during the action. Their bravery and daring saved many people from being hurt, and their sense of humor and 'camp' helped keep the crowds from getting nasty or too violent."

Despite their historic posture, the queens in the East remained largely shunned, economically and socially downcast, even by fellow gays. In San Francisco, the queens continued to provide much of the community nurturing and fundraising savvy needed to fuel the burgeoning movement—traditional feminine skills. But, for the most part, they remained resolutely middle class, even while a new and outwardly classless drag sensibility was beginning to assert itself.

By the late 1960s, a younger generation of gay men were learning how to organize themselves: Angry, well-educated and politically astute, often espousing socialist ideals, they viewed drag queens with resigned embarrassment—a barely understood social inheritance. San Francisco was then sweeping up the Haight-Ashbury neighborhood and its ragtag leftovers from the Summer of Love. And while drug dealers and runaway youths were clearly not welcomed, the gay people who had been such an integral part of the counterculture scene there simply moved elsewhere in the city. This was a decade before a frenzy of downtown highrise construction would inflate rents and living costs to a record level, making San Francisco one of the most expensive urban habitats in the nation. The city then was an enchanted place, still habitable for artists and free spirits of all stripes, alive with exploration on many fronts. The Cockettes were simply a group of gay men who decided to get together and put on a show.

"Their productions were transvestite-glitter-fairie-theatric masques," recalled Ginsberg. "Transsexual dressing is a gay contribution to the realization that we're not a hundred percent masculine or feminine, but a mixture of hormones—and not being afraid of that natural self which the hormones dictate. The Cockettes just brought out into the street what was in the closet, in terms of theatric dress and imaginative theater."

"I don't think any of us were aware of the politics of what we were doing," former Cockette John Rothermel told me some years later. "Since we were so open to interpretation, we were used by radical factions and distorted well beyond what our statement really was— that we were simply having a party. As a statement it was naïve, but it was oh, so fresh and very guileless. It took someone else to come along and say, 'Hey that's outrageous.' Because I think that in being truly outrageous you can't have a self-conscious attitude that betrays what you're doing. At that moment, you lose the spark."

It was only a matter of time before the international press descended on the colorful and irreverent troupe, issuing profiles, celebrity reviews and important magazine covers headlining the "decadence" of it all. Meanwhile, this small band of Aquarian-age drag queens went about their business; living freely, canvassing secondhand stores for props and costumes to adorn their midnight shows, and covering everything with a patina of glitter. "About the only thing we paid money for was the glitter," said Rothermel. "We ransacked the city for it.

"The glitter was about the idea of the ages of light. The whole thing was some sort of rainbow-colored depiction of what it's like to have hallucinogenic experience. It's what we were trying to exemplify in one way or another. We had had numerous enlightening experiences in our lifestyle, and people who have had such experiences usually say that when they find peace of mind or their greatest self-realization, something magical happens—like a great white light that descends upon them or exudes from them. It's sort of like that story about Jesus and the twelve disciples, when the flames appeared on their heads. It was like the idea of having a halo, of being aware of your aura, your magnetism."

The Cockettes were truly ingenuous, but the harsh glare of hype and expectation undermined their fragile magic. They gave their last performance in the autumn of 1972. "The time, the mood, the people were changing," said Worman. "The camaraderie started to deteriorate into dish. The light that had sailed cometlike across the San Francisco sky to illuminate the arrival of the new androgynous Aquarian Age was moving on."

Today, most gay men who remember the group view its ambiguous message as an anachronistic relic from another era—scarcely relevant. But the troupe's tinseled theatrics ignited imaginations, awakened a consciousness in all those they touched in their vain attempt to resurrect innocence, rearrange reality. No doubt unwittingly, they had probed a vital nerve, decorated a rite of passage still remembered and deeply felt by some.

Yet the tradition of radical drag persisted in the city with another group, the Angels of Light. More underground, and perhaps more serious minded about their craft, the Angels still used glitter and campy routines. But their shows seemed to have more of a point: Opposition to the ruling class was the message of their 1975 dada musical extravaganza, *Paris Sights under the Bourgeois Sea*; a warning about imperialism was implicit in *Sci-Clones*, an audacious and often breathtaking mix of Chinese folk opera, Balinese mask drama and science fiction epic; and themes of spiritual quest and attainment were interwoven with Hindu mythology and lavish song and dance routines in 1980's *Holy Cow!* Men and women in the group explained in 1979, "The Angels of Light are an expression that represents an inward dream and vision. It means a positiveness, an idea of sharing the things that are important in uplifting people." Employing great imagination and ingenuity over the years, the Angels' elaborate, baroque productions were mounted with little funds and offered to audiences without charge.

One of the most astute observations about the Angels' ability to move their audiences in ways rare to contemporary theater was offered to me by Adrian Brooks, a poet, novelist, performer and playwright-in-residence with the Angels of Light from 1975 to 1980. Six years after his principal involvement with the group had come to an end, Brooks had the following words to say about the spirit that resonated deep beneath the glitter: "Perhaps, in some way, the Angels of Light danced in the circus arena for all gay people and, in our own unique fashion, exhibited the joy of a spontaneous, childlike self-discovery that was illuminating. The fascination with everything incandescent and luminous, the glorification of the present tense, the suspension of disbelief in the melange of whirling colors and forms—all these things were more than individual creators, more than solo performers taking a star turn. It was its own self-evident proof of existence, its own tapestry and common parable. Not simply invented or used for effect, but gathered up as one collects ample harvest, arms full of the bounty, a tribal celebration that surpasses the mere fact of survival and becomes, in and of itself, a kind of ancient religion that must be discovered afresh by any mystic or dervish.

"We were all dervishes, then, and we knew it even at the time. The fact that the productions were complex but based on simple morality tales, meant that their very creation involved a synthesis which went far beyond the venue of a theatrical presentation. It was incumbent on me—as playwright-in-residence for the group—to suspend formal discipline, abandon judicious editing, circumvent the reflexive application of a writer in order not to impede the free flow of spirit. This was a choice, and it had to be made (and made again and again), despite academic criticism, despite reviewers who failed to understand that camp was taking its place beside other time-honored forms of theater: dance, mask drama, vaudeville, burlesque, commedia del l'arte, guignol. That it was a spirit beyond the rules and could only be entertained by creating a vehicle. Within that vessel, the whorl would come to pass. But if it was ever burdened (as it came to be) by spirit denial or self-consciousness, like love itself it would become crippled, mutant, deformed and lost in its own crazy-house mirror.

"Thus, both the theater and the participants themselves enacted a ritual spirit dance, most remarkable for the fact that it never sought to codify the soul life of the community but, rather, welcomed the outsider as insider and accepted the haphazard as synchronistic. In doing this, the actors themselves—and all who participated—performed offstage psychic roles as well as onstage characters. The most fascinating thing of all was that there was an inversion of self-portrayal, the shadow side of individuals, the minor mask of Janus flitting across the stage—directly contrary to the offstage personality and its effect on the theater as a company. Throughout the course of the theater's life, the company thus represented an intense experiment in self-discovery—for it had profound psychic resonance for the players that surpassed the public face presented. With this curious and mysterious loop, the Angels became as mystical and totemic for the people involved as the theater itself was for the community it served as beacon, spur, paper lantern and, ultimately, overburdened blossom."

Exploration around the issues of gender, dress and androgyny were not only being contained on the city's stages. In the late 1970s, a small circle of gay men came together to reclaim the powerful epithet of *sissy*. Chanted, implied and denied, few words in the male lexicon seem so universally to hit the emotional bottom line. It is a word most gay men grew up with, praying that it didn't mean them, although it usually did, leaving long-remembered wounds.

"It's important to break down sex roles," a member of the outspoken and visible circle said at the time, "and putting on a dress is one of the most obvious ways to do that. The first time I put one on was to attend a political rally." Another "sissy"-identified man told me, "The main reason I wear a dress is because I like the feel of it. I like expressing my kinship with the people I've learned from." But for those in the group there was a deeper meaning to cross-dressing, beyond political confrontation and gender solidarity.

"There's an historical precedent of effeminate men being spiritual leaders all over the world. People are just now becoming aware of that history," one of the men in the group said. "When a man is feminine and a woman masculine, I think that person is more in touch with the total range of human experience. They are more receptive, they have a broader range of sensibility and awareness. It goes far beyond the boundaries of sex roles.

"Sex roles are one of the primary ways in which we identify ourselves. If you could break out of that, I think it would be easy to see how you could break out of other restraints—to think that there is more to the world than what we can see. I'm learning to trust my feelings, and for me that's a spiritual development. That's what magic is. I see my life becoming increasingly shamanistic, but it's a quality that doesn't even apply to this culture."

By the early 1980s, the idea of applying spiritual purpose to cross-dressing was a concept seized, quite literally, by another group of gay men who dubbed themselves the Sisters of Perpetual Indulgence. Controversial even within the gay community and often provoking outrage, especially from the middle-aged burghers of the by-then well-entrenched gay commercial establishment, the Sisters flaunted themselves throughout the city in the distinctive black and white habits of nuns. "Our mission is much bigger than we could ever have imagined," the well-publicized group admitted in 1981. "Our ministry is one of public manifestation and habitual penetration. Our motto is 'Give up the guilt.' And we're going to do that through any form at our means—theater, dance, spiritual expression and therapy."

In the tradition of actual nuns, the Sisters dedicated themselves to service to their community: fundraising, educating on the issues of health and sexuality, staging public healing rituals and participating in political protest, including one demonstration honoring the slain nuns and laywomen of El Salvador. In fact, they involved themselves with the type of work that had always seemed the stock in trade of the city's queens. And like their predecessors, they found the greatest opposition to their cross-dressing coming from other gay men. At the Central American vigil, for instance, it was the gay monitors of the march who cajoled and threatened them to leave for fear of negative publicity. "One man said we were an embarrassment," a Sister said, "but I've been one most of my life anyway. They couldn't understand that we weren't making fun of nuns, that we're adding more to the nunhood than had been added in the recent past, and that it was an outreach toward the other Christian groups participating—who, by the way, made no comment on their own."

Keeping whimsy, mockery and outrage alive was probably the Sisters' most significant accomplishment—sustaining qualities that were rapidly diminishing as the gay community's self-consciousness and power grew. "So much of the political movement has become narrow," one of the Sisters said. "We might be the answer to the evolution of coming out as a gay person."

"Humor and sexuality are at the roots of spirituality," they explained to me. "They are the transcendental experiences that take us beyond morality. Through humor and sexuality we can realize visions and feelings beyond everyday life. The truest religion in the world is theater, or ritual. On a broad philosophical range, we are being religious in the truest sense, but merely by definition. Being nuns is a practical application of our spiritual feelings as gay men."

The Sisters of Perpetual Indulgence kept their communal vows for a few years, and then splintered. Some members continued to wear their habits, standing out against the city's changing panorama as lone—almost totemic—figures. Many of the Sisters were already active in the newly created fairie movement, where the interplay of ritual, androgyny and pagan spirituality seemed to be intuitively understood and less hidebound by cultural convention and dogma.

In this brief history, cross-dressed men appear as the rude and anarchical element disrupting the surface of society's status quo. And to all these men, one *feeling* has seemed central: that cross-dressing is a natural, almost instinctive gesture, a remnant of some misunderstood and long-forgotten tradition. When compared to the cross-dress of shamans in other cultures, the drag worn by the men described here could be viewed as a ritual-fetish-power object, enabling catharsis in themselves and others. Prescribed forms of dress codified around gender roles is the most pervasive means of social control—a tacit spell which cross-dressing immediately shatters.

But to understand this better, let's return to the stage of the Palace Theater and, in particular, a life. This young man is central to the legacy of radical drag on the West Coast, which he eventually left. So in spring 1981, I traveled to New York City to catch up with this errant angel of light, and here is his story.

He discovered his name in a Jean Cocteau novel. Somewhere, he says, there is a line about a blood-red hibiscus: a flower that blooms briefly and then shrivels. "That interested me very much."

I'm sitting on a park bench in Sheridan Square playing with the sound of the word, letting it pass between my lips. "Hi-bis-cus." The word has a powerful, almost passionate, connotation for me—representing, as it does, a fantastic period in gay history. A wrinkle in time that, sadly, bears as much relevance to the lives of gay people today as a chapter from *The Wizard of Oz*.

Hibiscus. Spawned in New York, bred in San Francisco and on the road in the rest of the world. I'm staring at his name now on a billboard high above the square, set in hundreds of tiny red sequins stitched in place by a team of elderly women in Brooklyn. The slightly ludicrous, and very gay, icon glitters over the blasé midday crowds, advertising a new act. The whole thing reminds me of a not-too-distant past when being gay meant something different. But I resist sentiment and remind myself that glitter—and all that it reflected—had its day. I express no laments but entertain a curiosity.

I find Hibiscus in a spacious West Village loft apartment littered with gaudy props, bamboo furniture from the 1940s and other nostalgic knickknacks. I'm startled when he answers the door. I did not expect this handsome young man, more likely to peer from the pages of a fashion magazine than down from a glittered billboard on Sheridan Square. He adjusts a wool cravat, and I wonder to what extent his dress and careful manner are calculated. I indulge a shift of setting and drag and—for a moment—am amused to find myself playing Louella Parsons to his Jayne Mansfield. "I've always been fascinated by her," he later admits. "I love her entire life. She had heart-shaped everything."

Like his environment, Hibiscus's life has been eclectic, a collection of odd events. He's been a performer all his life, a passion that has led him to some very strange places, from performing at Black Panther headquarters in blackface to singing and dancing "under a Mafia whip" in Paris.

"I was born in Bronxville, in Westchester," he begins. "Then my family moved to Florida. My parents lost everything in the subdivisions that sank." His father decided to pursue a career in acting and returned to New York. Eventually, the rest of the family followed and, "We lived in an apartment on First Avenue and Ninth Street that cost twenty-eight dollars a month and had sloping floors. We camped out in sleeping bags. It was interesting."

Both his parents became regulars at the Caffe Cino and other off-off-Broadway theaters. Hibiscus, then George Harris, worked as a child model in commercials and played bit parts at the Cino, La Mama and other showcases. It was the early 1960s. He was thirteen when he left home to live with another man. "My parents were very liberal and, considering the financial situation at the time, very understanding. There was never any question about my gayness. I mean, my mother told me that I was. I always knew that I was different."

According to Allen Ginsberg, the precocious young actor had a circle of friends that included Irving Rosenthal, who had edited William Burroughs's *Naked Lunch* at Grove Press, and filmmaker Jack Smith, whose *Flaming Creatures* remains a classic of independent cinema. Both men espoused controversial and visionary points of view through their work. "Jack Smith's film involved dressing people up in transsexual costumes with great adornment; veils and spangles and beautiful makeup. And Irving had the theory of having everything free," said Ginsberg. "So Hibiscus brought all that new culture west."

When he was seventeen, Hibiscus had an offer to drive to California with Peter Orlovsky and another friend. "I was still very Brooks Brothers—you know, short hair and lots of madras shirts. I was lucky to catch the whole love-child bit just in time.

"We arrived in San Francisco, and one of my friends decided he was going to start a printing commune in Japantown. I started to grow my hair and became a vegetarian. I lived the life of an angel there. I was celibate and started to wear long robes and headdresses. I'd go down to Union Square and pick roses out of the garbage and run around singing all my old Broadway favorites: 'You Are Beautiful,' 'If I Loved You.' " The headdresses kept getting bigger and bigger.

"Everything was free then. Free medical care; a free newspaper, *The Kaliflower*; and we even used to distribute free food to the needy. I had also been doing this show at various communes around town—the Kitchen Sluts Floor Show. I'd go with a couple of other friends and scrub down their entire kitchen, then present cum bread. The making of the bread was rather controversial. It was a whole spiritual thing for me at the time, although a lot of people didn't like it."

The city was alive with counterculture entertainment. The Grateful Dead and the Jefferson Airplane gave regular concerts in the parks, and groups like the Committee and the Floating Light Opera attracted large followings. A small movie theater in North Beach, the Palace, was also featuring Nocturnal Dream Shows at midnight. "I wanted to do a New Year's show," Hibiscus recalls, "and the Palace invited me to do it there. About eight of us—including Dusty Dawn, Scrumbly, Goldie Glitters and Kreemah Ritz—got up on the stage in drag and danced to an old recording of 'Honky Tonk Woman.' The audience surged toward the stage, screaming. I was dumbfounded." The 1970s had begun; the Cockettes were born.

A bit of worldly sophistication, a touch of transplanted glamour and years of practical experience—even at such an early age—were all elements of Hibiscus's carpetbag brought west. San Francisco then seemed like a romantic but somewhat faded European town. Lacking much formal education ("I went to the school of hard knocks"), Hibiscus nevertheless projected an undefinable authority through his soft-focus persona. "I feel that I have always had a certain energy at my fingertips, a spirit for bringing creative people together," he says. "It must have come from some other place. It's a well I've always drawn from."

The foundling troupe took its cue from Hibiscus and dipped into the inchoate pastiche of popular American culture, then so abundantly at their disposal. The Cockettes exposed and played with the sexual and cultural confusion of the times and emerged, if not with diamonds, then at least with rhinestones. "Our second show was *Paste on Paste*,"

Hibiscus recalls. "It opened with Kreemah Ritz showing a novice how to put on coconut breasts and closed with the entire cast singing 'You'll Never Walk Alone' to the Virgin Mary." The group staged one revue per week, usually with a budget of less than 20 dollars. Backdrops were painted sheets, sets were fashioned out of cardboard and castoff junk from the streets. "You could do things like that then."

Gone with the Showboat to Oklahoma, Myth Thing, Pearls Over Shanghai followed in rapid succession, and the group began to attract widespread attention. Janis Joplin, John Lennon and Truman Capote were among the celebrities who sent notes backstage. *Rolling Stone, Paris Match* and other major periodicals published feature articles; the troupe was featured in several underground movies; and the theater was packed to the chandeliers every Saturday night. "No one had seen anything like it before. It was totally freeform," explains Hibiscus. "Instead of dressing in drag, I was dressing more as gods. We were all creating mythic figures."

"It was a revolution in theater," recalls Sylvester, who left a church choir in nearby Oakland to join the motley group—a significant step toward his career as an international pop music star.

Smart-alecky pluck, a "let's-put-on-a-show" attitude and plenty of glitter: An ingenuous fantasy had fermented into a show-biz phenomenon. But the scene began to attract adults more stony than stoned out, and their somber appraisal of the group's commercial potential meant that Hibiscus's days at the Palace were numbered.

One night after a performance of *Madama Butterfly*, he came home to find his apartment building burned down. He took off for the country to recover from his loss, but stayed too long. Upon his return he discovered that he had been voted out of the troupe. His insistence that their shows be free did not agree with the group's newfound ambitions to seek fame and fortune in New York.

The Cockettes took off (with someone else dressed as their founding figure) and opened November 5, 1971 amid great hoopla at the Anderson Theater in the East Village. The group had been taken up by New York's cultural avant-garde, and even the *Washington Post* said that their debut was the biggest off-Broadway opening the city had ever seen. Still, the group failed miserably; a classic case of too much, too soon. It was while hastily exiting at intermission with other attending celebrities that Gore Vidal said, "No talent is not enough," offering a premonition of headlines to come: COAST TRANSVESTITE TROUPE A DRAG, FOR THIS THEY HAD TO COME FROM FRISCO? Other critics argued that their impact would be felt for decades. Nevertheless, the troupe soon returned home, and despite another year of performances for an enthusiastic hometown audience, its inner light was never to shine quite as bright.

Meanwhile, Hibiscus remained in San Francisco and continued to pursue his ideal of free theater. While in the mountains, he had met a stranger who had told him that he was an angel—or at least one in training—and so he called his new group the Angels of Light.

Their first performance was Christmas 1971 atop the city's staid Nob Hill. With he and a lover dressed as Mary and Joseph and friends dressed as angels, the troupe enacted a mock Nativity scene in Grace Cathedral, as a counterpoint to high mass. "Everyone there kind of liked us," Hibiscus explained, "but the police came anyway." It was the troupe's first show, and many others were to follow, including performances in ghetto neighborhoods where more than one rock was hurled through a theater window.

"We did shows like *Flamingo Stampede* and *Moroccan Operetta*, which was like *Kabuki* in Balinese drag. Allen Ginsberg did his first drag onstage in *Blue Angel Cabaret*." Ginsberg remembers that performance well. "I dressed up as a sort of Shakespearean nurse with a long cone hat with the moon and stars pasted on it and a blue gown, which was appropriate to Blake's 'Nurse's Song.' Hibiscus and I were lovers at the time. He was a very beautiful man, was very kind to me, and gave me a place to do an act—to sing Blake, actually. He had a kind of angelic imagination."

Eventually Hibiscus left San Francisco and returned home to New York, where he was reunited with his family. With parents, siblings and a lover, Angel Jack (discovered while hanging from a cross), Hibiscus began to perform as an East Coast incarnation of the Angels. Once again he attracted notoriety, including the interest of Belgian choreographer Maurice Bejart, who financed the group's first European tour. The troupe spent much of the rest of the 1970s traveling throughout the continent in various shows and configurations, always with a strong cult following.

He's been back on home ground for some time now, determined to stay put with a new cabaret act—at least for a while. The concept of free theater is still a precious one for him, but these are leaner times than the late 1960s. Today, even sparkle has its price.

For Hibiscus, the world is a somewhat more serious place. Gaiety, in all senses of the word, and especially within the homosexual milieu, seems posed on the edge of exhaustion. "I'm afraid I'll slip and say something that will outrage a million mad queens," he suddenly blurts out in the middle of the interview. An impish grin interjects. "But then, there aren't many mad queens left anymore." There's something happening within the gay movement today that worries him, a growing attitude almost too intangible for him to express satisfactorily.

"I don't know if I'm going to say this right, but I have to: I'm scared to death of what's emerging in the gay middle class. I was at the Saint [a trendy, high-tech disco] in costume the other night and I was petrified. I felt like Jezebel when she came into the room with a scarlet dress. No one wanted to go near me. Everyone was so afraid to be different. I call it a gay middle-class vacuum. This conformity is a dangerous thing.

"I think that people who are gay verge on being angels, or wayward angels. Gayness is a gift. I know a lot of people who feel that gay men, in particular, can be the most powerful force for transformation within our society. Gay men have often pushed society to new limits, such as with the Cockettes. All I really want to say is that the gay middle class can track you down."

Try as they may, it would be a futile task for anyone to track down Hibiscus. "My idea is to be a 1950s drag queen for today," he says in a sudden change of mood, "a kind of Liberace for the 1980s. I want to take the act back to Europe. And, of course, to San Francisco; I lived so intensely there, every street has a haunting memory. I guess I still have a semiaudience out there, although most of them seem to have moved to Oregon."

Most creative people know that to dissect inner compulsions is to destroy the soul of their work. The content of Hibiscus's art seems ephemeral: camp humor, secondhand glamour and a child's perennial delight. He may be a trickster with a tacky mirror, but somehow it's impossible not to take a look.

I had planned to return for another visit after our first talk that April afternoon, but I never got the chance. A year later, in May 1982, George Harris was dead. He was among the first in a legion of angels to die from AIDS.

WILL ROSCOE

LIVING

THE TRADITION:

GAY AMERICAN

INDIANS

Gay people today, in their search for self-definition, have turned to other cultures for a reflection of themselves. This inquiry into the legends, literature and art of other places and times has resulted in the creation of a new myth—the idea of a global gay heritage. For gay Americans, this willful act of re-creation has begun on home ground, nourished by the rich vein of fable and folklore peculiar to the peoples who have inhabited the continent before and since European colonization.

During the past decade, gay American Indians have begun to reexamine those once-honored traditions and reclaim the roles they played in tribal life. In doing so, as the following chapter shows, they contribute new insight into the potential roles and identities gay people can fulfill in their communities. As Jonathan Katz points out in Gay American History, *the recovery of the history of gay roles in traditional American societies "is a task in which both gay and Native peoples have a common interest."*

Rocks crunch under boots as the small group of dark-skinned men and women and their light-skinned friends make their way up the trail. At daybreak on a crisp October morning, they have convened atop the Bay Area's Mount Tamalpais for a very special occasion.

"This is far enough," says a young woman, and the group huddles on a bend in the trail. She lays down her bundle and begins unwrapping its contents.

The sky is brilliantly blue. Below us, a sea of fog obliterates all signs of the great city nearby.

The delicious smell of burning sweetgrass—the cool, smooth surface of a clay pipe—the dark, rich pungency of native tobacco. She sings, in another tongue, verses to the four directions. The pipe goes around the circle twice. Each takes a blessing from its smoke, some with prayers in yet other tongues, all praying, hoping, thinking together for a brief period.

And in moments it's done. The group straggles down the mountain, relinquishing the trail to tourists and sightseers.

Yet this simple ceremony marked a momentous victory in the history of lesbian and gay people. Gay American Indians are restoring the spiritual and cultural role they once held throughout this continent, in the time before the white men came.

———————

The modern emergence of gay American Indians can be traced largely to the founding of the Gay American Indian organization (GAI), conceived in 1975 by Barbara Cameron (Lakota Sioux) and Randy Burns (Northern Paiute) in San Francisco. In the years that followed, GAI grew from a social club into a national organization, and individual gay Indians came out on the reservation and in the city, gaining recognition as artists, writers, professionals and community workers—visible members of both Indian and gay communities.

In 1985, with some six hundred members, Burns could claim, "GAI is the oldest ongoing organization of dark-skinned gay people here in the Bay Area still breaking down racism in our community."

"It's taken more generations for us to get to where we're at now," says Erna Pahe (Navajo), who has served as president of the GAI board of directors, "but we've found a new tool now and that tool is speaking out."

"Times have changed," says Burns. "I see gay Indian people in key positions in our Indian community, getting appointed to city government. I'm seeing ourselves like the Harvey Milk or Alice B. Toklas political clubs; I think down the road we will have an impact, both in the Indian community and the gay and lesbian community."

But gay American Indians are asserting more than their political rights. They are forging an "Indian" definition of gay identity that is at once contemporary yet drawn from tradition.

"We are special!" declares Maurice Kenny (Mohawk) in his poem "Winkte." The word comes up frequently when gay American Indians talk about their past and present roles in society.

"The tradition of the gay Indian has always been a real special one," says writer Beth Brant (Mohawk). "Like someone who is touched by something special."

"Gay Indians were special to a lot of tribal groups," says Burns. "It's not just a sexual thing. It's that we have roots here in North America."

The place of American Indians in white cultural awareness has always been disproportionate to their numbers. In *The Primal Mind*, Jamake Highwater describes the impact of nonindustrialized peoples on Western art and culture as "the ultimate irony of our era: Those who have been most utterly defeated have become most influential."

If this is true, then the struggles and victories of this tiny band of American Indians may indeed influence how all of us come to view gay identity.

Realities

"My parents were forced to go to BIA [Bureau of Indian Affairs] school. If they were caught speaking their tribal language they were punished. They couldn't practice their religion. They had to go to church every Sunday. And when you're at BIA school nine months out of the year it rubs off."

—Randy Burns

When contemporary gay American Indians took their first tentative steps out of the closet, they encountered homophobia of surprising vehemence among nongay Indians. "We do not want to receive your publications," wrote the editor of a national Indian journal to *RFD* (an alternative gay men's magazine) in 1977, "because they encourage a kind of behavior which our elders consider not normal and a detriment to our way of life."

Paula Gunn Allen (Laguna Pueblo/Sioux) debated for a year before publishing her essay on Native American lesbianism, "Beloved Women," in 1981. "I decided I could take the risk—I don't live there. But there are young gay Indians who do and they have to hear this."

According to Allen, traditional leaders are afraid of homosexuality being used as an excuse to take away their lands, homes, or children. In the 1920s, the Bureau of Indian Affairs did indeed gather pornographic gossip about the Pueblo Indians to win support for legislation unfavorable to Pueblo land claims. Burns also blames government policies, along with "the Christian influence with our people."

Whatever the cause of Native homophobia, the consequence for gay Indians is aptly termed "double oppression"—rejection from other Indians for being gay, discrimination in the white world for being Indian. Gay Indians in contemporary America have won their self-esteem through ongoing confrontation with racial discrimination, homophobia and isolation. The story begins, for many, "on the rez"—the Indian reservations and reserves scattered throughout rural America.

"Before Alcatraz it was just about impossible to stand up and say who you were," explains Kenny, referring to the occupation of that island by Indian activists in 1969. "If you had a job you'd get fired. Your family might disown you. You certainly would be ridiculed."

Burns's own experience on the Pyramid Lake reservation in Nevada bears this out. "I was always, constantly challenged to fight, to be a man. That went on until I was in tenth grade.

"We've even had incidents where gay Indian people have been murdered, sadistically, on our reservations. When you read it in the local news it doesn't say 'gay Indian person,' but other contacts we have say, 'That brother was gay.' "

When not confronted with open hostility, gay Indians face silence and invisibility. As Erna Pahe explains, "Even when I go back home now, we never talk about it. It's the activities or ceremonies that our family is going to. The spiritual way is always put as a priority. Your personal side of life is a little different."

For many gay Indians, the path to a positive self-image begins with a break from reservation and family. "When I came out to California I finally got that feeling that I had control over my own life," says Pahe. "When I did go back to the reservation I was ready to deal with, 'Hey, I'm just me, but I'm independent and I do have my life to live, whichever way I choose to live it.' "

Traditions

> In traditional Indian societies, berdaches were respected, perhaps feared, because their condition manifested power given them by the super-natural.
>
> —C. Callender and L. Kochems

Between the homophobia of missionaries and government agents and that of Christianized Indians themselves, memory of the traditional part of gay people among Native America tribes has been lost, denied or repressed. The link to the past on which gay Indians are building an identity today often resides on dusty library shelves: in old accounts by missionaries and explorers; in dry, technical journals by anthropologists.

The earliest observers used the French term *berdache* to describe the men they saw who "did woman's work and wore woman's dress." They also learned of women who excelled in male activities, as hunters, warriors, chiefs and healers. Today, new scholarly interest has revealed a surprisingly widespread distribution of these roles, from the Arctic Circle to Central America. GAI's own history project has compiled a computerized data base of references on the *berdache* in over 130 North American societies.

Cross-dressing has always drawn the greatest attention from Western observers. Over the past hundred years, anthropologists have introduced a variety of terms to classify the *berdache*—"hermaphrodite," "trans-vestite," "gender-crossing"—all focusing on the (presumed) desire or intention to change gender. In fact, this has led many to ask, with theorist Kenneth Plummer, "Why should one even begin to contemplate the notion that the *berdache* has anything at all to do with homosexuality in our terms?"

Other observers, however, have focused on the roles *berdaches* played in their communities. Among the Kutenai of Montana, for example, women sometimes gained fame as warriors and guides. Among the Mohave, women known as *hwame* were powerful shamans and healers. The male *berdache*, on the other hand, often specialized in the arts and crafts of his tribe—pottery, basketry, weaving, bead- and leatherwork—activities that were traditionally the work of women.

In the 1920s, the anthropologist Ruth Benedict described *berdache* roles as niches that tribal societies created for individuals who, in another time and place, might be labeled "deviants" or "homosexuals." In her often reprinted book *Patterns of Culture*, Benedict wrote, "The possible usefulness of 'abnormal' types is illustrated from every part of the world."

A lively debate has erupted on the relationship of the *berdache* to contemporary gay identity. At the core of the problem are the differences in world view that have underscored the conflict between Indians and Europeans for centuries. In the case of sex roles, anthropologists Callender and Kochems conclude: "North American Indian definitions of gender generally reversed the criteria used in Western societies: They emphasized occupational pursuits and social behavior rather than choice of sexual object."

In the flurry of words, few seem to have noticed the absence of the one voice most qualified to speak on the meaning of Indian traditions—that of Indians themselves.

Connections

To the question—what does the *berdache* have to do with gay people today?—gay American Indians have a positive response. "It has everything to do with who we are now," says Brant. "As gay Indians, we feel that connection with our ancestors."

"We are living in the spirit of our traditional gay Indian people," claims Burns. "The gay Indian person is probably more traditional and spiritual and more creative than his or her straight counterpart because that was the traditional role we played. The old people, women especially, will tell you that."

Allen points out that every Indian tribe had its own word for the "special" men and women who preferred the activities of the opposite sex. *Homosexual* is not useful because it focuses on sexuality, whereas most tribes consider role and occupation more important. *Gay* is Allen's choice because it includes men and women and has come to mean a "lifestyle" as well as a sexual pattern.

Navajo mythology tells of a supernatural *berdache* who helps the men and women reunite after a quarrel has led them to live on separate sides of a river. Pahe's own philosophy reflects some of the traditional wisdom in this story. "The straight community is so worried about staying within their little box and making sure that I look like a female or that I really play the role of a male image. In our culture, in our gay world, anybody can do anything. We can sympathize, we can really feel how the other sex feels." Pahe sees gay Indians as "the one group of people that can really understand both cultures. We are special— because we're able to deal with all of life in general."

For Brant the connections are spiritual as well. "If there is a spiritual awakening for Indian people, it may be the gay Indians who are seeing the visions. At least, I feel that way myself. Why was I touched in this way? Why do I have this power? I know why: I have to go out and share it."

Helping "our people," serving the community, contributing skills —this is what gay Indians see themselves as having in common with the *berdache* of past times. "Gay Indian people are taking care of their community," says Burns. What gives this claim credence is the response of Indian leaders and elders who now appear willing to accept openly gay Indians as legitimate members of the Indian community.

"One of the most positive things we've done," explains Pahe, "is to be aware of other programs' problems. When their funds are being cut and what they really need is a whole bunch of Indians to go over there at City Hall to speak up, the agencies say, 'If you want people to come out there, call GAI.' "

In the same spirit, the organization sponsors the annual Honoring American Indian Women awards dinner, to acknowledge the contributions of local Indian women active in community affairs. At a recent event, attended by some two hundred Bay Area Indians, Burns and Pahe awarded certificates of appreciation while children ran up and down the aisles and nongay elders mixed comfortably with young gay Indians, who served generous slices of a giant banquet cake decorated with GAI's logo.

Outreach such as this has paid off. Because of their access to the political networks of the San Francisco gay community, nongay Indian leaders have begun to seek GAI's help in making contact with local politicians. Burns sees this as another role based on Indian tradition. "In many tribes, we were the go-betweens. Because of our skill and our education today, we are the go-betweens between the Indian community and the governmental bodies."

Salyoqah Channey (Seminole), a nongay elder who has been active in both East and West Coast American Indian organizations, recently joined the GAI board of directors. Why is a grandmother working with gay Indians? "I think they're being very, very helpful because they're enlightening non-Indians to our needs. They're doing a real civic duty. They're trying very hard to help our people and that's why I'm involved."

By drawing on such traditional Indian values as community service, mutual aid, and respect for elders, Burns believes that GAI has fostered a new attitude among nongay Indians. "When you have elders coming to us, asking us to be part of their ceremony, that's spiritual, that's cultural, that's Indian."

Identity

The day I saw a poster declaring the existence of an organization of Gay American Indians, I put my face into my hands and sobbed with relief. . . . I understood then that being gay is a universal quality.

—Judy Grahn

If the men skilled at women's work and the women who became hunters and chiefs were fulfilling "gay roles," as gay American Indians claim, we might well question the assumption in Western society that being gay is only a matter of sexual preference. After all, American Indian societies supported their gay people and, perhaps for millennia, observed them sympathetically. These many tribes, who viewed gay people in terms of social roles as well as sexuality, may indeed have had the greater insight into our nature.

What does it mean to have a history, to be able to say, "We have roots here in North America"—to feel yourself part of a tradition?

Among the Cheyenne Indians, gay men were called *hemaneh*. Sometimes the *hemaneh* went with the other men on war parties, dressed in his best finery and totally unarmed. He charged the enemy first, alone, galloping at full speed. The Cheyenne believed that the sight of their fearless gay brother would surprise the enemy into wasting bullets, leaving them defenseless in the ensuing attack. As for the *hemaneh*—his magic would protect him.

This is what it means to have roots—to know you're not alone and not the first; to know you have, like the *hemaneh*, sources of inner strength to overcome obstacles and to do it, in gay fashion, with a flair.

Allen hints at a bond that Indian and non-Indian gay people share, as the "special" people of their respective cultures. "It all has to do with spirit," she says, "with restoring an awareness of our spirituality as gay people."

Gay American Indians are offering us a chance to share in their tradition, to make their history a part of ours—or as Allen put it, speaking at the 1979 Gay March on Washington, "I welcome all of you who have come here as old souls, returning to restore to this land the gayness it once had."

MALCOLM BOYD

TELLING A LIE

FOR CHRIST?

There is no relationship more curious than the one that exists between gay people and organized religion, for they have long been among its greatest sufferers and saints. The Christian churches, for example, have cast gay people from grace—these faggots and crones, survivors of burning times past—yet, over the centuries, gay people have continuously found ways to integrate themselves into their very heart: the "profane" made sacred, in a circuitous dance, until one has been rendered indistinguishable from the other. To its very marrow, the church has been informed by gay spiritual energy.

This is a paradox, of course, given the historic persecution of sexual minorities in religion's name and the unequivocal rejection of the church by them. Yet, there is a quality about gay people that is spirit, that is religion, only they have been denied experience of it, and so, in turn, tragically deny it to themselves. A circle completes itself: the "sacred" made profane.

While the story of gay people and the church has been essentially one of betrayal from the fourteenth century to now, gay spirituality continues to reveal itself in many forms. These representative words from the diverse participants at a first-ever conference on gay spirituality held in Berkeley, California, January 1986, are telling about the urgency of the gay message to traditional Western religion: "Gay people hold the key to the next stage of human evolution—a world in which it is possible to cooperate without competing," said a teacher of meditation. "We stress that gay people are different and that if we deny this we become second-class nongay people—that is, homosexuals," declared a Buddhist priest. "We're different, a germ of an androgynous tradition," explained an Anglican scholar. "Being gay is about being in the world in a different and essential way. Androgyny permits all things," said a lesbian psychic. "There's something about gay people that goes beyond sexual orientation. All throughout history we've been very different from heterosexual people. I believe there is something about gay people that is profoundly religious," said a shaman. "A gay person cannot live an unexamined life," concluded a poet.

In the following chapter, Malcolm Boyd, an openly gay Episcopal priest, says that gay people must have "the courage and audacity to create our own theology." Boyd, widely known for his many books and outspoken activism in the civil rights and peace movements, feels that gay people "are a broken people who understand the brokenness of others. We need to claim God and morality, rather than let either be used oppressively against us." He argues that, despite its apparent hostility, the church has actually attracted disproportionally high numbers of gay people to it; a refuge and vibrant world filled with the art, ritual, mystery, ideals, and many others like themselves.

"Gay men and lesbians are a deeply moral people," Boyd says, even while recognizing morality as the most effective weapon used against them. It is an awareness made all the more poignant by his own experience. Ordained a priest in 1955, Boyd publicly declared his sexual orientation over twenty years later in the pages of The New York Times. *As a result, he was shunned and denounced by many from within the church. But no reaction cut as deep as the one he received the very next day when a trusted friend burned every one of his books in her backyard.*

E dward Carpenter wrote that the "real significance of the homosexual temperament" is that "the non-warlike man and the nondomestic woman . . . sought new outlets for their energies . . . different occupations." So, they became "the initiators of new activities," especially in the arts and crafts, spirituality, shamanism and priesthood.

Homosexuals have long sought a refuge within the church, only to be rebuffed or injured by it. Yet there seemed, for a long while, no *better* place to be. For single men could hide under the complex but convenient label of "celibacy"; also, the church afforded an ambiance of "high culture." Here, one found music, art, theater, performance —as well as the highest reaches of intellectual life in the form of theology.

In 1951, when I departed a Hollywood career for the Episcopal priesthood, I felt the strong attraction of precisely these qualities within the church. My unmarried status would presumably henceforth go largely unnoticed; or, at least, it would be cast in a traditional framework of social acceptance. "Father Boyd is, well, a priest. No, he isn't married. He's a *priest.*" Too, I could work and live with a large number of other homosexuals as closeted as myself. Liturgical drama and music, ritual and its high and colorful accouterments, would surround me.

The homophobia within this very structure, however, deeply shocked me as I gradually became aware of its hard reality. It was due to the self-hatred, the low esteem generated by closeted homosexuals who were both my leaders and my peers. So, instead of joy, I discovered cynicism, bitterness, frustration, and considerable anguish. There was an underlying emphasis on Good Friday's suffering and sacrifice; one identified strongly with *it*, while the liberation of Easter was fraught with fantasy and remained distant.

Homosexual life within the structure of the church was intricate and coded as society seems to have been, say, in the Ming Dynasty. Hiddenness was the name of the game. Two men could live together openly—two priests or a priest and a layman—but such a relationship must abide by the strictest rules of "correct" public behavior. Not only was there no security in such a relationship; there was also no peace. I know, because I lived in one. The tensions created and exacerbated by the situation were as corrosive to love as acid to substance.

The negative stereotypes of traditional churchly homophobia were constantly served and reinforced. As a consequence, it was deadly for a priest to be open in the underground homosexual community of his city or town. Blackmail was a ready weapon; the insinuation of the possibility was even worse.

Many gay priests were beloved within their parishes for their sensitivity, androgyny, gaiety of spirit, wisdom, wit and sophistication. They tended to be lovers of the arts and brought unusual openness, imagination and flair to the pursuit of their tasks.

Yet at the least suggestion of homosexuality, they could be simply and peremptorily dismissed. Within a matter of hours, many were sent on their way into ignominious exile. For numerous older men it was too late to start a new career; their "security" was smashed by rumor and angry retaliation, leaving a gay priest without resources, mercy or love.

The church remains today as closeted a community as any other major social institution, but with an unusually high proportion of homosexuals. Some sources within the church say that at least a third, if not more, of the hierarchy and clergy are gay.

In my first parish as a young priest, I knew instantly who were the other gay men present. Two of them became my closest friends. Their home was the place I could go to let my hair down, be myself, take a lover visiting from out of town, and find an occasion of unabashed joy. Of course, these two friends were closeted, too, anxious that no one suspect their sexual orientation. Yet one of them was unquestionably the best cook in the entire parish. His casseroles were the most sought-after dishes at our parish potluck suppers.

I noticed how church membership seemed to provide a semblance of needed structure and support for their relationship. They worked hard for the church, were genuinely loved and accepted, participated in a wide variety of activities. But years later, after my departure, a homophobic priest (in their view) arrived and forced them out. They were deeply hurt by his seemingly capricious use of priestly power to humiliate and banish them.

Another gay man in our parish was the church organist. On some Sunday mornings he was absent without an explanation. This remained a mystery to most of the congregation. But we gays shared the secret knowledge of his serious alcohol problem. He was absolutely closeted—except at the baths.

A priest who lived nearby came out to me as a gay man, and we had sex on several occasions. He took great risks, I remember, by picking up sailors and bringing them home to the rectory. Later, he wondered why he had never been made a bishop.

One of the richest men in the city was a church member at a posh, elitist parish on the other side of town. He used to invite me to lunch at his home. He was also a closeted homosexual with a drinking problem. He "came out" one night when, dressed in women's clothing and driving his car at a high speed, he killed a pedestrian. It was our understanding in the gay community that a settlement of 1 million dollars was allegedly required to get him off.

A beloved older priest in another parish was murdered one night— and his name splashed over the front pages of the newspaper next day. The priest's bloody body was found stark naked except for a T-shirt, we read. He had been stabbed to death by what police called an itinerant. Homosexuality was not mentioned in the story, but it was a sensational subliminal reality and became a hot piece of gossip hawked at nearly every gathering in the city.

When I was called to be a college chaplain at a Midwestern university campus and to head a church in the community, I found homosexuality honeycombed virtually *everywhere* . . . and absolutely hidden. A dozen men in the town had tried meeting secretly once a week to have sex and share their hidden lives, but the police found them out—on a tip from one of their wives. Their probation was: Never do anything like that again. Now they were *really* on puppets' strings, operated by their confused and angry wives.

A male student on the campus came to see me one day. He had been drinking a beer in a bar when a couple of fraternity men invited him back to their Greek house. Upon arriving there, they took him into a room, locked the door, stripped him, held a revolver to his head, and demanded that he suck their cocks—and those of another half-dozen men who had crowded into the room. He appeared homosexual to the fraternity men because he had long hair, wore unconventional garb, and liked poetry.

I slept with a number of priests, but it was better for me when I found a part-time lover who was a waiter and a short-order cook in a nearby city. I could relax with him and share warm intimacy, whereas there was always a high stress involved in relationships with other closeted priests who were as worried about disclosure as I was and had a tendency to feel guilty because of the savage contradictions between their public images and personal truths.

My life was split down the middle. Friday nights, I had sex with my lover in a motel. Sunday morning, I conducted church services for people who were predominantly members of nuclear families—and would have been shocked beyond belief if they had known about the *other* side of my life. Sometimes I drank too much when the pressure of my hiddenness was too hard to bear. One night when I was driving and drunk, cops who stopped me—and saw my clerical collar—said, "Go home, Father. We're not going to take you in because, if we did, you'd be destroyed. Please, just go home, Father." I did.

Once, a gay man was deeply in love with me, and I with him. But I could no more have lived an open life with him—worked out a really honest, naturally productive, good relationship—than I could, under the circumstances, have rocketed to the moon. We parted. He became an alcoholic; I continued my lonely, driven, utterly incomplete life. Yes, we *could* have shared a full, realized, meaningful life together, *but* it would have required that I leave the priesthood. I was unable to contemplate it then. Incidentally, he was also a member of the church.

The church has generally been an alien environment for gay people. There are exceptional parishes that have been accepting, warm and healthy, but they are few and far between. "Telling a lie for Christ" has sadly been a requirement that not only killed much of gay spirituality, but seriously maimed any kind of spirituality. This has been a real plague in seminary life. And it is the closeted ecclesiastical figures in high places who surround patriarchal hierarchies, creating a climate of lies and misunderstanding, preventing honesty and truth.

Organized religion of any kind presents hard problems for an individual. Great spiritual truths get waylaid amid cold bureaucracy, selfish careerism, the primacy of materialism, and sacrifice of original ideals. Yet it is necessary to engage in an ever-present struggle for the cleansing and reawakening of organized religion. When its soul is tarnished, political ramifications lead to antijustice authoritarianism and cruel persecution. Gay people have much to teach organized religion about unconditional love in openness and vulnerability, the truth of human diversity and reality, and the nature of God as the Creator of diversity, the Lover who created life.

We gay people, in our diversity, will never follow simply one path in spirituality. We will be everywhere—into major Christian denominations and the fairie movement, new spiritual movements and leather, Judaism and Islam and Eastern religions, agnosticism and paganism and cults. We will follow many different paths—and, ideally, respect and support each other in our separate journeys toward the truth we seek.

We gay people have deep spiritual needs that cry out to be met: ecstasy, openness/honesty, an awareness of mystery, the clear expression of social justice, ritual rooted in community.

As a people we *are* queer. We *are* different. This is a part of our God-given creation and gifts. Our spiritual needs cry out to be met, honestly and fully, integrated with our sexual and other needs. We are a deeply moral people, yet we have dumbly accepted moral censure of ourselves by demagogues and zealots of hate. So, responding to their pronouncements of rejection—in the same way that gay people accepted a label of *homosexual* from a homophobic culture—we have too often simply cast away our claims upon both morality and a loving relationship with God. When we did this, it was in an excess of low self-esteem; we *reacted* to hate instead of insisting upon our *action* of self-affirmation. Our scripture-quoting, gay-hating, politically self-serving enemies do not "own" God! Why have we reacted in a paranoid way that suggests we think they do? The time has come to *claim* our moral posture in society, to *claim* our beloved relationship with God.

We need to be open to a spectrum of alternatives. I explore a rich variety of sources, including the ritual of the Eucharist, corporate and personal prayer, dream analysis, dance, hiking, examining and respecting other religious traditions, participating in encounter groups, and nurturing the mysterious border area where love and sexuality meet.

We must become familiar with risk. Let me share with you an experience that shattered conformity in my life, allowed me to grow spiritually in ways I would not have dreamed possible.

I was living and working on black voter registration in summer 1965 in rural Alabama and Mississippi with four black men, all of them young, yet veterans of the freedom movement with the Student Nonviolent Coordinating Committee. The five of us had shared a good deal of life for the few past weeks: poverty, hunger, fatigue, police harassment, threats to our lives by white supremacists, and the seemingly endless rebukes of white people in ways large and small—the stare of hate, the refusal to grant permission to drink out of a public fountain or to use filling-station rest-room facilities, the smiling insult spoken as if to a child. Now I wondered if we might conceivably share the Mass.

We had spent the night in a rural shack made available to us by a poor black family. I got up early, found moldy bread and a bottle of beer in the icebox, placed them on a wooden table in the living room, and waited for the others to awaken. One man had spent the night with a white woman student he had brought back with him; he had to leave immediately to take her home, for it would be dangerous for them to be seen together any later in the morning. They departed in the car that we used for travel. Another set out along a nearby highway to buy groceries.

I was left in the shack with two men and a young black woman who had spent the night with one of them. As we talked leisurely over cups of coffee, I said that I hoped we might share the action of the Mass and communion. I proposed to do this after the other two returned. The woman said she could not participate because, in her belief, communion was holy—to be received only once or twice a year; sex was dirty, including the intercourse she had engaged in during the past night; she had been taught to keep communion and sex separated from each other. Soon one of the men became worried about the delayed return of the man who had gone to buy food, and he set out to find him. Three of us remained. Then the man with the car came back. Another man in our group angrily attacked him for returning so late. The two swore at each other and fought in the room of that shack.

The wooden table was overturned, the beer spilling on the floor. The man who had returned with the car asked why the beer had been on the table. He knelt down, picked up the piece of bread, and tearing off the mold, ate it. I explained that I had wanted to share with them *this* part of *my* life, as I had shared so many parts of their lives with them. There seemed to be a feeling of sympathy for me. Not only was I white and older, but there was this *other* separation, too, this obsolete, or archaic, business of being a priest, something that none of them could talk about.

The others returned, peace was quickly made; I was once again absorbed into our fragile but very real community, as if I were not separated at all ("You'll have to be a nigger like we are," one of them had said to me at the outset); and our common life continued as we ate toast and drank coffee. It seemed to me that, in a way I had neither designed nor sought, we received communion. But I wondered how I could relate this experience to that other part of my life in the church and the world as an ordained and functioning priest. Church rules and regulations—indeed, the middle-class white cultural mores that were inseparable from them—seemed as remote as another century.

But what of my "role"? Would the institutional church feel this entire experience, including what I had wished to do with the bread and the beer, was wrong or illegal or blasphemous or merely sadly isolated from reality? I was being changed; could I go back as if I were unchanged? I had been absorbed momentarily into a community that would shortly not exist for me, yet a terribly real one (and, if I died here, the last one I would know). Now I wondered if the community to which I would return—a parish church—could possess such intimate involvement (including the sweat, warts and tensions), depth of fellowship, or a kind of unnamed love that offered the totally shared experience of mutual risk in danger as well as a genuine caring for each other. For *here* we were prepared to die together in the cause of human liberation. My friends in the parish church would not, I believe, understand or readily express openness to these new and present friends, with their methods, language, attitudes and lifestyle.

This raw experience led me to write the following meditation. Its publication resulted in genuine controversy.

Jesus Had a Penis

In his thirty-three years on earth, Jesus had shoulders, a stomach, penis, legs and feet. What's shocking about this? The reaction of certain people to it.

First, some people consider penis *a dirty word; in polite "Christian" society one is not supposed to acknowledge physical realities, only spiritual ones. Taking this point of view, Christianity is not concerned with society, politics, economics, the arts or sociology; it is about "religion."*

Second, some people consider Jesus to be God but not man. Well, yes, maybe Man, but not man. "He could never have had a penis" —though the Latin American church observes a day of the holy foreskin. "Okay, maybe he did have a penis, but don't talk about it."

Don't talk about Jesus as real. Keep him up there in the sky where he's uninvolved in real, raw life.

The opposite of "telling a lie for Christ" is the truth. Let's look at an analogy in the black experience.

In the 1920s, during the Harlem Renaissance, "New Negro Writers" appeared and represented "in art what the race militants had represented in politics—not an appeal to compassion and social redress but a bold assertion of self." ("That Was New York—Harlem, What a City," by Jervis Anderson). The New Negro Writers included Langston Hughes, Countee Cullen, Arna Bontemps, Wallace Thurman, Rudolph Fisher and Zora Neale Hurston.

"We younger Negro artists who create now intend to express our individual dark-skinned selves without fear or shame," Hughes wrote in the *Nation* in 1926. "If white people are pleased, we are glad. If they are not, it doesn't matter. We know we are beautiful. And ugly, too. The tom-tom cries and the tom-tom laughs. If colored people are pleased, we are glad. If they are not, their displeasure doesn't matter either."

In other words, truth is truth, not propaganda. The truth must be expressed, let out of the bag, written, sung, acted, danced.

Now, our gay stories must be told in all their beauty, ugliness, diversity, shadings and stark truth. And this includes our gay spiritual stories. Yes, the untold stories of gay saints. The time has come for their telling.

TOBIAS SCHNEEBAUM
WE, THE FAIRY
HEADHUNTERS

In the following chapter, Tobias Schneebaum, a writer, accomplished painter and world traveler, examines the compassionate nature of "the other." He also extends his discussion beyond traditional religious precepts, literally to their other side. Instead of denying sexuality, he embraces it as a life-affirming source. Rather than contain spirituality within rigid codes, he explores a world where spirit is immanent in all things.

In Keep the River on Your Right *(Grove Press, 1969), Schneebaum describes the eight months he lived with the Akaramas people, a Stone Age tribe of the remote jungles of Peru who practice homosexuality and cannibalism. Schneebaum was fully accepted into their way of life, as he was among the Asmat, a New Guinea tribe with similar rites among whom he spent time a few years later. These powerful experiences changed the way he views the world of the senses and of spirit. "I was cutting away all that I knew about myself. I was removing my own reflection, and as I walked on, I walked into an incarnation of myself that had always been there, so hidden it had never reached the outer layers of my soul," he wrote.*

It was a spiritual journey nurtured through open brothership, as the following adventure with the Asmat testifies. One hot day, Schneebaum says, he and men from the tribe were on an expedition down a river. "We noticed a mud mound close to shore. The leader pointed us there, and after banking the canoes, everyone dove headlong into the mud. What an orgy we had, you can't imagine! It was sexy and sensual, and we were all screaming with joy. That was ecstasy on everybody's part."

Recently, I received a letter from one of my oldest and closest friends. "I went to the park several nights running," it began, "scored several times, sucked four and got fucked by three. The one afternoon I was out by myself in Paris, I went to a porno movie house and had seven more. Then, two in Colmar. Over three nights, seven again. Six I sucked off and one fucked me. The latter was really a doll, as were many of the others. Five in Little Horn a few weeks ago here and seven in Bagby one evening last week. What do you suppose happened to me? Should I worry about it? Perhaps it's part of the process of reconciling my body and soul, which have often been at odds with each other. It doesn't interfere with my studying the mystics or my going to church and I don't feel hypocritical about it. It's the duty of all of us to try to become saints, and the only way we can do that is by using the selves that we have, however ordinary or out-of-the-ordinary those selves may be. Modes and patterns be damned! My euphoria doesn't make values." The letter ended, "Honey, I hope you won't think the less of me over my recent activities."

The last sentence upset me, not for the obvious reasons of jealousy or because I could see clearly that my friend had intended to turn me on (which he did) but because the letter evoked so many of my own concerns about homosexuality and its accepted definition in our society.

George (not his real name, of course) was a great beauty when I met him in New York thirty years ago. He is still exceptionally attractive. During that early time, he was going through a period of intense and painful self-examination. He was trying to deny his sexuality, calling his body's demands evil. He was so deeply troubled he thought his only salvation was through religion. He began to take instruction in becoming a Catholic, thinking he would thereby become celibate and saintly. In those days, I was working at a job that meant getting up at six in the morning, while George was living on unemployment insurance. Despite my own physical fatigue, we talked into the night, every night, going over his life detail by detail, beginning with his first sexual experience at the age of nine on the altar of the church in his hometown, when he was fucked in the ass by a priest.

George's sexual encounters had been varied but remained within the framework of homosexuality. In spite or because of his great sexual energy, or because it harked back to that early contact with the church, he always carried within him a disposition and yearning toward mystical life and often thought of becoming a religious himself. I, too, had thought in that direction and, by the time we met, had already stuffed my brain with philosophies of the East. When we met in 1952, I had just returned from several years in Mexico, where I had been painting in a small village on Lake Chapala. I had traveled throughout the country and, on a walking trip across the Yucatan Peninsula, had met a Catholic priest lying in his hammock reading T. S. Eliot, a fact that endeared him to me instantly. I stayed at his small house, working with him for several weeks and, good Jewish boy that I am, even painted the Stations of the Cross in one of his churches in the jungle before going on to Chetumal, on the east coast of Quintana Roo. The priest had been a rare human being, a truly good man in all senses of the word, for it was obvious that for him missionizing did not mean converting numbers of pagans to Catholicism but instead helping them in every way possible. When I left, he said, "If you ever come across someone interested in doing lay missionary work here, please send him down."

George was fascinated with the idea of being a missionary in Mexico and decided to go down as soon as he was baptized. We both wrote to the priest, who agreed to give George a trial. The only immediate problem was financing a bus trip. A letter from the priest suggested getting in touch with Dorothy Day at the *Catholic Worker* in the hope that she would fund the ticket. George was terrified of meeting this extraordinary woman, so I was delegated to make the request.

My appointment with Miss Day was memorable—memorable and disappointing. I had had a fixed, romantic, idealized image of the Great Lady, but she seemed, in the flesh, a typical professional Catholic do-gooder with limited vision and unpleasantly affected mannerisms, not the least of which was the conspicuous austerity of her dress, contradicted by the huge, dazzling cross dangling from her bosom.

The priest had written to her from Mexico, so she recognized George's name and was aware of the problems and circumstances. Yet, her questions betrayed a holier-than-thou attitude, like Katharine Hepburn in the first part of *The African Queen*, as if she were certain that George had done something intolerably evil and was guilty of abominations too offensive to describe. "He must be a drunk," she said, without asking whether or not he drank. "But what has he done that he finds it necessary to escape from the United States?" Unnerved by her questions and her ways, I left in a state of depression, trying to excuse her behavior by comparison to Japanese Zen masters who encourage discipline in novices through rudeness and physical abuse.

George and I managed to raise the money without her help, and he went off to the remote village of Bacalar. Some months later, his first letter arrived, full of enthusiasm and delight with himself and all that was happening around him. A letter from the priest confirmed that George was loved by everyone and was doing an excellent job; he was just the sort of person the priest was looking for. George stayed there two years before falling seriously ill with hepatitis and returning to the States for treatment. I may say here that George was indeed celibate during his stay there, though his letters indicated he might easily have succumbed to the many temptations around him.

After three months in the hospital in the Southwest, George went back to school, took a master's degree in library science, and proceeded to make a name for himself in the world of cataloguing. Throughout the 1960s and 1970s, he was in love with and lived with a priest who died in 1980. It was twenty months after his death that George wrote the letter ending, "Honey, I hope you won't think the less of me over my recent activities."

Yesterday, I answered the letter at length but kept no copy. It is just as well, for it forced me into thinking about a subject that has been troubling me for years: the antagonism of most of the straight world for the homosexual, the inability of the homosexual to know how to express himself in our society, the lack of knowledge and understanding in the Western world in general concerning homosexuals and/or sexual acts between men, and the lack of knowledge concerning the sexual interaction between men in some Eastern and Oceanic societies. (I use the example of men here because I do not know enough about sexual activity between women.) Damnit! Why should George have to feel guilty about his return to an overtly active and multi-partnered sexual life? Why should he think that a mystical or saintly life is necessarily at odds with sexual activity? He no longer feels guilty about his homosexuality, but he does feel guilty about the quantity and quality of his encounters, as if they had anything to do with morality or loyalty or faith.

It is understandable that, as he approaches the age of sixty, George would begin to worry about his attractiveness to others, about becoming old and unwanted. It is a time when most men and women feel their sexual life waning or coming to an end, whatever their glands might tell them to the contrary. We are conditioned throughout our lives to believe that aging means a lessening of sexual drive and desire. I myself, at sixty-one, am more content within myself than at any other time of my life and find that younger men turn to me in a way that has never happened before. It does not matter how this change came about, that it might have been necessary to go through various painful rites of passage; the fact is that, at least for the present, my life is reaping a bit of what it has sown.

George was not faithful to his priest/lover; he had his occasional one-night stands, knowing that they had nothing to do with the basic relationship between him and his friend. He was, however, limited in his affairs by the simple matter that his lover was a priest, a fact that dictated circumspection on the part of both of them, particularly when the priest was wearing his collar and, in the presence of parishioners, when he was in mufti—though surely some members of the church knew of their connection.

It is not surprising that, after the months of mourning his friend's death, George would find a need for coming out and testing his wings again. He compares his recent experiences with those of the protagonist in John Rechy's *Numbers*, trying to prove himself still attractive, even at what he calls his "advanced age." Then, too, his inability and his need to reconcile his sexual episodes with what he calls sainthood have been a recurrent theme in his life. I am against neither sainthood nor sleeping around—although I am involved in neither—and I believe that conflict between the two pursuits need not necessarily arise.

The dried-up, asexual character of Dorothy Day does not imply that saintly people are good people or that celibacy determines saintliness. Dorothy Day was probably a better human being in her younger, more openly sensual days. For centuries, people have been writing books about sex and the church, denying that a connection between the two could be fruitful or life-enhancing, but little has been written in the West about what other religions have to say on this subject. There are esoteric books available, of course, but, generally speaking, our society rarely reads them or misunderstands what they have to say. In *The Tantric Mysticism of Tibet*, John Blofeld writes: "The unhealthy attitude bred by our Puritan ancestors' disgust with the body has made it difficult for many Westerners to take a balanced view of the sublime teaching of the Tantras which, since they are concerned with winning full control over the body, speech and mind, provide guidance for dealing with the whole of human experience."

In his *Tantra*, Philip Rawson says, "Tantra asserts that instead of suppressing pleasure, vision and ecstasy, they should be cultivated. Tantra distinguishes sharply between the beastlike man in bondage to appetites, who seeks pleasure only for the sake of experiencing the ecstasies they offer, and the committed Tantrik, who treats his senses and emotions as assets to be turned to a special kind of account."

Rawson continues, "No Tantrik rite can work unless the enjoyment and desire are there. It is absurd to pretend that such a rite can be undertaken in the spirit of mere cold duty. To begin with, no man can get the necessary erection for a sexual rite unless his body can both be possessed with normal instinctual response, and can also expect, on the basis of past experience, that the desire will be consummated in some way."

Tantric Buddhism believes in using orgasm as a medium toward enlightenment. It must be used in a special, controlled way, so that the adept, as he approaches enlightenment, learns that the physical orgasm is no longer necessary and he uses its energy to achieve complete fulfillment. The final phase of retaining the orgasm must be similar to the way of those medieval mystics and saints who tried desperately to control all passion, even wet dreams, in order to attain godliness in their quest for spirituality. Yet even George—who has read widely on these subjects—is limited by the world in which he physically lives and cannot accept the possible compatibility of these apparently opposing ideas.

Blofeld indicates that the sexual activity within the Tantric monasteries was (is) only between men and women, that it is through the union of opposites that the energy needed in the search for enlightenment can be created. A friend of mine questioned his guru on this matter; his immediate response was one of laughter, as if such contacts were of no importance. He went on to say that homosexual relationships alone did not lead beyond the first stages on the road toward Nirvana, but that the adept had to perform with women as well. On the other hand, a mutual acquaintance's serious experiences—sexual and otherwise—within monasteries in West Tibet were necessarily limited to men, which was the normal way there.

Our world, our Western world, teaches us only one path to righteousness, though other ideals have begun to filter through the Judeo-Christian system of ethics. Other cultures have much to teach us if we are open to them and, most importantly, if they are made known to us. A great part of Hinduism, Buddhism and other religions (usually referred to in the West as "occult") has been hidden within circumlocutions that make it impossible to understand them in the way they were originally meant to be understood. Blofeld says, "Among other causes which lead to misunderstandings regarding Tantric Buddhism are: the secrecy which has traditionally surrounded the inner core of the doctrines; the sexual symbolism employed in Tantric texts and iconography; and the appalling misrepresentations put about by certain Christian missionaries. . . ."

Which barely begins to touch on the subject. In his essay, "Native American Transvestism," historian Martin Bauml Duberman writes, "Traditional (heterosexist-dominated) anthropology has long avoided data relating to sexuality of any kind and especially of the 'deviant' variety." A few anthropologists have published works that are not obscure and are not hidden away in archives in remote corners of remote libraries, but in the main, discussion is so limited that there might as well be a world conspiracy to suppress what little research is accomplished. It is as though there were a general agreement that "the sexual life of the savages" must be discussed only within certain limited circles, and then must always be couched in anthropological or medical language not generally accessible to a public whose interest would only be prurient and must surely lead to great evil.

In many non-European societies, homosexuality is normal among young men; moreover, it is *necessary* to them and to their way of life. They would be horrified to learn that our young men cohabit with members of the opposite sex before marriage, for that is the way to femininity. We are taught to believe that only heterosexuality is acceptable, but there are others who believe quite differently. We are taught that those who practice homosexuality are "queers," "fairies," effeminate men who really would prefer to be women. We believe that the dominant member of a relationship is the more masculine of the two, whether he commits sodomy or is fellated; a passive partner is looked (down) upon as feminine, one who takes a wifely role. Yet on the other side of the world, among certain groups in New Guinea, lo and behold! the opposite is true. The way to manhood is by opening your mouth and/or your asshole. To accept a penis into your mouth or anus is the *only* way toward masculinity. It is only by absorbing semen from one more powerful that the young become men.

During rites of passage among the Marind-Anim (*Dema*, by J. Van Baal, Martinus Nijhoff, 1966), the initiate, around the age nine, is sodomized by his mother's eldest brother and then in turn by the rest of the men in the clubhouse. The semen introduced into his anus is what makes him grow into manhood, makes him rugged and brave. Without it, he would remain puny, without the strength necessary to become a fierce headhunter, without even the ability to harden his penis. The more semen he is able to accept, the more quickly will his body grow into that of a great warrior. So, too, among the Sambia (*Guardians of the Flutes: Idioms of Masculinity*, by Gilbert H. Herdt, New York: McGraw-Hill, 1981), who practice fellatio in this same way, believe that the more semen a young man swallows, the stronger and taller he will grow. To ensure masculinity, he fellates as many older youths as possible; he is therefore intensely promiscuous, seeking out one partner after another.

It is interesting to note that although the initiate is assigned a partner older than himself with whom he forms an affectionate relationship (and sometimes loves), the initiate's promiscuity seems to bother no one. It is an accepted fact that he will perform sexually with as many partners as he is capable of taking on. It is also intensely interesting to note that within these two societies (and there are many others in Melanesia), the young boys and bachelors are forbidden all contact with members of the opposite sex from the time they leave their mother's house to enter the men's house until after they get married. The first Sambian heterosexual experiences are often frightening affairs for both partners and are usually consummated in the manner preferred by the groom—by the woman fellating him. Eventually, most of the men settle into what we would term a normal, married life. Many of the young men retain their homosexual attachments and are bisexual for some years after marriage; some men, taught to be terrified of any contact with women, remain unmarried and continue only homosexual relationships. No stigma is attached to this, although an older man will be the butt of jokes if caught committing fellatio or being sodomized by a younger man.

George's guilt concerning what he refers to as his promiscuity—guilt that is a product of our Western moral system—might not have developed or might not have been so deeply felt had he been aware of the attitudes toward promiscuity in other societies. This promiscuousness might appear undirected, as if the youths were out for any and every man, but, like those of us who limit ourselves to younger (or older) partners or to those with huge penises or good builds or pretty hands, these youths (beginning at age eight or nine) must make sexual contact with certain men, preferably those who are not friends, perhaps with those who might even be their enemies. Seduction becomes a challenge, and it is possible that scores are kept there, too. Of course, Melanesian men also suffer sex-related feelings of guilt, although the word *guilt* should be replaced by *fear* or *terror*.

Other tribal groups employ sadomasochistic rites that would make even the most experienced leather men pale. The Fore and related people of the New Guinea Highlands (*Excess and Restraint*, by Ronald M. Berndt, Chicago: University of Chicago Press, 1962) have a particularly difficult road to adulthood, commencing with their first initiations by periodically having wild cane thrust up their nostrils and having their tongues scraped with coarse leaves until the blood flows freely, and continuing into adulthood with an elder inserting spear grass into the penile duct and twirling it around until both blood and semen gush out; then, replacing the spear grass in succeeding weeks with a twig covered with salt and, still later, with special leaves bunched together and pushed into the urethra and again twirled until the blood and sperm flow. How many of us could bear that pain to prove our masculinity? And how many of us would *enjoy* the pain enough to reach orgasm?

My own recent studies in New Guinea have brought forth information that may be unique. Among the people with whom I have been living on and off since 1973, certain groups have a relationship between two men called *mbai*, formed around the age of two. Although the men claim to form the attachment themselves, it is more likely to have been arranged by the families of the boys in order to strengthen clan ties. As children, they play together in a normal way and examine and pull on each other's penises. Girls may be included in early sexual play, particularly when bathing in mixed groups, when the boys will insert a finger or two into a girl's vagina and the girls will play with a boy's penis; the boys, when alone, insert fingers into each other's anuses. As they get older, sexual play between the *mbai* becomes increasingly complicated, until it involves fellatio and sodomy. The *mbai* relationship lasts until the death of one of the men and may be more binding than marriage. A wife, little more than a commodity purchased with axes and knives, spears and bows and arrows, may be discarded at any time, but *mbai* are permanent friends.

I asked Akatpitsjin, the headman of one of the villages, "What happens if you come upon your wife having sexual intercourse with another man?"

"Oh!" he said, "I beat her up!"

"What happens," I continued, "if you catch your *mbai* having sexual intercourse with another man?"

"Oh!" said Akatpitsjin, "I beat up the other man!"

"Not your *mbai*?" I asked ingenuously.

"Oh, no! He is my *mbai*!" he said, shocked that I could think otherwise.

Although a man may have a serious love affair with another woman, he may not do so with another man. He may, however, have sexual contact with other men, and frequently does. The men might masturbate together, even with the *mbai* of one or both looking on. On rare occasions, the *mbai* might even take part. The unrelated men might suck one another's penises but never to orgasm. Fellatio and sodomy to orgasm are reserved only for the *mbai*.

It is also interesting to note that there is no such thing as a passive or active partner in the Western sense, except for the actual moment of sexual intercourse. The relationship between the two men is always balanced; when one *mbai* performs fellatio or sodomy on another, the roles are invariably reversed immediately after orgasm.

In his youth (or even now) George would not have sought to emulate a cannibalistic, headhunting people such as this group, but they obviously have something to teach us about tolerance and role playing. I wouldn't for a moment suggest that they are the Noble Savage: They have as many sexual taboos as we do; theirs are different, concerning themselves primarily with incest between males and females. But what different attitudes we might all have about sex in all of its manifestations had we more knowledge of other cultures. George and others might have been saved from years of guilt—by far the more fearsome of the two major varieties of headhunter.

GEOFF MAINS
URBAN ABORIGINALS
AND THE
CELEBRATION OF
LEATHER MAGIC

In American culture—where eros has been cynically used to greater effect, and lesser meaning, than in any other—the relationship between sex and spirit is barely comprehended. When seriously wrapped in black leather, it is scarcely tolerated. Yet one leather man living in San Francisco could tell me that "We're the new American shamans. It's a fellowship without a church."

It is an international fellowship with specific rites of initiation: where playing outlaw, rather than victim, is preferred; complex needs are negotiated, and met; and where some men perceive sexuality inextricably linked to their own spirituality, pointing to a new religious direction. The surfaces of leather may seem simplistic, easily deduced. But its inner reality, if properly channeled, is descent to a world of primal feelings and shadows, transcendence to ecstasy, and then, perhaps, beyond.

Leather men remain iconoclasts; practitioners of a powerful ritual magic and healing art. At the core of their experience lies one of the most significant statements made thus far by the gay movement: the liberation of sexual energy. The transformation of sexuality into a vital, positive force is an evolutionary act. And all judgments aside, it may be the celebration of the pagan, anarchistic pleasures of radical sexuality that will, in part, make it so.

In his book Urban Aboriginals: A Celebration of Leathersexuality (*Gay Sunshine Press, 1984*), *Canadian author Geoff Mains takes forms of radical sexuality to an important new depth of understanding. Mains, a biochemist by training, scraps fearsome old myths. Instead, he compares the experiences of contemporary leather men (primarily those in the Pacific Northwest) with similar sexual and spiritual activities found in other cultures. Using current medical research into the biochemical effects of physical sensation, he explores the possible physiological basis for these ecstatic, cultural journeys.*

In the following chapter, Mains reveals what most experienced leather men already know: that radical sexuality is a subtle interplay of mind, body and spirit; a soulful charging of each; an exploration of the capacities of the total self. "Within leather," states Mains, "humanity attempts to redress the animal. It is not the only way, but one, perhaps, from which the rest of the world has something to learn."

In all the worlds, in all the immensity of time, there is no other like each of these streams, rising cold out of the earth where no eye sees it; running through the sunlight and the darkness to the sea. Deep are the springs of being, deeper than life, than death . . .

—Ursula Le Guin,
The Furthest Shore[1]

The magic that springs within each of us is often hidden from sight but wells forth from deep fonts. Those of us who seek to tap this magic find new insights and perspectives, rejuvenation, and even apotheosis.

Urban Aboriginals is a work about leather people and the magic of their experience. It began as a project to document a subculture variably called leather or S/M. This project focused on the reasons its adherents believe in what they do, some reasoning about how it worked, and the satisfactions leather people gain from their interplay. As the investigation proceeded, it became clear to me that, despite its many different approaches, leather experience was a special form of that magic sought by human cultures everywhere. In their craft, leather men and women touch on some of the deepest and most hidden aspects of human existence. Through leather, its participants can seek compassionate revelation. And through its spells, leather experience can in turn provide a form of power over existence.

I could have begun *Urban Aboriginals* by challenging the misconceptions outsiders hold about leather: that people who practice it are abusive, brutal, crude and dangerous. Or that leather acts are blatant statements of autocracy, violence, hatred and self-contempt. I could even have spent time arguing, perhaps even refuting, the lore of the now sanctified: Freud, Reik, Krafft-Ebing and others. I could also have addressed the allusions and innuendo that so ignites the popular press on the subject, whether *Newsweek*, the *New York Native* or the *New York Post*.

But this approach would have given undue credence to the unapologetically ignorant. It would focus my work on the motives of the attacker rather than attacked, overemphasizing defense at the sacrifice of exploration. And, as a result of this, my work might have slipped into a negative stance. More than anything, such an analysis would have detracted from the magic that people seek through leather. The magic qualities of experience tend to be ignored by so-called rational and often culturally indoctrinated researchers. And because *magic* of experience is so difficult to defend or to justify to many Westerners, adopting a posture of defense in dealing with leather might place the emphasis of my research on human rights and not on human interaction.

Instead, *Urban Aboriginals* explores leather culture from within, drawing on people's experience and using modern science to shed light on this. The book, for example, examines recent research on opioids, that family of nerve transmitters found naturally throughout the animal kingdom and chemically analogous to plant-derived drugs such as opium, codeine and morphine. Current understanding of these substances and their functions provide unique insights about the interplay between pain and pleasure, reward, and altered states of consciousness. Yet while this development of scientific knowledge lends important understanding to leather, the tenor of *Urban Aboriginals* alternately draws on those people that live its craft.

There is, in many minds, an association between leather and extreme, even abusive, dominance and submission. Two things need to be said about this as preamble to the following excerpts. First, while dominance/submission, even in strong forms, flavors many leather scenes, such acts are not universal: Many leather people explore scenes such as pain/pleasure, bondage and fisting without sexual role-play. Second, where this role-play occurs, it is usually on quite different grounds than generally conceived. Says one man: "Absolute dominance is not the symbol. It's dominance given in trust and received voluntarily. It's dominance tempered by an understanding of limits. It's dominance given with humility and as love."

Of an importance here is a requirement for a sense of humility: a sign, particularly in the top [the person taking the leading role], of a mind that, if it has not been there itself, at least knows and respects the space that its partner is about to enter. Through many leather scenes, both top and bottom give hard and second thought to the chains of their reality. Arrogance and insensitivity have little place in this searching. Comments Jason Klein: "A master can be destroyed as readily by an intelligent slave as a slave can be destroyed by a stupid sadist."[2]

Despite certain common outcomes, those streams of consciousness that comprise leather are as diverse as the people who practice it and their sexual and social customs. These practices, in many combinations and with shifting emphasis, can take on quite different meanings. The *details* of leather role play provide no simple generalizations. Partaking of these rituals are individuals with a diversity of attitudes, tastes and capacities. Some men search for security and self-affirmation. Others desire contrasts, exhilaration or pure enjoyment. Some search for all of these. The nature of personal relationships varies with individual, with acculturation, and apparently with physical capacity. Something as fundamental to leather as the pain/pleasure barrier and its impact on mind space varies considerably between people and thus between relationships.

Pain as Authority

Despite occasional homage to democracy, we experience a world in which aggression is to large extent the currency of law and order. Who benefits, whether individual or society, and which concept of morality is upheld, is not the question here. The spanked child, the battered spouse, the victim of a mugging, or the apprehended insurrector—all of these people alike suffer pain as an expression of social power. The involuntary and aggressive use of pain is a major tool in the maintenance of human dominance, despite the efforts of some cultures to put limits on this abuse of authority.

Involuntary pain as an expression of power is common not only in the West, in dictatorships, or in the military or the prisons. Aboriginal ritual widely uses pain as expression of social or religious authority. The boy at puberty may be pinned down and circumcised. Youths of either sex may be beaten, their ears or noses pierced, or forms of skin gouging or tattoo applied. These rites may involve intense, cathartic pain/pleasure experience. Preceding rituals of separation such as fasting, solitary confinement, exhaustive dancing or sleepless vigil could well generate opioid highs. And yet, while these mind spaces may lend to the spiritual authority of the experience, they are not essential. These rituals are one-shot; they mark a special passage in an individual's life and are statements of the tribe's sanction of that passage. Pain is a means of exerting the authority of the tribe and of driving the message home. The products of pain, whether tattoo or piercing, are an ongoing statement of this newfound status.

Another and second kind of pain ritual is quite different from this first. This ritual is voluntary, often communal, and repeated many times in a lifetime. These are rituals found not only among aboriginal peoples but also among subcultures in Asia, Europe and the Americas. Most often these rituals have strong spiritual contexts. Pain becomes a symbol of sacrifice as well as a submission to divine authority. Take, for example, the Kavadi dancers, who, surrounded by crowds of friends, make their way through the streets of Penang and Singapore on Thaipusam Day. Each man, as he dances, carries on his shoulders a heavy yoke of steel and wood that is connected to his flesh by hundreds of tiny steel hooks; the yokes are highly decorated for the festive occasion.[3] Compare these rituals with those reported among Mayan tribes. Here, each of a group of dancers is pierced with thorns or wooden skewers through various body parts—tongues, cheeks, earlobes, legs and genitals. Each of these piercings is linked with those of other participants by a web of ropes. The group dances itself into states of ecstasy.[4] Consider the firewalkers of Singapore who whip each other to banish fear before their passage across the red hot coals.[5] And more familiar than any of these are the recent images from Iran: penitent Shi'ite Moslems flogging themselves and each other in the streets.

In these latter forms of pain experience, it seems likely that the mechanisms of the pain/pleasure barrier come into play. Here, pain becomes a symbol of authority to whom submission is demanded, albeit a divine one. But submission is voluntary, and the eventual and ecstatic release that is obtained, both through the release of opioids and a shift of consciousness, is a reward to the faithful. Here also is an incentive to repeat performance. The pain/pleasure rituals of leather, often enacted in voluntary submission to a trusted dominance, share strong similarities with these latter experiences.

Getting There

Consider the preferred conditions of a leather scene. There is darkness and isolation. The many, complex and often shifting sensations of the outside world are excluded. There is little room for distraction, frill, or fancy music. If present, music is chosen to fit the scene; often it is repetitious, even monotonous. Sometimes it can be spacy. Walls and floor are often bare and black. The direct focus of everything is the individuals; men are measured by themselves, not by pictures on the wall. Toys, chains or other equipment, if present, add to the focus of the action. Leather is austere and its direction is its head trip. Piss scenes or fisting can be undertaken in rococo chambers, but here the scenery may contradict the state of mind. It distracts from the direction and, often, something seems wrong.

Charles Tart suggests that in inducing a shift of mind, there are three steps.[6] The first of these is a disruption of the existing state of ordinary consciousness. The second, through the application of forces that destabilize the existing state, directs the mind toward the altered state. The third step destabilizes this new state.

Set against the austerity of the play area is a form of human interaction requiring total absorption. This interaction is ritualistic and is full of overtones of the socially forbidden. It might involve boot licking, restraint or the greasing of a butthole. Everyday world and actions are outside, new forms of commitment and response are implicated. Together with the backdrop, the conditions of interaction focus the mind, disconnecting it from its workaday world. Role-playing, if it takes place, often plays on the themes of buried or frustrated emotions; this again is a direction away from ordinary, repressive reality.

Physical actions, as well as environment and social interaction, contribute to this first step of disrupting ordinary reality. Many leather practices are well known in other contexts as means of disrupting ordinary consciousness. Hooding, bondage, periods of confinement and other forms of sensory deprivation may be followed with episodes of overload—for example, humiliation or paddling. These actions direct the mind away from the outside world and create a heightened awareness of the body, its limits, and its instincts. Actions like those of a paddle or a moving hand are often measured and repetitive. Such actions (like those of a moving watch, a mantric chant or a drumbeat) are recognized tools in trance induction. Still further activities stretch muscle or erogenous tissue, activate pain-bearing nerves, and alter the pain/pleasure barrier. And actions such as tit play, C/B [cock/ball] torture or whipping may also cause an increase in the opioid levels of brain and blood. Applied alone, alternately or together, various combinations of these techniques can induce nonhurtful pain, sensory overload or deprivation, and physical stress. All of these have been linked with shifts in consciousness.[7] Success in applying these techniques is a product of the skill of the top. Success is measured in the contrast or richness of the scene and in the mental energy or "high" that is released.

If focus, attitude and play in a leather scene provide the first step of consciousness shift, then the play also acts as a patterning agent in directing the mind to new states. Play acts to switch on certain mental substructures and to turn off others. In scenes that involve role-play, instincts of dominance and submission are turned on. The mind relaxes into and enjoys repressed or hidden capacities: the thrill of pain/pleasure from flagellation; the peace of restraint in bondage; or the overwhelming and indulgent joy of ass play. Fears and inhibitions are abandoned. Hidden motives and instincts emerge. Reality becomes a sounding board for the exercise of fantasy. In the state of mind that comes to be, outside reality almost totally ceases to exist. All is rooted in the rich dynamics of the participants.

These dynamics provide the third element required to bring about mind shift. Anxieties and rewards that both negatively and positively support an ordinary state of mind have been cut. Salaries, ambitions, material rewards and blackmail have come to mean little or nothing. Instead, they are replaced with a world of utmost reliability based on a strong personal intimacy that in trust and care, even if only for the duration of a scene, far exceeds in intensity that encountered in the other world. Here is the confidence between slave and master; the give and take between mutual fisters; the intuition shared between bondage tops and bottoms. Concern and affection that modulate leather scenes act to smooth out any underlying anxiety. And the passionate commitment, along with the sexual and emotional release, provide positive payoffs. Together, all of these attributes of leather scenes help to stabilize the altered state of mind.

Human Strength and Human Frailty

David's first steps into the new year are measured and into himself. He has a mantra that he often uses when he goes into bondage, and as he waits for John, he sits quietly repeating it. He prepares for a scene that could be two hours or ten—a decision that is not for him to make. Later, John will light the work area. For now, the darkness is calming.

When John arrives to take control, David is ready. Alpha brain waves already predominate in his mind, and except for the continuous mantric repetition, the thinking and memory-saturated hemispheres of David's brain have almost shut down. He rises slowly and to an upright position in front of John. The actions are secure and flow like liquid. His head is slightly bowed, humble yet expectant.

There is a sense of ritual that is played out in the images. In the dimness John appears to have grown in size. The ominous black of boots, chaps and jacket gleams slightly. Visor and peak of cap and dark lines of beard cage John's face: Here is a man who has touched the power of the soul in hidden places and knows how to speak with it. In contrast David mimes the diminutive. He, too, is in leather, but in chaps and boots only. His cock and ass hang free and vulnerable.

The hooding that immediately follows John's arrival acts to close in David's world. Eyes, face and neck are wrapped in black leather and laced up the back; there are holes for the nostrils and mouth. Then, to complete the enclosure, John puts his own jacket on David, zips the front, and handcuffs him behind the back.

What follows is rough and sudden: statement of the power of master and outside world. While it temporarily wrenches David from his alpha state, it is a supreme gesture. John shoves his lover to his knees, stuffs his cock in the exposed mouth. And pisses.

In what will be an eight-hour voyage, this is the most blatant action. What follows on the part of John are undertakings that are meticulous and measured. A harness made of the leather that is used to subdue horses is strapped about David's waist and shoulders. The use of this type of leather may be a symbolic overstatement of the voluntary submission it encloses, but it is also functional. In time, as chains are first hooked in the harness and then attached to rings in the ceiling and walls, the body it contains will eventually slant forward and then float free.

David is adrift well before his body. In slow, practiced steps, he has turned away the outside world, passing the reins of control to a man who knows him more than any other: a man who for this occasion has assumed the metaphor of God and creator. David's anxieties and frustrations have been left outside—a step itself that many Westerners find difficult to achieve. Even in periods of rest, the hyperactive and adrenergically motivated computers that form our thinking minds continually regurgitate and evaluate the figments of our lives. Yet with some self-taught training, David has learned to focus through meditation so that his mind lifts away on the inside from that world that John rebuilds on the out.

As he works, John directs himself totally to his craft; to the power within his fingers that shapes the outer form that his lover is to take. With additional straps about the legs and arms and thick laundry cord, he immobilizes the limbs so that they are held by counteracting ropes positioned in opposing directions. As he fastens new straps, or makes or adjusts knots, he is always careful to avoid constriction and uneven tension. The sculpture as a whole must flow evenly and harmoniously, and the man within it must remain a comfortable part of the harmony.

From time to time John stops and watches his work, always silent. At some point he rests for ten or fifteen minutes. Finally, the head itself is encased with rope tied over the hood and then immobilized. For a long instant the frenetic anguish of David's life has been stilled and the often contracting forces that pull and tug across it have been frozen.

Here is an image of human strength and human frailty. The inescapable frailty of the human condition, of a man who is bound and stilled as any of us can be, at any moment. For the David who has moved outward, this bound body speaks ironically of peace and freedom. In that body John sees his own frailty, intrinsically tied to his own strength. The strength of his creation, a human sculpture built of another man's frailty and another man's conviction. The strength of a human body frozen in its glory. Bondage in its fullest is no mere pastime. Like all forms of leather, bondage can be apotheosis.

David is conscious of his outer world during all of this, and he is aware of the actions that free him temporarily from his dependence on it. But for this long instant, such perceptions are largely peripheral. In a focused meditative state of mind, he reaches across the wall that has closed behind him to a light that is shining through him. That wall is solid, physical and erotic. John has anchored his bonds to the conscious reality of David's psyche: his hopes and frustrations. These include a need to be totally possessed by another man. Occasionally, as David's focus dips downward and deep into the motivations of his brainstem, he brushes with the sexual power of the scene and the strong role that power plays in his life. In David, as in many of us, this power is linked as much to a need to dominate as a need to be dominated. For David, that erotic power has been locked into the wall behind him. When he eventually shifts his focus back to his body, or when John brings him downward, David will confront not his ordinary, but a very different form of reality.

John takes several hours to complete his handiwork. Finally satisfied, he quietly leaves the room to return with a beer. In some scenes this part of the trip is an ultimate statement of the dependence of slave on master. As Jack Fritscher writes in *Drummer*: "When a man is immobile for eight hours he learns to know his place."[8] He may gain a sense of stability, a sense of humility, or a respect for a master. For John and David, each of whom switch roles with some regularity, bondage yields perspective of their own lives set within the human condition. A day earlier John had spoken with David about David's wishes in the matter. They could very well have decided to go the other way. David had wanted a prolonged trip but did not specify the precise time. Now, knowing David's limits, John waits in silent vigil, a devotee before an altar.

Recognition by Infringement

"No, it doesn't frighten me that it might be dangerous with his hand inside me. It feels good and I'm as secure as ever. He's touching at the core of my strength."

Territory is recognized by infringement. Definition of self and of community come through interaction with other individuals. A step toward or across an established boundary generates perspectives on both territory and its implications.

Along with all of its other attributes, leather play is territorial. Through mutual invitation, its players explore a variety of aspects of physical and mental territory. This is a process in which, as Jack Fritscher puts it, a man "stakes out progressive ownership of the territory of his own body."[9]

In bondage, the physical and psychological territory of movement are restricted and a man comes to better understand the map of his own body. He learns how every movement of limb or face is reactive to personal feeling. He learns, from the frustrations that develop over this lack of self-control, the degree to which actions are self-seeking in purpose. In bondage men expand their facilities of communication, learning to talk through the slightest quiver of muscle or the slightest touch. In some scenes communication may be nonverbal and even extrasensory. And in the peace of bondage men can learn something of that delicate interplay between physical and mental territory. In immobilization, the mind of dreams, memories and aspirations takes new balance against that world we record at any moment through the senses.

If bondage puts a certain emphasis on mental territory, play with pain/pleasure clearly puts weight on the physical dimension. Here is a test of limits, of taking the body to its known boundaries and beyond. Here, men move out into new terrains and pleasures. Through physical distortion they activate deepseated emotion to learn of the interplay of fear and trust. And yet, despite its use of the physical, this play also brings forth relations between mind, body and well-being; it embraces the mental euphoria at the edge of physical limits; and it exposes the cultural manipulation of physical and mental capacities.

In the course of mutual and sexual role-play, men chart the territories of ego. A top can help a bottom to understand both himself and his own limits; through reflection the top can come to similar ends. In a contractual adoption of roles, each man may limit his options, while at the same time a spectrum of new choices becomes apparent. What may not have been possible previously can now be explored on defined ground. Through this form of constrained interaction a cajoling takes place. The bottom can do things not believed possible but desired of himself. The top may question his own ambitions in the face of the limits of his partner in trust. The bottom searches within himself for consensus and rationale and finds solace in gut emotional release. The top, always conscious of his partner's condition, questions himself, his own motivations, and his own capacities. The men that emerge from this voluntary role-play view the demands of social convention with detachment if not distrust.

Water sports also engage elements of territory, much of it animal. While role-play explores the innuendoes of dominance and submission, water sports explore repressions of physical function. Men pissing on each other are at once marking territory and taking possession of their friends. There is a wisdom and a relaxing that grows out of such play. Men who can live freely and happily within themselves, who are able to accept and to express animal function within a human context, and who can combine such varied and human functions as repairing machinery, ministering to the needs of the sick, and baptizing a buddy with their own piss, have achieved a remarkable sense of balance.

Fisting involves all of these elements of territorial excursion: constraint and self-control, physical limit, pain/pleasure, and mental/physical balance. But it does something much closer to reality: It walks the frontier between life and death. A man brings another deep into his own territory to give him the gift of himself. As an animal he is most secure at the center of the territory he defends; to invite another man to enter this territory and to touch the strength is a considerable gift of love.

In their commitment to one another, humans have a strong need to put their lives symbolically on the line. Doing so is a path toward self-definition. Leather play is a form of that process, and the fraternal and trusting atmosphere that exists between its players makes it all the more possible and all the more rewarding.

The Fortune of Being Blessed

It would seem that only in the worldwide unification of consciousness and its absorption of a growing diversity of behavioral potentials can the genius of our species accumulate, synthesize, and enrich its awareness of itself and the cosmos that harbors it.

—Jason Klein[10]

The men of leather space encompass a dichotomy.

On the one hand are men with strongly religious backgrounds and/or current affiliations. Former monks into whipping and pain/pleasure. Anglican priests into water sports and bondage. Catholic priests into fisting. Ex-ministers or seminarians who are leather/Levi club members or bikers. The presence of these affiliations within the leather community is conspicuous; their numbers are greater than expected by chance.

In contrast with these men are a large number with no connections to organized religion and often strongly negative reactions toward it. These men tend to view religious authority as repressive, misguided and dogmatic. Many of these individuals have rarely attended a church and have no desire to begin.

Despite these apparent differences, the leather community is hardly rocked with religious dissension. Leather men tend to be highly tolerant of each other's spiritual or personal convictions, despite the personal differences that occasionally appear in that community. But more influential perhaps than respect for conviction is a shared form of experience. Leather men share a common spirituality that emerges from the space itself. For the religious, this spirituality is a natural complement of both the symbolism of play and of deep emotions and trust that move it. For the distrustful, this spirituality is an important element of the scene that conventional religions have seemed unable to provide. The spiritual leanings of leather space are not surprising; many of its elements are shared in common with religious experience.

Leather experience can provide self-definition. "I've discovered more of myself through probing and playing in leather scenes," notes one man, "than was ever possible in either straight or gay life. Because of that discovery, I'm a happier, sounder person." As detailed earlier, leather play is often an improvisation based on character fantasy. This process, sooner or later, and more than often sooner, can bring one in conflict with one's personal and psychological limits, including hangups and emotional conflicts. Acting to confront reality with the fantasy of our lives and to confront our fantasies with yet others, leather space brings forth our mechanisms of defense and our repressed emotion. Then stripping these bare of their cultural trappings, it ends with a fundamental form of love.

Leather experience can create strong catharsis and emotional release. It allows the expression of hidden instinctive and often forbidden motivations in ways that are pleasurable, caring experiences. While these acts hardly conform to the rituals of romantic eroticism, they are rooted in an intense emotional power that can heal and bring peace. Through escape from the tensions of everyday reality orientation, leather permits an acting out of inner conflict and social tension. In releasing these socially tightened springs, leather play can purge tension to create an increased awareness of personal strength. And from all of these experiences, there is a sense of well-being that persists long after the experience.

Self-definition and catharsis are complemented by a sense of fraternity that is spiritual and social. Men who have put their lives on the line for their partners share a special attachment to those who would do the same. That fraternity is expressed through a broad anarchistic network reflective of this process of self-definition. Members of this fraternity, like the disciples of a religious order, are remarkably open to one another in discussing the details of personal experience. Points out one individual: "I'd been out in the gay world for many years before I became associated with the leather scene. I couldn't believe the sense of warmth and openness that existed. Of people who liked each other as a people. Of friendships that went on for years."

These elements are reinforced in yet one further way. In many scenes the participants reach altered states of mind or even trance. These mind shifts have strong spiritual qualities. Purusha Larkin, for example, has written powerfully of the spiritual overtones that are linked with pain/pleasure experience and fisting.[11] "Communion with body consciousness" and "cosmic erotic awareness" may be outcomes of radical sexual experience, and Larkin draws connections between these and the many forms of religious ecstasy. There also seems to be little doubt that these experiences are similar to those pursued by various aboriginal and Oriental cultures.

The rewards of this spirituality are not only personal, but tribal. Trance and catharsis define a form of shared mental territory in affirming what are perhaps some fundamental human qualities—the need to give oneself fully and in trust, the need to approach and respect one's limits as part of self-realization, and the need to fully live the human animal.

Like words and acts of shamans, the spiritual utterances of leather men can take on special importance to the fellow members of their tribe. These are men who have put their lives on the line, who have really been there. For any tribe that has been either actively oppressed or is in a marginal social position, these words and acts help in building cultural security.

There is something holy in a leather scene—something about which writers such as Arnie Kantrowitz, unafraid of the implications of radical sexuality, are emphatic.[12] In a locale such as the Catacombs [in San Francisco], there is a friendly, caring aura that extends between people, a sort of sharing in the fortune that comes from being blessed. "The needs of the tribe," writes Ludwig, "are met through identification with the entranced person, who not only derives great personal satisfaction from divine possession, but also acts out certain ritualized group conflicts such as the theme of death and resurrection."[13]

The man in the sling at the Catacombs is a symbol to his brothers. Most of them have been there and all would like to go there. In the raw, powerful beauty of his being fisted, of living that process that only a women can know as birth, are a fire and joy that binds men together. In each other's hands and each other's trust, leather men enact the very themes of life.

Cultures That Dream

In her now classic book *Patterns of Culture*, Ruth Benedict describes two fundamental variants of culture: the Dionysian and the Apollonian.[14] Subsequent research suggests that cultural typing is more complex than this, but Benedict's patterns are still relevant and especially so to leather space.*

Dionysian societies seek to cross the bounds of ordinary existence. Illumination is sought in forms of altered consciousness, and the heavy and often turbulent experiences that bring such transcendence are not only valued but institutionalized. Individuals in Dionysian society seek these experiences alone or in small groups. Interactions with the powers of the universe are intensely personal. Culture provides the avenues, but it does not presume to step between a person and the gods. Among those described as Dionysian are many aboriginal cultures, including

---

*The terms *Apollonian* and *Dionysian* should not be interpreted too rigidly. There are elements of both experiences in many societies. Highly ordered and bureaucratic Asian cultures live side by side with religions such as Buddhism, for example, which, while hardly indulgent, stress the use of transcendental mind states. Ancient Greek cultures were often a remarkable blend of the two forms of experience. These terms are appropriately used here because Western culture, perhaps unlike many others in history, is strongly and almost exclusively Apollonian.

most North American tribes, many Eastern religious sects such as the dervishes, and strong elements of classical Greek culture (hence Dionysus or Bacchus, the god of wine and ecstatic rites).

Apollonian societies in contrast know but one law: moderation. They are distrustful of excess and they restrain life within what they regard as reasonable, rational existence. Apollonians are suspicious of altered consciousness. Often, they do everything within their power to outlaw any tendency toward Dionysian experience. Apollonian cultures tend to be highly focused power structures, whether or not these are democratic. They include most of the cultures of Europe, North America, and many in the Orient. Apollonian cultures are relatively rare among aboriginal peoples, although Benedict points to the Zuni of southwestern North America as a strong exception.

Leather space is an exploration of the frontiers of the human experience conducted alone or in small groups. It employs pain/pleasure, catharsis, coordinated forms of physical and mental stress, and sensual, indulgent experience to yield, on occasion, transcendence. These intensely euphoric, even ecstatic experiences parallel the Dionysian practices in aboriginal cultures. The gratification of leather, like the gratification of Dionysian experience, may be shared within the tribe, but the catharsis and energy it brings are highly personal.

The culture of leather has emerged in the midst of a society that, despite guilt or status-driven indulgence, is strongly Apollonian. Western society is to the core *middle* class, puritan and wedded to the supremacy of the rational mind. It misunderstands any form of emotional release except aggressive violence, and it forbids alternate states of consciousness: In this ordered, Western world, ecstasy awaits us as a reward after death. This is our payoff for what is regarded as a chaste, moral existence. Apollonian society, by way of the rational mind, determines gods and rewards. Contact with the supernatural is strictly regulated by the moral guardians of Apollonian society. Often, the ends of God and society become indistinguishable. In the West, particularly, we are expected to sacrifice many forms of satisfaction so that we can both meet our Creator on good terms when we pass on and ensure that the economy grows while we live.

With the terrible onslaught of AIDS, parts of the gay community look with even greater distrust at leather experience. Leather is alluded to as cause of this health crisis; there are attempts to sanitize the gay movement by purging it of these so-called extremes. Yet leather experience did not create the LAV/ARC/HTLV-III virus, and there is no evidence that leather men have been affected to a greater degree than any other gay subgroup. In terms of safety, many leather practices (for example, role-play, whipping, pain/pleasure, bondage) are probably less likely to pass on viral agents than even conventional sex. Some, like fisting, have been proscribed as unsafe, at least in part because medical science is uncomfortable, if not unfamiliar, with the full range of human capacities. That apart, most leather men (fisters included) make special efforts to undertake their magic with care and responsibility, and this is even more so today.

Now, more than at any other time, those who use leather to explore transcendent experience need its revitalization, its special magic and its powers. In courting these, leather people have something to give both themselves and a world thriving on distrust and disbelief. The heart that screams ecstasy through pain/pleasure speaks directly to both its soul and God. The body, immobile in the peace of bondage, momentarily clears its burdens and gains new strength. The mind that rediscovers in its own body the strength of carnal delight finds new joy and sees in new ways. Gay suspicion of leather experience manifests an Apollonian and puritanical upbringing, a distrust of anything but the rational and the "moderate," and a condemnation of those who dare to explore beyond it. The magic of leather, like all magic that moves through ritual and mind play, moves best from person to person. This magic carries participants to the edge of their experience and their limits in the manner of shamanic journeys. In achieving this magic, individuals are required to give and trust and be humble. These are all things, perhaps, we could learn more of today.

Ursula Le Guin, who writes profoundly of magic, puts it another way[15]: "Who knows a man's name, holds that life in his keeping." Leather magic is a knowing of hidden names and a cherished giving and holding of human souls.

References

1. Ursula Le Guin, *The Furthest Shore* (New York: Bantam, 1975).
2. Jason Klein, *Drummer* 44 (1981): 16.
3. M. Ratram, *Penang* (W. D. Andreol, 1973). Also described by B. Finer, "Report of the Dahlem Workshops, Berlin, 1979" in H. W. Kosterlitz and L. Y. Terenius, eds., *Pain ans Society* (Weinheim: Verlag Chemie, 1980): 223–227.
4. P. T. Furst, in N. E. Zinburg, ed., *Alternate States of Consciousness* (New York: Free Press, Collier-MacMillan, 1977): 53.
5. A. Weill, *The Marriage of Sun and Moon* (Boston: Houghton-Mifflin, 1980): 254.
6. C. T. Tart, *States of Consciousness* (New York: Free Press, Collier-MacMillan, 1970).
7. A. M. Ludwig, *Archives of General Psychiatry* 15 (1976): 225–234.
8. Jack Fritscher, *Drummer* 24 (1978): 16.
9. Jack Fritscher, *Drummer* 30 (1978): 13.
10. Jason Klein, *Drummer* 44 (1981): 21.
11. Purusha Larkin, *The Divine Androgyne* (San Diego: Sanctuary Publications, 1981).
12. See, for example, Arnie Kantrowitz, "The Synagogue, The Saint and The Mine Shaft," *Advocate* 15 (April 1982): 32.
13. A. M. Ludwig, *Archives of General Psychiatry* 15 (1976): 225–234. Copyright 1976, American Medical Association; quotation reprinted with permission.
14. Ruth Benedict, *Patterns of Culture* (Boston: Houghton-Mifflin, 1934).
15. Ursula Le Guin, *A Wizard of Earthsea* (New York: Bantam, 1975).

Above: Collaborators in art and life: Christopher Isherwood (left) and Don Bachardy. (Photo by Stephen Stewart.) Left: José Sarria in 1986 as ''the Widow Norton,'' a drag persona inspired by the Emperor Norton, a real-life eccentric who lived in San Francisco nearly a century before and who consequently became a part of the region's enduring folklore—as has Sarria himself. (Rink Foto.)

Above: Clothes make the man: Cross-dressed members of San Francisco's ''Royal Court'' assemble before a Coronation Ball in 1975. (Photo by Crawford Barton.) Left: An Angel of Light, early 1970s. (Photo by Dennis Forbes.)

Hibiscus in a Cockettes production, 1970. "We were creating mythic figures."

Angel Jack and Hibiscus.

Angel Jack and Hibiscus.

Above: Hibiscus in 1981: "A Fifties queen for today." Right: George Harris, a.k.a. Hibiscus, shortly before his death in May of 1982. (Photo by Marjori.)

The Cockettes as they appeared in Steve Arnold's 1971 film, *Luminous Procuress*.

Above: Goldie Glitters as ''The Tinsel Queen'' in the 1971 Cockettes production, *Pearl Over Shanghai.* (Photo by Karma Patrol.) Right: Shaman drag: An Angel of Light performs in a 1980s Hindu extravaganza, *Holy Cow!* (Photo by Ron Blanchette.)

Sisters of Perpetual Indulgence proclaim ''Give up the guilt!'' (Photo by Greg Day.)

Urban aboriginals in their native dress. (Photo by Robert Pruzan.)

PART 2

The World Within Ourselves: Voices and Visions

DON KILHEFNER
GAY PEOPLE AT
A CRITICAL
CROSSROAD:
ASSIMILATION OR
AFFIRMATION?

Don Kilhefner sits at the edge of the gay village: reflective, troubled and, in his own way, gently subversive. He has played a quiet but pivotal role in the creation of the gay liberation movement on the West Coast, one facet of the intelligent and heartfelt commitment to social change he has felt throughout his life.

Born and raised in a Pennsylvania Amish/Mennonite community, he spent his first seventeen years in an environment sparse with material comforts but abundant in its respect for nature. Even then, "I had a very innate and early awareness that I was different from my brothers and sister," Kilhefner recalls, "a sense that I really didn't see the world the same way they did. This frightened me at the time."

After graduation from college in 1960, he was struck by Kennedy–New Frontier idealism and got involved with one of the first voter registration projects in the South. The Peace Corps and work on its front lines in a remote and isolated Ethiopian village followed. Later came years of antiwar activism and, finally, the rumblings of Stonewall, with its anger and assaults. A generation was growing up gay, and lessons of survival were quickly learned. "We were a people with nothing to take care of ourselves with —except each other." So Kilhefner withdrew from a UCLA doctoral program to work full time for gay liberation. He laid groundwork for the nation's first gay and lesbian community services center in Los Angeles and, as its first executive director, developed it into the largest and most successful organization of its kind in the world. He founded the first residential alcoholism and drug treatment program for gay people, created alternative means by which to explore the dynamics of gay consciousness—involved himself, in fact, in all areas of his community. Still, after all of this, Kilhefner came to believe that something, somehow had failed.

He raised questions few wanted to hear. "It's not the what, *but the* who," *he explains. "Our community looks at* what *institutions we've created and* what *titles we hold, rather than* who *we've become as human beings. The word* community *has become a shibboleth, a weight around our necks. We have a community that is not a community, despite its social complexity. Something on an inner level has failed. Where is the soul of our movement?"*

Dissatisfied and disillusioned, yet hopefully searching, Kilhefner left Los Angeles in 1977 and began a long trek—a gay vision quest—that would take him through the northwest and southwest regions of the United States and also into previously hidden reaches of his own psyche. "The exterior and interior search began at about the same time," he explains, "but the inner journey was ultimately the more important one, because it forced me to confront my own inner darkness and assimilate it into my total being."

He met others who felt as he did. Kilhefner had known for some time that there was another dimension to being gay, a different reality not acknowledged by a rapidly assimilating subculture. Research into gay consciousness that he had been involved in since the early 1970s now began to form a unified picture—a new model by which the history of gay people could be reenvisioned. He also began to understand that a succession of visionary poets and mystics had talked about this other quality, their words constituting a gay spiritual tradition.

Kilhefner returned to Southern California in 1978. Through a series of "gay voices and visions" groups, he began to share his realization, this lineage of writers who had found words to articulate profound, inner aspects of the gay experience: Walt Whitman, Edward Carpenter, Gerald Heard, Harry Hay, Llee Heflin, Mitch Walker, Arthur Evans, and others. The following chapters reflect Kilhefner's important work; writings that have directly affected the way many gay men view themselves. To begin, however, Kilhefner summarizes his own feelings in an article, written in 1979, stating that gay people are at a "critical crossroads," facing the choice of "assimilation or affirmation."

He has continued his pioneering work over the years and is currently exploring and documenting "the anatomy of gay men's psyches as seen through the phenomenology of their dreams." In his own search for meaning, Don Kilhefner continues to rediscover and reinvent, presenting a radical reconceptualization of what it might mean to be gay. He believes that his current investigation—and the similar work of others—"is as full of implications for the future of gay consciousness as the paradigmatic shift from Newton's view of the universe to Einstein's."

Invocation

There was a time when you were not a slave,
    remember that.
You say you have lost all recollection of it, remember. . . .
You say there are no words to describe it.
You say it does not exist.
But remember. Make an effort to remember.
Or, failing that, invent.

—Monique Wittig

These notes are not about the historical roots of the American gay movement. Instead, they address an increasingly critical, but virtually ignored, dilemma faced by gay people—our assimilation into the mainstream versus our enspiritment as a people. It represents a topic that the current leadership of the gay community, for reasons of class self-interest or a newly acquired sense of identity, refuses to address. I am talking about nothing less than *reinventing* ourselves as gay people.

For most gay men—and I feel qualified to speak only of gay men —the idea, much less the exploration, of gay-centered and defined spirit/politics/healing is a new one. It is full of revelation/revolution.

A valuable place to begin is a careful examination of the three basic questions put forward to gay people in the early 1950s by the original Mattachine Society: "Who are we?" "Where do we come from?" and "What are we for?" The search for the answers to these questions is even more relevant today to the existential reality and well-being of gay people than when they were first advanced thirty-five years ago.

At this point it is easier to state who gay people are *not*—we are not *homosexuals*. The concept of a *homosexual* is a modern, Western phenomenon. In 1869 a male physician first coined the word to define a person by sexual attraction toward another person of the same gender. Since then, hetero-male culture has used this concept to control gay people, not only on the physical but on the mental and spiritual levels of our being as well. It is essential to recognize that this hetero-created Myth of the Homosexual is just that—a *myth*. But like all social myth structures, it has painfully shaped and controlled our unfoldment as a people during the past century as we internalized its negative implications of sin and sickness.

Virtually all of the hard and imaginative work of the homophile-gay movement during the past three decades has been directed toward this myth. At this point, the major accomplishment of our movement has been to replace the *negative* Myth of the Homosexual with a *positive* one by denying the sense of perversity and by refuting effeminate stereotypes. But the myth remains hetero-originated and defined, nevertheless.

Today, regardless of the gay movement's sociopolitical rhetoric, *homosexual* and *gay* are virtually synonymous (for a brief period between 1970 and 1973, this was not true). No matter how liberated and progressive our self-image as gay men might be, most of us still lead our lives within the matrix of the Myth of the Homosexual—albeit on subtle levels, sometimes. Our so-called gay identity is still largely hetero-male derived and defined. For example, the plethora of conferences in recent years aimed at "developing a positive gay identity" are really aimed at learning more positive ways of coping with the homosexual myth structure in which we still find ourselves enmeshed. They have very little to do with discovering our true-self identity as a people. Our minds have been colonized well.

When we try to share with our dominant society just who we think we are as gay people, we find ourselves simply feeding back to them permutated definitions of the sexual orientation myth they originally fed to us. This process, of course, is not unique to gay men. Mary Daly's *Gyn/Ecology*, for example, provides a brilliant analysis of a similar predicament in relation to the emergence of a truly woman-centered identity for women.

The past decades of gay activism have given us a little time to contemplate deeper questions about ourselves. This has placed gay men at a critical juncture in our process of true-self discovery outside the Myth of the Homosexual. This new matrix has major implications for our future evolution as a people and for the "re-visioning" of our movement as a self-defined movement.

We now stand at the metaphorical fork in the road. I refer to one path as *gay assimilation*. It is based on the positive Myth of the Homosexual, a largely unexamined, underlying assumption that "we're no different from anybody else except for what we do in bed." Other than our choice of sex partners, we're just like heterosexuals.

For the gay assimilationists, civil rights and acceptance by heterosexuals are panaceas. Personal identities and life plans are based on heterosexual models of respectability and upward class mobility. Nongay, Caucasian physical attributes and behavior are emulated. For the gay assimilationists, political success means gay people becoming as power-oriented, manipulative, and competitive as hetero men in playing the game of electoral and community politics. At present the gay movement and media are dominated by gay assimilationists. And it's one of the reasons we can't trust our leaders.

As a result, what passes for "gay" politics, "gay" religion, "gay" psychology, et cetera, is really little more than hetero-male evolved politics, religion, and psychology, with the word *gay* mindlessly or opportunistically prefixed. So-called gay churches and synagogues are based largely on the same structures, values and consciousness as their patriarchally possessed prototypes. A "gay" bagman for the Democrat or Republican party is indistinguishable from his nongay counterpart. At the base level, what passes for "gay" therapy differs little from what heterosexual therapists do. After all, if we really are just like they are, why shouldn't gays become a mirror imitation of heterosexual society?

When I'm around gay assimilationists, I often feel like I'm associating with straight men, and I'm reminded of gay author James Baldwin's warning that when a minority group attempts to assimilate, it always does so *totally* on the terms of the dominant culture. And gay men are being accepted by hetero culture to the extent that they look, behave and think just like straight men, in the process becoming despirited people.

Blacks have their "oreos" (people black on the outside, white on the inside). Native Americans have their "apples" (people red on the outside, white on the inside). A friend suggested recently the appellation "wax fruit" to describe similarly acculturated individuals among gays. In any case, I frequently come away from my interactions with gay assimilationists feeling spiritually raped.

At the metaphorical fork in the road where we now find ourselves, an alternative possibility is available to us as gay men. I refer to it as the path of *gay enspiritment*. It is less well surveyed at this point, but across the country, this alternative is increasingly being explored by a new generation of gay men, many of whom had ventured down the gay assimilation road, only to find the price too high for their souls.

This other possibility says that there is a reality to being gay that is radically *different* from being straight (note: *different*, not better or worse). This gay reality is inside of us, and it is substantial and meaningful. It is real. We can feel it in our hearts and in our guts. And it has nothing to do with hetero mythologies, either negative or positive, about what it means to be gay.

People coming out of a cultural tradition different from our own have acknowledged this difference. The anthropological literature is full of examples. For instance, the Crow Indians traditionally used the concept *bote* to describe us—"notMan/notWoman but Other." Young children also see the difference. Recently, I overheard a three-year-old friend admonishing her preschool classmates: "Don is *not* a man!"

As gay men continue to reclaim our cultural and spiritual history outside of the Myth of the Homosexual, we are discovering a rich historical lineage pointing toward the current emergence of gay consciousness. During the past century this gay spirit has been identified, nurtured, deepened and passed on by an incredible line of gay mystics and visionaries—Walt Whitman, Edward Carpenter, Gerald Heard and Harry Hay, to mention one such lineage.

Walt Whitman (1819–1892), the poet of America, is particularly central to the emergence of gay consciousness. By contrasting individuals as being either of an "adhesive" (gay) or "amatory" (hetero) nature, *for the first time in recorded history* Whitman's *Leaves of Grass* defined us as a people with a particular vision and spiritual essence, and not solely as a sexual act. For gay men of that time there was an immediate, deep spirit connection with Whitman's visionary poetry, which has continued undiminished to the present day.

Profoundly influenced by Whitman, noted British socialist Edward Carpenter (1844–1929) enlarged Whitman's opening even further with his pioneering writings about the "intermediate type" (gays). Specially significant was his research into the important role gay people have played traditionally in non-Western cultures throughout the world— shamans, healers, priests, magicmakers, mediators, seers, and innovators in the arts and crafts.

Carpenter's far-reaching observations about the unique functional roles of gay people in society have recently been reiterated and enlarged upon by Harvard's E. O. Wilson, the founder of the new academic field of sociobiology. In his *On Human Nature*, Wilson concludes: "There is . . . a strong possibility that homosexuality is a distinctive beneficent behavior that evolved as an important element of early human social organization. Homosexuals may be the genetic carriers of some of mankind's most altruistic impulses."

Gerald Heard (1890–1971), a longtime resident of Los Angeles, was a prolific author, anthropologist, philosopher of history, BBC commentator on science, Vedantist and science-fiction writer, in addition to being a considerable influence on many of the outstanding British intellectuals of his day. For the first time, Heard began to deal with our difference—our "otherness"—as gay people (he called us *isophyls*) within the context of evolutionary biology. He felt it was gay people within the human species who best represented the biological concept of neoteny—prolonged youth. Our neotenous nature allows gay people to be open and growing and mobile and exploring long after our heterosexual age peers have been forced to settle down into the specialization and stability required of parenthood and so-called maturity. It is because of our neotenous nonspecialization, Heard contended, that gay people have been able to make such a rich contribution to human culture.

Heard was the precursor to the innovative work done by human ethologist Dr. Charlotte Bach (1920–1981), who lectured at London University. One of the lessons of the history of science, as Bach recognized, is that getting the right answer is often a matter of asking the right question: "Why are there 'gays' at all?" and "Why hasn't evolution eliminated 'gayness' millions of years ago?" Like Heard, she says the answer is simple—gayness is an indispensable evolutionary factor in our species.

Where Heard uses the concept of neoteny to characterize gay people, Bach used the term *sexually ambiguous* in her publications. Using an evolutionary emergent model for our species, Bach claimed it is the heterosexual majority that provides the stable, generally conservative, base that is necessary for our species's ongoing reproductive survival, while it is the sexually ambiguous minority (gays) that provides for the evolutionary significant behavior changes that in due course trigger evolutionarily significant anatomical changes.

In Bach's view: "Gay people are needed to the survival of our species as much as so-called straight people. 'Gays' and 'straights,' far from being opposed ends of a polarity, are complementary constituents of a unity, namely, the unity of the human species."

This helps to explain why gayness has always survived and our persecutors have always gone down the drain of history.

Whitman, Carpenter and Heard, among others, wondrously blazed the trail of gay enspiritment, and today that work continues by a new generation of gay men following in their footsteps. This path involves completely redefining ourselves, our history and our culture outside of the Myth of the Homosexual and beyond gay assimilation. Gay men still do not have an adequate language to describe much of this paradigm shift in consciousness, but from all over the land there is significant movement in that direction.

Historian Arthur Evans provided a major revisionist approach to gay historiography in 1978 with his daring book *Witchcraft and the Gay Counterculture*, subtitled "A Radical View of Western Civilization and

Some of the People It Has Tried to Destroy." And in *The Night Sun*, San Francisco poet Aaron Shurin sings new possibilities for gay men in his healing chants.

Mitch Walker, in *Visionary Love*, has guided us much further down this path of gay enspiritment by inventing concepts and terminology more in keeping with the way gay men see and feel and move in the world.

Harry Hay and this writer, following the pioneering efforts of Arthur Evans and others, have done important breakthrough work in gay consciousness by reclaiming a fairie archetype to probe at the mystery. At 1979's seminal Spiritual Gathering for Radical Fairies, over two hundred gay men from all over North America found their way to a remote spot in the Arizona desert to experience a brief taste of true-self identity. They were invited "to tear off the ugly green frog skin of hetero-male imitation to reveal the beautiful Fairy Prince hidden beneath."

Hay is a pivotal figure in the growth of the gay movement in this country. Moving out into new dimensions of gay spirituality, Hay calls upon all people to recognize that there is a qualitative difference between gay consciousness and hetero consciousness. Gay people have a different window on the world, our own way of seeing, our own vision. This difference in essential vision Hay has called *subject–subject* consciousness in contrast to the *subject–object* consciousness of the hetero-male culture around us.

Gay men have a unique potential within them to experience nature and other beings not as "objects" to be manipulated and mastered, but as "subjects," like themselves, to be respected and cherished. Thinking in terms of opportunism, power, competitiveness and self-advantage arises out of a subject–object consciousness. The gift of subject–subject relationships is equal-sharing and loving-healing.

For a long time gays have been trying to *minimize* our differences from heteros *as an act of survival*. But now, for the first time in history, gay people are being urged to begin *maximizing* our differences from straights *as an act of love*—to ourselves and to them.

Maximizing our differences does not mean *us versus them*. It is not a call for gay separatism or elitist groupings. It does mean, however, that gay people must begin a radical new process of self-discovery that starts with what is inside of us; we must begin to discover who we really are, and we must begin inventing a language capable of revealing these essential differences to our dominant culture. In the process, we will become a mirror that will allow heteros to see themselves and their culture in ways heretofore unavailable to them. At a time when hetero-male culture has become lethal to the continued survival of our species and other beings on this planet, what greater act of loving kindness could gay people perform? This is a contribution gays have been making all along. Now, however, there is the potential for doing our dharmic dance with a level of awareness and compassion never before available either to gays or straights.

We must learn to honor, not hide, our being different; affirm and celebrate our gayness in original and playful ways; acknowledge a rich hidden heritage both within and outside of us; and find new models to explain the body of information and intuitive knowledge we have been carrying for a long time but that had no way to get out.

So, my evocation to gay people is to keep moving beyond the Myth of the Homosexual. Understand that being gay is not the same thing as being homosexual. A new wave in gay liberation is forming. In deep and profound ways, none of us has really "come out" yet.

WILLIAM MORITZ
SEVEN GLIMPSES OF
WALT WHITMAN

Although Walt Whitman has been relentlessly examined, as poet and scholar William Moritz explains in the following chapter, he has seldom been observed as he really was or for the full truth of his loving. And despite the powerful visions revealed in his poetry, even he must have realized its certain fragility; disguising and revising his own true feelings, yet leaving signs of them, like markers on a trail, for likeminded men. Walt Whitman remains the wellspring of gay male consciousness in our modern era; capable, as few others, of making so deep a journey into the most expansive regions of his soul.

Walt Whitman is universally recognized as one of the greatest authors of the modern era, a man who revolutionized poetry—indeed, almost created modern poetry single-handedly with the impressive organic free verse of his *Leaves of Grass*. Bibliographies list thousands of books and critical articles about him and his work—more than anyone could reasonably be asked to read. Since 1955, a magazine devoted exclusively to Walt Whitman studies has appeared under the various titles of *Walt Whitman Newsletter*, *Walt Whitman Review*, and *Walt Whitman Quarterly Review*.[1]

All critics agree that one of the greatest aspects of the magnificent *Leaves of Grass* is its spiritual vision—the "cosmic consciousness" identified by Whitman's friend, the psychologist Dr. Richard Maurice Bucke[2]—and that Whitman's mystical experience is inextricably entwined with sexuality. The most recent biographers have accepted the fact that Whitman was "homoerotic."[3] (More about that later.)

In this brief space, I cannot hope to give you more than a few hints about how to approach Whitman, which may help you to a deeper, more sensitive understanding of Whitman's own words. Please remember that no amount of criticism can substitute for reading *Leaves of Grass* itself: Whitman's poetry constitutes his great legacy to you.

I. "Faint Clews and Indirections"

Walt Whitman, born May 31, 1819, on Long Island (he preferred the Indian name Paumanok), New York, was the second of nine children. His ancestors were Dutch, Welsh and English. His father, never quite successful, worked mostly as a carpenter and house builder (with occasional interludes of farming) until his death in 1855, just a few days after the publication of the first edition of *Leaves of Grass*. His mother, of Quaker stock, a simple but loving housewife, lived until 1873. Several of his brothers and sisters led sickly or troubled lives, and Walt contributed to the family welfare throughout his life.

Walt attended grammar school in Brooklyn for only five years, from 1825 to 1830, and then was apprenticed as an office boy, where his education began in earnest when a kindly lawyer subscribed to a lending library for him. He switched to the printing business, where he worked until the great fire of 1835 decimated the New York business area. He returned to Long Island, where he was an itinerant schoolteacher in nine different country schools between his seventeenth and twenty-second years, from 1836 to 1841. Against the standards of the time, Walt refused to beat the children but rather tried to induce them to learn with games. He may have been dismissed from one job for undue familiarity with a male pupil. In 1841 he returned to New York, where he wrote articles and edited several different papers in New York and Brooklyn. In 1848 he traveled down the Mississippi to New Orleans for a three-month stint editing a newspaper there, but he was fired and returned to Brooklyn, where he worked in journalism until 1859.

Since the 1830s, he avidly attended theater and opera. Beginning in the mid-1840s, he actually wrote some opera reviews, and by the end of that decade became such an opera fan that he attended performances every night they were offered—for weeks on end.

In 1854 and 1855, around age thirty-five, in a sudden flurry of inspiration, he wrote and published *Leaves of Grass*, which appeared in a deluxe first edition on July 4, 1855. It met with moderate success, and great praise from Ralph Waldo Emerson. A second, more modest edition, with some new poems added, appeared in 1856, but Whitman continued to work as a newspaper editor until 1859. In 1860, he published a third edition, much enlarged and including a section, "Calamus," exclusively celebrating "manly love" and the "dear love of comrades."

In December 1862, he went to Washington, D.C., to visit his brother George, who had been wounded in the Civil War. He stayed on to nurse the many convalescent soldiers and worked part time as a copyist in the army paymaster's office. His work as a "wound-dresser" was deeply rewarding, and he found many friendships among the young soldiers. In January 1865, he was appointed to a better job in the Department of the Interior, Office of Indian Affairs. He also met a streetcar driver, Peter Doyle, who would remain his intimate friend for about ten years.

In June 1865, Secretary of the Interior James Harlan discovered a copy of the 1860 *Leaves of Grass* in Whitman's desk at work and fired Walt as the author of an indecent book. Through influence of friends, he was "transferred" to the attorney general's office, where he worked until 1873. In 1866, William O'Connor published a booklet, *The Good Grey Poet*, defending Whitman against charges of immorality and in fact praising his spiritual values, comparing him to Shakespeare, Dante and Homer. After the publication of the 1868 edition of *Leaves of Grass* (including war poems and the great elegy for the death of Lincoln, "When Lilacs Last in the Dooryard Bloom'd"), as well as an expurgated British edition, Whitman's literary reputation began to soar; and over the next decades he would receive praise from such poets as Algernon Swinburne and Alfred Lord Tennyson, and would be visited by adoring young writers such as Oscar Wilde and Edward Carpenter.

In January 1873, at age fifty-four, Whitman was partially paralyzed by a stroke. His mother died four months later. Forced to give up work, he moved to Camden, New Jersey, where his brother George (and wife) would take care of him. Despite occasional improvements, he was mostly delicate and suffered other strokes during the remaining nineteen years of his life. Defying his ill health, he gave frequent lectures on Lincoln and managed to travel to Colorado in 1879 and to Canada to visit Dr. Bucke in 1880. He also prepared several new editions of his poetry (the 1881 *Leaves of Grass* was banned in Boston) and the fine prose memoir *Specimen Days*. His books sold well enough that in 1884, at age sixty-five, he bought a modest house in Camden, the first time he had ever lived in his own home—and now, ironically, with a housekeeper and nurse because of his failing condition. During his last years, a neighbor, Horace Traubel, recorded almost daily conversations with Walt; and at Whitman's death in March 1892, Traubel, Dr. Bucke and the lawyer Thomas Harned became his literary executors, seeing through the press an edition of his writings, as well as volumes of his letters and conversations.

II. Narcissus

Few public figures of the nineteenth century were photographed more than Walt Whitman, whose appearance attracted as much attention as his "indecent" book. He dressed almost like a common working man—not any one specific type of laborer but, rather, a synthesis of characteristics that caught Walt's fancy: boots with his trouser legs tucked into them, shirt open at the neck to show a little of the hair on his chest, a broad-brimmed hat—perhaps the equivalent of the modern Levis and logger shirts.

Since Whitman himself put such stock in his image, you should take the trouble to hunt down one of the better collections of Walt Whitman photographs. Although all of his biographies have some illustrations (and the older ones usually have better-quality images), the best collection of high-quality reproductions can be found in the 1971 Godine edition of Walt Whitman's *Specimen Days*, with sixty-four portraits. [4] Another valuable collection is Gay Wilson Allen's *Walt Whitman* (New York: Grove Press, 1961). [5] *Walt Whitman Quarterly Review* has also announced a forthcoming publication of the complete photographs of Walt Whitman.

As you leaf through the various poses, the most striking impression that exudes from them all is the overwhelming loving warmth of the man—and the possible source of that warmth, his gaze: He most often looks directly at you, inviting, scrutinizing, offering; open and smiling. Even when his eyes are turned away from you, they seem to be communing with some other space in which you would be equally welcome.

Whitman redefines the ancient myth of Narcissus for us: His face radiates a kind of joy that comes from appreciating the beauty of one's own face, not as an imitation of some standard supposed perfection but rather as an instrument for communicating loving emotion. Whitman is at peace with his own soul, and greets all creation as a comrade. Whitman has looked into his own face and found it mirrored in the faces of others, and he is happy to short-circuit hostility with a smile. Whitman's dear friend John Burroughs corroborates for us what we can see with our own eyes:

> The atmosphere of Whitman personally was that of a large, tolerant, tender, sympathetic, restful man, easy of approach, . . . regarding you from the start for yourself alone. . . . His personal magnetism was very great, and was warming and cheering. . . . His eye was not piercing, but absorbing,—"draining" is the word happily used by William O'Connor; the soul back of it drew things to himself, and entered and possessed them through sympathy and personal force and magnetism, rather than through mere intellectual force.[6]

This portrait of a man who shares his spiritual serenity openly, equally, without prejudice, with respect for the identity of all things; this image will reappear later in this book (for example, as the subject–subject consciousness of Harry Hay), but perhaps it appeared first in the person of Walt Whitman.

> You give me the pleasure of your eyes, face, flesh, as
> we pass—you take of my beard, breast, hands,
> in return . . .
> —"Calamus" No. 22 (1860 edition)

III. Opera Queen

> But for the opera, I could never have written *Leaves of Grass*.[7]

On more than one occasion, Whitman openly acknowledged his debt to grand opera in the formation of the style of *Leaves of Grass*. An entire book, Robert Faner's *Walt Whitman and Opera*, presents detailed lists of Whitman's references to opera and analyzes how the operatic format of recitative and aria contributed to the structure of Whitman's lines of poetry, as well as poems as organic units.[8]

Looking at the 1841 photo of Whitman (the frontispiece of Gay Allen Wilson's profile, *Walt Whitman*), with his natty velvet coat, bowtie, walking stick and dapper tilted hat, and the languorous gaze, it is hard not to think of him as a modern "opera queen." Undoubtedly there is some basic truth to this, for the total aesthetic experience of opera, so sensitive and emotional, attracts a disproportionately large number of gay men. But again, it's important to keep a sense of perspective. In Whitman's day, opera was the popular mass entertainment—Whitman insists he sat in the gallery among appreciative common working people. In a land flooded with international immigrants, opera was the closest thing to a universal entertainment, since the pageantry, mime and music provided emotional cues and coding that transcended language. This cross-cultural popularity of opera was only superseded by the silent movie, which adopted wholesale its aesthetic: melodrama and spectacle with continual musical accompaniment. So perhaps the opera was to Whitman somewhat as the movies are to people today.

Faner's book unfortunately appeared just on the eve of Maria Callas's stardom, which marked a radical change in attitude toward the classical operatic repertoire. Faner speaks in a semivacuum about operas that had not seen the stage for decades, but now you can buy "private" recordings of recent stage revivals of all but one or two of the operas Whitman knew.

During the dozen years before the first edition of *Leaves of Grass*, Whitman saw almost exclusively Italian and French operas, with Rossini, Bellini, Donizetti and Meyerbeer the dominant composers. Verdi's early works *Nabucco, I Lombardi* and *Ernani* were well known to Whitman, but *Rigoletto* and *Il Trovatore* made their New York debuts only in February and May, 1855—too close to the publication of *Leaves of Grass* to have been much influence. Wagner and lush romanticism were unknown to Whitman, whose opera was classic *bel canto*, with stirring overtures, melodic arias, grand ensembles and ballets. At an 1853 production of Meyerbeer's *Le Prophète*, in addition to seven star singers and the usual chorus and orchestra, it took a full ballet, two hundred extras and a military band for the coronation scene, and people on roller-skates simulating ice skating, in order to tell the historical tale of a country innkeeper, overcome by religious visions, who becomes crowned king of Germany only to succumb to corruption, from which he is rescued by his faithful, strong mother.

Among Whitman's other favorite operas we find Rossini's *Guillaume Tell* and Auber's *La Muette de Portici* (in which common people revolt against tyranny), Donizetti's *Poliuto* (in which Roman converts to Christianity die in the arena rather than renounce their faith), Donizetti's *La Favorita* (in which a monk gives up his vows for the love of a beautiful woman) and Meyerbeer's *Les Huguenots* (in which Catholics massacre Protestants). In Donizetti's *Marino Faliero*, the Doge tries to overthrow his country because they have not sentenced one of his enemies severely enough; and in Meyerbeer's *L'Etoile du Nord*, Peter the Great disguises himself as a carpenter to learn more about his subjects and falls in love with a commoner. So there were strong elements of Romantic, historical/political and spiritual idealism in the plots of Whitman's operas—and a great deal of passionate love, from the noble though illicit love of the Druid priestess in Bellini's *Norma* to the vexations of Bellini's *La Sonnambula* (*Sleepwalker*) who finds herself in the wrong man's bedroom. And Whitman was also especially moved by such scenes as the duet in Bellini's *I Puritani* in which two soldiers swear to fight and die together for liberty and their religious ideals.

But above all, what must have impressed Whitman—and what grips the opera queen today—is the complete possession, through the power of the music, of the listener by the characters:

> I hear the trained soprano—she convulses me like
> the climax of my love-grip;

The orchestra wrenches such ardors from me, I did
    not know I possessed them,
It throbs me to gulps of the farthest down horror,
It sails me—I dab with bare feet—they are licked
    by the indolent waves,
I am exposed, cut by bitter and angry hail,
Steeped amid honeyed morphine, my windpipe throt-
    tled in fakes of death,
At length let up again to feel the puzzle of puzzles,
And that we call BEING.

The great Marietta Alboni (apparently a finer singer than anyone
we have heard in our day) appeared to Walt not just as the woman
she portrayed, but as all women, as the Great Goddess herself:

The teeming lady comes,
The lustrous orb, Venus contralto, the blooming mother,
Sister of loftiest gods, Alboni's self I hear.

This ability to see into the souls of others, to identify and commune
with them—what Harry Hay has called subject—subject consciousness—was one of Walt Whitman's great gifts; one of his goals for
Leaves of Grass as a revolutionary, universal masterpiece; and, perhaps,
one of the perceptions he learned as an opera queen.

IV. Adhesive!

For the one I love most lay sleeping by me
    under the same cover in the cool night,
In the stillness, in the autumn moonbeams, his
    face was inclined toward me,
And his arm lay lightly around my breast—
    And that night I was happy.
                    —"Calamus," No. 11 (1860)

A modern reader of *Leaves of Grass*, and particularly a gay reader, will have little doubt that Whitman himself was homosexual. But we must proceed with caution. Walt Whitman lived in an environment that was in some ways quite different from ours. In 1855, no modern word for love between men had been coined—only such legal terms as *sodomy*, *pederasty* and *buggery* designated crimes with names from biblical, classical Greek and medieval eras. In 1864, four years after Whitman's "Calamus," a gay German lawyer, Karl Ulrichs, would coin the word *Uranian* or *Urning* for a "female soul in a male body," basing his term on Plato's *Symposium*, which identifies Aphrodite Urania as the patron goddess of men who love men.[9] In 1869, fourteen years after the first edition of *Leaves of Grass*, a gay Hungarian, Dr. Karoly Benkert, coined the German word *homosexualität* (translated as "homosexuality" some dozen years later), which remains a standard tool for stigmatizing male–male love as an abnormality or psychological disease.

Whitman himself used the term *adhesive*, which he borrowed from the discipline of phrenology; and Robert Martin, in *The Homosexual Tradition in American Poetry*, has shown in detail how Whitman carefully adapted the term with the intent of giving gay people a name so that they could come together as a vital part of American society.[10]

Phrenology is almost unknown today, but in the mid-1800s, at the height of its popularity, intellectuals as well as common people accepted its teachings as scientific fact—much as we today assume that the new discipline of psychology (Freud died less than 50 years ago) is utter truth, while children and laymen with no real knowledge of Freud and Jung bandy about terms like *neurotic* and *schizo*. Phrenology was based on the revolutionary scientific discovery that different areas of the brain are responsible for different kinds of mental functions; but it went wrong in assuming that, therefore, the areas that were most developed would be larger and push the skull out slightly so that a trained technician could feel the slight bumps, thus "reading" a person's character by "mapping" his skull—an idea accepted and used not only by Whitman but also by Poe, Hawthorne and Melville, Coleridge, Charlotte Brontë and George Eliot, Balzac, Baudelaire and George Sand, much as modern authors use psychology.[11]

But phrenology was more than "reading bumps": It advocated a total health regimen with sunlight, fresh air and exercise, vegetarianism, health food and temperance, sex education, dress reform and women's rights.[12] Orson Fowler, the leading New York phrenologist (and distributor of the first edition of *Leaves of Grass*), promoted in 1848 a modern architecture using concrete for construction materials, all rooms having windows, and many other visionary improvements that would become common as "inventions" of our own century. This holistic approach to health and good consciousness attracted the best minds of its times, among them Whitman, who regularly exercised, sought fresh air, and practiced other phrenological prescriptions for his own good.

This holistic idealism is also crucial to understanding Whitman as a gay man. He conceived of himself as "a Kosmos," a unity with all of his experience—the central metaphor of *Leaves of Grass*—which included the passions of everyone he observed and identified with. This made him plan *Leaves of Grass* carefully to represent a fair, complete, proportionate spectrum of people, among whom women are frequently praised and encouraged—to the point that, for the sake of balance, Walt changed the pronouns on some poems he had written about men (for example, "Once I Passed through a Populous City") that could equally well apply to women; considering the number of overtly gay poems he republished, it could not have been for the purpose of concealing his identity, but rather of reaching the widest audience.

The arguments about Whitman's sexuality have centered largely around the prominence women and straight sex hold in *Leaves of Grass*. Many assume he must have had sex with women to have written this way (often simultaneously failing to assume that he must have had sex with men to have written "Calamus")—and they assume that, if he did have sex with women, therefore he could not be gay. These assumptions don't hold up. Whitman, a keen and sensitive observer, could well have written almost anything from imagination or extrapolation of his equivalent experiences. He may have had some sexual encounters with women but could still have been quintessentially gay in preference, usual activity or desire—remember, many famous gay men, such as Oscar Wilde, were married, with children (and even some of the authors in this book are fathers!).

In fact, we possess a "sexual pedigree" for Whitman.[13] Gavin Arthur wrote Allen Ginsberg about Edward Carpenter making love to him in the same manner Whitman had made love to Carpenter: *karezza*, the long, tender touching of bodies, kissing and caressing not necessarily aimed at quick orgasm but rather, as in Indian Tantric yoga, at sustained physical and spiritual ecstasy—a style of lovemaking, by the way, recommended by the phrenologists and other nineteenth-century sexologists. Arthur also says Whitman had some experiences with women and had some children—but, we must remember, Arthur's 1966 book, *Circle of Sex*, strongly favors bisexuality or "ambigenic love," as he calls it.

Arthur might also have been influenced by the famous letter Whitman wrote to John Addington Symonds in 1890, when the seventy-one-year-old poet lay on his deathbed, surrounded by straight people, including his literary executors. Symonds had been writing Walt for twenty years asking for a clarification, a precise public statement on the real meaning of the "Calamus" poems; and Symonds also made it clear from his own verse and writings that he was interested in pederasty as a Greek ideal. Whitman avoided answering this oft-repeated question until 1890 (possibly under the influence of his own literary executors), when he finally wrote rejecting Symonds's "morbid inferences," insisting that *"Leaves of Grass* is only to be rightly construed by and with its own atmosphere and essential character."[14] He then chides Symonds for a lack of "restraint," saying that Walt, at least, only loses his restraint in his poems! He reiterates that "I wholly stand by *Leaves of Grass* as it is, as long as all parts and pages are construed as I said by their own ensemble, spirit and atmosphere." Then, noting that he is seventy-two (when he was actually seventy-one), concludes with a claim that "tho' always unmarried, I have had six children. . . ."

Symonds, who had never met Whitman personally, took the letter at face value—indeed, regarded it almost as an anomaly that the man who wrote "Calamus" could be so "pure" or naïve.[15] Edward Carpenter, who had slept with Whitman, said in a lecture: "Personally, having known Whitman fairly intimately, I do not lay any great stress on that letter," and adds, "We must remember, too, how different the atmosphere on all these matters was then (especially in the U.S.A.) . . ."[16] Perhaps Whitman, who had been fired (maybe more than once) for being "indecent" and had seen his books banned, seriously worried about their survival and lied to avoid further discrimination. Those who have studied Whitman most also tend to dismiss the letter; for example, the New York University Press's new *Collected Writings of Walt Whitman* calls it "a monumental fib."[17]

But the letter does tell us some very important things about Whitman's ideals: *Leaves of Grass* must be viewed as a unit, since everything belongs in its proper context. Anything isolated and carried to an extreme becomes morbid. For example, the "sick-gray faces of onanists" in "The Sleepers" does not speak against masturbation but rather against the obsessed person whose sole "profession" has become onanism. Perhaps Whitman also looked askance at the Greek ideal of pederasty, since it implies an unequal, possibly exploitative relationship, rather than the man-to-man comradeship Walt promoted. And perhaps Walt disliked anal intercourse: for despite Robert Martin's ingenious "decipherings" of Whitman's erotic descriptions, the fact remains that Walt purposely contrived such descriptions as vague and ambiguous so that they could excite every reader's imagination—not as a one-to-one code to be "broken"! The only way to approach the issue is as a Platonic dialogue, as Jim Kepner did in his excellent pioneer article "In Paths Untrodden."[18]

The specific truth of details in Walt Whitman's life may never be known, but the glorious poems he wrote remain as an inspiration to us. Whitman probably lived in a kind of vacuum—Jonathan Katz's *Gay American History* books provide few details about any "gay life" in the New York or Washington, D.C., of the mid-nineteenth century.[19] Although H. Montgomery Hyde's *The Love That Dared Not Speak Its Name* documents "gay bars" in England since the early 1700s,[20] these, like the earliest documented American clubs of the 1890s, suggest heavy transvestite role-playing, which Whitman would not have liked. But Whitman saw a social phenomenon—male pair-bonded workers, settlers, adventurers—looked into his own heart, and had the genius to know that he could name them *adhesive* (comrades who "stick together") and call them (by "The Institution of the Dear Love of Comrades") to a vital role in the society at large: the shaman of "The Sleepers," the nurse of "The Wound-Dresser," as well as the trappers, laborers and loafers. The call was to realize your self as a significant, integrated part of creation, blessed with an exceptional, sexually reinforced perception that all humans are brothers and sisters—a call we are still learning to answer a century later.

V. Sweet Flag and Live Oak Moss

One of the great delights of reading Whitman's poetry is comparing the different versions. The 1855 first edition is the most exciting book as a conceptual unit; no author's name, no individual poem titles— utterly novel. Several modern facsimiles reproduce the volume in its original format, and it is worth looking for one just to hold it and feel it. You should also read the text through all at once, if you can. A Penguin paperback makes the 1855 text easily available for study.[21]

The 1860 edition in which "Calamus" first appeared is also available in a facsimile of a unique copy with Whitman's handwritten revisions[22]; and the original manuscript versions of most "Calamus" poems were published by Fredson Bowers,[23] who shows that Walt originally called the "Calamus" poems by the title "Live Oak With Moss," drawn from his wonderful poem "I Saw in Louisiana a Live-Oak Growing"—a poem often neglected in discussions of Whitman's sexuality, for it implies that Walt had a lover in Brooklyn before going to Louisiana in 1848.

The New York University Press's monumental *Collected Writings of Walt Whitman* also provides fascinating detective possibilities, since every scrap of his notes, diaries, address lists, and correspondence are transcribed and annotated. Some are, naturally, quite uninteresting, but among them are notes about men he "slept with" and many sketches for poems that reveal ideas he cleverly concealed in the final polished version. For example, we find a first draft for the delicious Section 24 of the 1855 *Leaves of Grass*:

> If I worship any particular thing, it shall be
> some of the spread of my body . . .
> Root of washed sweet-flag, timorous pond-snipe
> nest of duplicate eggs, it shall be you,
> Mixed tussled hay of head and beard and brawn
> it shall be you,
> Trickling sap of maple, fibre of manly wheat,
> it shall be you. . . .

The sketch makes it clear that "sweet-flag" is already "Calamus" before 1855, and the textual variations make the sexual and spiritual implications quite obvious (calamus root, by the way, is a mild psychedelic drug):

> Calamus sweet-green bulb and melons with bulbs
> grateful to the hand/
> I am a mystic in a trance exaltation
> something wild and untamed—half savage . . .
> Trickling sap flows from the end of the manly
> maple tooth of delight . . .
> Living bulbs, melons with polished rinds that
> smooth to the reached hand
> Bulbs of life-lillies, polished melons
> flavored for the gentlest/mildest hand
> that shall reach . . .[24]

You can also find the full text of a famous notebook entry in which Walt worried about whether Peter Doyle really loved him.[25] The text is followed by a sensitive biography of Peter Doyle. A photo reproduction of the actual notebook page also appears.[26]

VI. "Whoever You Are Holding Me Now in Hand"

> Doubtless I could not have perceived the universe,
> or written one of my poems, if I had not freely
> given myself to comrades, to love.
> "Calamus," No. 39 (1860)

At the root of *Leaves of Grass* lies a conceptual nexus that gives the book such power and resonance. The prophet Isaiah proclaimed (Isa. 40:6): "All flesh is grass"; and Whitman, in the book he meant as a "bible" for the new democracy (the loving comrades and free men and women of America), makes the prophecy ricochet, for each leaf of his book of poems is the flesh of the poet and the flesh of all his experiences.

> What I assume, you shall assume,
> For every atom belonging to me, as good belongs
> to you.

No author's name appeared on the title page of the first edition— only an engraving of him looking at you, as you must look at him and at yourself, mirrored in him.

> And now it seems to me the beautiful uncut hair of
> graves.
> Tenderly will I use you, curling grass,
> It may be you transpire from the breasts of young
> men,
> It may be if I had known them I would have loved
> them . . .

In the long enumerations, in the little scenes (of the woman watching the soldiers swim, the man being buried, and others), Walt enters completely the soul of the subject of each event.

> I am the man—I suffered—I was there.

In "The Sleepers," he does this overtly as a shaman,[27] and he risks the splendors and miseries of the traveler in the land of dreams:

> I am curious to know where my feet stand and
>   what is this flooding me, childhood or manhood
>   and the hunger that crosses the bridge between.

Because the poetry resonates between a whole man writing his truth and the whole of creation mirrored in it, the book transcends its creator just as you, the reader, can transcend it and yourself by expanding your consciousness.

> Have you practised so long to learn to read?
> Have you felt so proud to get at the meaning of
>   poems?
> Stop this day and night with me, and you shall
>   possess the origin of all poems,
> You shall possess the good of the earth and sun—
>   there are millions of suns left,
> You shall no longer take things at second or third
>   hand. . . . nor look through the eyes of the
>   dead,
>   nor feed on the spectres in books,
> You shall not look through my eyes either, nor
>   take things from me,
> You shall listen to all sides, and filter them from
>   yourself.

As Whitman enlarged *Leaves of Grass* over the years, this vision remained intact.

> Loafe with me on the grass—loose the stop from
>   your throat,
> Not words, not music or rhyme I want—not custom
>   or lecture, not even the best,
> Only the lull I like, the hum of your valved voice.

One of the finest examples of this reflexive perspective is the thread that runs through the "Calamus" poems, warning the reader in No. 3 of the 1860 edition of his unreliability (but asking to be thrust beneath your clothing so he can feel the throb of your heart, or rest upon your hip); warning the new person in No. 12, "Have you no thought, O dreamer, that it may be all maya, illusion?"; demanding in No. 16, "Who is now reading this?"; in No. 28 Walt reads someone else's book and "hastily puts down the book, and walks away, filled with the bitterest envy"; in No. 32 he asks what you think he means to do with his writing; in No. 36 he confesses a love affair with an athlete, but admits that "I dare not tell it in words—not even in these songs"; and in the closing poem, No. 45, he returns to the "whoever you are now holding me in hand" with a serene perspective on life, death, and the gift of wisdom across time.

> When you read these, I, that was visible, am become
>   invisible,
> Now it is you, compact, visible, realizing my poems,
>   seeking me,
> Fancying how happy you were, if I could be with
>   you, and become your lover;
> Be it as if I were with you. Be not too certain but I
>   am now with you.

This careful ribbon binding these "leaves of joy" confirms what Walt says in *Calamus*, No. 39, that his mystical vision and his poetic art are a special product of his gay consciousness.

VII. "Good-Bye, My Fancy . . ."

> It is to the development, identification, and general prevalence of that fervid comradeship (the adhesive love . . .) that I look for the counterbalance and offset of our materialistic and vulgar American democracy, and for the spiritualization thereof.
>   —*Democratic Vistas*, 1867

We must return again to the little room on Mickle Street in Camden, New Jersey, where Walt Whitman spent the last lonely decade of his life. He had called for an army of gay lovers to follow him, but none came. At the end, he was surrounded by straight people who made him their own. Peter Doyle gradually stopped coming to see him because, as he explained, "I know he wondered why I saw so little of him the three or four years before he died, but when I explained it to him he understood. Nevertheless, I am sorry for it now. The obstacles were too small to have made the difference I allowed. It was only this: In the old days I had always open doors to Walt—going, coming, staying, as I chose. Now, I had to run the gauntlet of Mrs. Davis and a nurse and whatnot. Somehow, I could not do it. It seemed as if things were not as they should have been. Then I had a mad impulse to go over and nurse him. I was his proper nurse—he understood me, I understood him. We loved each other deeply. But there were things preventing that, too. I saw them. I should have gone to see him, at least, in spite of everything. . . ."[28]

June 10, 1888: Traubel records Whitman lamenting, "Where are you, Pete? Oh! I'm feeling rather kinky—not at all peart, Pete—not at all."[29]

January 16, 1889: Thomas Harned and Horace Traubel turn up the 1865 photo of Walt and Pete Doyle in Washington. Traubel notes, "Doyle with a sickly smile on his face . . . the two looking at each other rather stagily, almost sheepishly." Walt laughed heartily when Traubel picked up the photo, but Harned ridiculed him by mimicking Doyle's expression. Walt asked, "What do I look like there? Is it seriosity?" Harned suggested: "Fondness, and Doyle should be a girl."[30]

I always loved that photo. To me, Peter Doyle looks very happy— a little shy or modest at being posed for a photograph, but gleaming with genuine joy to be watching Walt. And Walt seems rather amused by Pete's discomfort mixed with pride. And Walt seems so benign.

And I love that other photo of Peter Doyle at fifty-seven in Binns's *Life of Walt Whitman*,[31] because I can see him as Dr. Bucke describes him.

{Pete goes to the closet and gets out Walt's old raglan overcoat and puts it on}: I now and then put it on, lay down, think I am in the old times. Then he is with me again. It's the only thing I kept amongst many old things. When I get it on and stretched out on the old sofa I am very well contented. It is like Aladdin's lamp. I do not ever for a minute lose the old man. He is always near by. When I am in trouble—in a crisis—I ask myself, "What would Walt have done under these circumstances?" and whatever I decide Walt would have done, that I do.[32]

When will we learn to love enough to take care of each other until death parts us?

References

1. *Walt Whitman Quarterly Review*, 308 EPB, University of Iowa, Iowa City, Iowa 52242. Subscriptions are $10 per year.

2. Richard Maurice Bucke, M.D., *Cosmic Consciousness* (New York: E.P. Dutton, 1901), still in print.

3. Justin Kaplan, *Walt Whitman: A Life* (New York: Simon & Schuster/ Bantam, 1980). Gay Wilson Allen's *The Solitary Singer* has gone through three editions (Macmillan, 1955; New York University Press, 1967; and University of Chicago Press, 1985), remaining the best and most thorough.

4. Walt Whitman, *Specimen Days* (Boston: David R. Godine, 1971).

5. Gay Wilson Allen, *Walt Whitman* (New York: Grove Press, Evergreen Profile Book No. 19, 1961). Copies of this are still available from the *Walt Whitman Quarterly Review*.

6. John Burroughs, *Whitman, A Study* (Boston: Houghton Mifflin, 1896): 61–62.

7. John Trowbridge, "Reminiscences of Walt Whitman," *Atlantic Monthly* (February 1902): 166.

8. Robert D. Faner, *Walt Whitman and Opera* (Philadelphia: University of Pennsylvania Press, 1951).

9. James D. Steakley, *The Homosexual Emancipation Movement in Germany* (New York: Arno, 1975).

10. Robert K. Martin, *The Homosexual Tradition in American Poetry* (Austin: University of Texas Press, 1979): 33–47. See also Joseph Casy, "Not

Happy in the Capitol: Homosexuality and the *Calamus* Poems," *American Studies* 19 (no. 12, Fall 1978): 5–22.

11. Roger Cooter, *The Cultural Meaning of Popular Science* (Cambridge University Press, 1984): 7, 303–304, et seq.

12. Carl Carmer, "The Fowlers, Practical Phrenologists," *The New Yorker* (February 13, 1937): 22–27.

13. Gavin Arthur, "Document Received from the Hands of Gavin Arthur & Its Authenticity Vouched for by Allen Ginsberg, San Francisco, 1967 [previously unpublished]," *Gay Sunshine* (no. 35, Winter 1978): 29.

14. Walt Whitman, *The Correspondence*, vol. 5: 1880–1892 (New York: New York University Press, 1969): 72–73.

15. John Addington Symonds, *Walt Whitman, A Study* (New York: E.P. Dutton, 1893): 98–99.

16. Edward Carpenter, *Some Friends of Walt Whitman: A Study in Sex-Psychology* (The British Society for the Study of Sex Psychology publication no. 13, 1924; reprint, Norwood Editions, 1978): 13. See also Carpenter's *Days With Walt Whitman* (London: George Allen, 1906; reprint, Ams, 1983).

17. Walt Whitman, *The Correspondence*, vol. 6: *A Supplement with a Composite Index* (New York: New York University Press, 1977): 53.

18. David Russell and Dalvan McIntire (pseudonym for James Kepner), "In Paths Untrodden: A Study of Walt Whitman," ONE, *the Homosexual Magazine* 2 (no. 7, July 1954): 4–15.

19. Jonathan Katz, *Gay American History* (New York: Crowell, 1976). Jonathan Katz, *Gay/Lesbian Almanac* (New York: Harper & Row, 1983).

20. H. Montgomery Hyde, *The Love That Dared Not Speak Its Name* (Boston: Little, Brown, 1970): 63 ff.

21. Walt Whitman, *Leaves of Grass, The First (1855) Edition*, ed. Malcolm Cowley (Penguin, 1976).

22. Walt Whitman, *Blue Book. The 1860–61 Leaves of Grass Containing His Manuscript Additions and Revisions*, vol. 1, Facsimile of the unique copy in the Oscar Lion Collection of the New York Public Library; vol. 2, Textual analysis by Arthur Golden, New York Public Library, 1968.

23. Fredson Bowers, *Whitman's Manuscripts: Leaves of Grass (1860), A Parallel Text* (Chicago: University of Chicago Press, 1955).

24. Walt Whitman, *Notebooks and Unpublished Prose Manuscripts*, vol. 1: *Family Notes and Autobiography, Brooklyn and New York* (New York: New York University Press, 1984): 194.

25. Walt Whitman, *Notebooks and Unpublished Prose Manuscripts*, vol. 2, *Washington* (New York: New York University Press, 1984): 885–894.

26. Walt Whitman, *Notebooks and Unpublished Prose Manuscripts,* vol. 3, *Camden* (New York: New York University Press, 1984), two plates following 1110.

27. George Hutchinson, "Parallels to Shamanism in 'The Sleepers,' " *Walt Whitman Review* 26 (no. 2, June 1980): 43–52.

28. *Calamus: A Series of Letters Written During the Years 1868–1880 by Walt Whitman to a Young Friend (Peter Doyle), Edited and With an Introduction by Richard Maurice Bucke, M.D., One of Whitman's Literary Executors.* (Boston: Small Maynard, 1897; reprint, Folcroft: 1972): 32–33.

29. Horace Traubel, *With Walt Whitman in Camden,* vol. 1, *March 28–July 14, 1888* (Boston: Small Maynard, 1906; reprint, Rowan and Littlefield, 1961): 298.

30. Horace Traubel, *With Walt Whitman in Camden,* vol. 3, *November 1, 1888–January 20, 1889* (New York: Mitchell Kennerley, 1914; reprint, Rowan & Littlefield, 1961): 542–543.

31. Henry Bryan Binns, *A Life of Walt Whitman* (London: Methuen, 1905): 232–233.

32. Bucke, *Calamus*: 29.

EDWARD CARPENTER
SELECTED INSIGHTS

Although seldom read today, the many volumes of Edward Carpenter's collected work represent an extraordinary canon of social criticism and visionary thought. Born in Brighton, England, in 1844 and raised in a large upper-middle-class family, Carpenter grew to become one of the most influential authors and speakers of his day. He remained on the forefront of progressive social change—an advocate of feminism, socialism, the labor movement, and the newly defined class of "intermediate types" with an informed and eloquent voice—until his death in 1929. And while he occupied a central place in the era's radical consciousness, his influence waned in the harsher reality of post–World War I society, during which many of his ideas were borne out by the course of actual events. Yet his thesis that intermediate types (or Uranians, as they were also known) "might possibly fulfill a positive and useful function" in human society is an idea that has only recently been grasped and expanded upon by some intermediate types for themselves—people whom we now call gay. Carpenter's legacy to us is an enormous one.

Carpenter came of age during a time of revived interest in Hellenism. Its basic tenets, especially those about male love, were reclaimed by the first generation of artists and intellectuals in contemporary society to explore homosexual passion and imagination openly. In delving to the source of their feelings, John Addington Symonds, Havelock Ellis, Karl Ulrichs and many others were inevitably led to the source of Western civilization—classical Greek literature and, in particular, Plato's Symposium. *It was there that the natural variation of humankind was most sublimely expressed, including the differentness of men inspired (according to Plato's legend) by Heavenly Aphrodite, daughter of Uranus.* This love was idealized by the Greeks (and much*

---

*Plato suggested that there were two kinds of love, the other known as Common Aphrodite: "Its marks are, first, that it is directed toward women quite as much as young men; second, that in either case it is physical rather than spiritual; third, that it prefers that its objects should be as unintelligent as possible, because its only aim is the satisfaction of its desires, and it takes no account of the manner in which this is achieved. That is why its effect is purely a matter of chance, and quite as often bad as good."

later by others who referred to it as Uranian*) and encompassed those "whose creative desire is of the soul, and who will long to beget spiritually, not physically, the progeny which it is the nature of the soul to create and bring to birth. . . . The partnership between them will be far closer and the bond of affection far stronger than between ordinary parents, because the children that they share surpass human children by being immortal as well as more beautiful."*

There is no doubt that Carpenter had this philosophy at the root of his consciousness when he wrote that Uranians, seeking "new outlet for their energies," became "students of life and nature, inventors and teachers of arts and crafts . . . revealers of the gods and religion . . . became medicine-men and healers . . . and so ultimately laid the foundation of the priesthood, and of science, literature and art." Furthermore, said Carpenter, by rejecting traditional gender roles, some Uranians combined masculine and feminine traits in themselves, thus expanding their capacities and creating a sort of magical, androgynous "cosmic consciousness," which further served the creative, forward spin of human evolution.

Carpenter based his idealism on dedicated study and observation but, unlike many of his contemporaries, practiced direct application of his ideals as well. He believed in a life of simplicity, working hard and living unpretentiously on his small country farm, Millthorpe. He spent many years there, composing his books, educating a constant stream of international visitors and sharing his life openly with male lovers. Carpenter was honest—when so many other homosexuals of the day were not—and persisted in the search for deeper meanings about his existence. He traveled twice to America to visit Walt Whitman, whose poetry had profoundly inspired him; and it was there with his mentor, and while in the company of other dear comrades throughout a pioneering life, that Carpenter experienced his greatest resonance as a gay man—in turn, passing these found truths on to a future generation.

*The following excerpts provide a brief sampling of Carpenters's perceptions about gay people, their place and possible function in human culture. And while most of his classic works have long been out of print—*Towards Democracy *(1883),* Civilization: Its Cause and Cure *(1889),* Love's Coming of Age *(1896),* The Intermediate Sex *(1908), and of particular interest to us today,* Intermediate Types Among Primitive Folk *(1914)—a new generation of gay readers has brought revived attention in Carpenter. As a result, some of his most important writing is now available in inexpensive editions; his words once again urging us to "sail swift and light through the universe . . . and seek the knowledge of all mysteries."*

It is possible that the Uranian spirit may lead to something like a general enthusiasm of humanity, and that the Uranian people may be destined to form the advance guard of that great movement which will one day transform the common life by substituting the bond of personal affection and compassion for the monetary, legal and other external ties which now control and confine society.

More than thirty years ago [1864], an Austrian writer, K. H. Ulrichs, drew attention in a series of pamphlets (*Memnon, Ara Spei, Inclusa,* et cetera) to the existence of a class of people who strongly illustrate the above remark. . . . He pointed out that there were people born in such a position—as it were on the dividing line between the sexes—that while belonging distinctly to one sex as far as their bodies are concerned they may be said to belong *mentally* and *emotionally* to the other; that there were men, for instance, who might be described as of feminine soul enclosed in a male body (*anima muliebris in corpore virili inclusa*) or, in other cases, women whose definition would be just the reverse. And he maintained that this doubleness of nature was to a great extent proved by the special direction of their love-sentiment. For in such cases, as indeed might be expected, the (apparently) masculine person instead of forming a love union with a female tended to contract romantic friendships with one of his own sex; while the apparently feminine would instead of marrying in the usual way, devote herself to the love of another feminine.

People of this kind (that is, having this special variation of the love-sentiment) he called Urnings; and though we are not obliged to accept his theory about the crosswise connection between "soul" and "body," since at best these words are somewhat vague and indefinite; yet his work was important because it was one of the first attempts, in modern times, to recognize the existence of what might be called an inter-mediate sex, and to give at any rate *some* explanation of it.

The instinctive artistic nature of the male of this class, his sensitive spirit, his wavelike emotional temperament, combined with hardihood of intellect and body; and the frank, free nature of the female, her masculine independence and strength wedded to thoroughly feminine grace of form and manner may be said to give them both, through their double nature, command of life in all its phases and a certain freemasonry of the secrets of the two sexes which may well favor their function as reconcilers and interpreters. Certainly it is remarkable that some of the world's greatest leaders and artists have been dowered either wholly or in part with the Uranian temperament—as in the cases of Michelangelo, Shakespeare, Marlowe, Alexander the Great, Julius Caeser; or, among women, Christine of Sweden, Sappho the poetess, and others.

But while the Uranian temperament has, in cases, specially fitted its possessors to become distinguished in art or education or war or administration and enabled them to do valuable work in these fields, it remains perhaps true that above all it has fitted them, and fits them, for distinction and service in affairs of the heart.

It is hard to imagine human beings more skilled in these matters than are the intermediates. For indeed, no one else can possibly respond to and understand, as they do, all the fluctuations and interactions of the masculine and feminine in human life. The pretensive coyness and passivity of women, the rude invasiveness of men; lust, brutality, secret tears, the bleeding heart; renunciation, motherhood, finesse, romance, angelic devotion—all these things lie slumbering in the Uranian soul, ready on occasion for expression; and, if they are not always expressed, are always there for purposes of divination or interpretation.

Anyhow, with their extraordinary gift for, and experience in, affairs of the heart—from the double point of view, both of the man and of the woman—it is not difficult to see that these people have a special work to do as reconcilers and interpreters of the two sexes to each other. . . . It is probable that the superior Urnings will become, in affairs of the heart, to a large extent the teachers of the future society; and if so that their influence will tend to the realization and expression of an attachment less exclusively sensual than the average of today and to the diffusion of this in all directions.

It certainly does not seem impossible to suppose that as the ordinary love has a special function in the propagation of the race, so the other has its special function in social and heroic work and in the generation not of bodily children but of those children of the mind—the philosophical conceptions and ideals which transform our lives and those of society.

Eros is a great leveler. Perhaps the true democracy rests, more firmly than anywhere else, on a sentiment which easily passes the bounds of class and caste and unites in the closest affection the most estranged ranks of society.

For if the slaughter of tyrants is not the chief social duty nowadays, we have with us hydra-headed monsters at least as numerous as the tyrants of old, and more difficult to deal with, and requiring no little courage to encounter. And beyond the extirpation of evils we have solid work waiting to be done in the patient and lifelong building up of new forms of society, new orders of thought and new institutions of human solidarity—all of which in their genesis must meet with opposition, ridicule, hatred and even violence.

Walt Whitman, the inaugurator, it may almost be said, of a new world of democratic ideals and literature, and—as one of the best of our critics has remarked—the most Greek in spirit and in performance of modern writers, insists continually on this social function of "intense and loving comradeship, the personal and passionate attachment of man to man." "I will make," he says, "the most splendid race the sun over shone upon, I will make divine magnetic lands. . . . I will make inseparable cities with their arms about each others' necks, by the love of comrades." And again, in *Democratic Vistas*, "It is to the development, identification and general prevalence of that fervid comradship (the adhesive love at least rivaling the amative love hitherto possessing imaginative literature, if not going beyond it), that I look for the counterbalance and offset of materialistic and vulgar American democracy, and for the spiritualization thereof. . . . I say democracy infers such loving comradeship, as its most inevitable twin or counterpart, without which it will be incomplete, in vain, and incapable of perpetuating itself."

The homogenic attachment, left unrecognized, easily loses some of its best quality and becomes an ephemeral or corrupt thing.

Unwilling as the world at large is to credit what I am about to say, and great as are the current misunderstandings on the subject, I believe it is true that Uranian men are superior to the normal men in this respect—in respect for their love-feeling—which is gentler, more sympathetic, more considerate, more a matter of the heart and less one of mere physical satisfaction than that of ordinary men.

—from *The Intermediate Sex*, 1908

The Uranian temperament in man closely resembles the normal temperament of women in this respect—that in both love, in some form or other, is the main object of life. In the normal man, ambition, moneymaking, business, adventure, et cetera, play their part—love is, as a rule, a secondary matter. The majority of men (for whom the physical side of sex, if needed, is easily accessible) do not for a moment realize the griefs endured by thousands of girls and women—in the drying up of the wellsprings of affection as well as in the crucifixion of their physical needs. But as these sufferings of women, of one kind or another, have been the great inspiring cause and impetus of the women's movement—a movement which is already having a great influence in the reorganization of society—so I do not practically doubt that the similar sufferings of the Uranian class of men are destined in their turn to lead to another wide-reaching social organization and forward movement in the direction of art and human compassion.

—from *My Days and Dreams*, 1916

If I had thought before (and I do not know that I had) that Whitman was eccentric, unbalanced, violent, my first interview certainly produced quite a contrary effect. No one could be more considerate, I may almost say courteous; no one could have more simplicity of manner and freedom from egotistic wrigglings; and I never met any one who gave me more the impression of knowing what he was doing than he did. Yet, away and beyond all this, I was aware of a certain radiant power in him, a large benign effluence and inclusiveness, as of the sun, which filled out the place where he was—yet with something of reserve and sadness in it, too, and a sense of remoteness and inaccessibility.

Some such impressions, at any rate, I gathered in the first interview [in 1877]. I remember how I was most struck, in his face, by the high arch of the eyebrows, giving a touch of childlike wonder and contemplation to his expression; yet his eyes, though full of a kind of wistful tenderness, were essentially not contemplative but perceptive—active rather than receptive—lying far back, steady, clear, with small definite pupils and heavy lids of passion and experience. A face of majestic simple proportion, like a Greek temple as some one has said; the nose Greek in outline, straight (but not at all thin or narrow—rather, the contrary), broad between the brows, and meeting the line of the forehead without any great change of direction; the forehead high, with horizontal furrows, but not excessively high; the head domed and rising to a great height in the middle, above the ears—not projecting behind; ears large and finely formed; mouth full, but almost quite concealed by hair. A head altogether impressing one by its height and by a certain untamed "wild hawk" look not uncommon among Americans.

—from *Days With Walt Whitman*, 1906

The following excerpt is the third of eight chapters from Carpenter's cross-cultural study, Intermediate Types Among Primitive Folk. *The preceding chapters discuss gay people "as Prophet or Priest" and "as Wizard or Witch."*

As Inventors of the Arts and Crafts

I have already said that I think there is an original connection of some kind between homosexuality and divination; but in saying this, of course, I do not mean that everywhere and always the one is associated with the other or that the relationship between the two is extremely well marked; but I contend that a connection can be traced and that on a priori grounds its existence is quite probable.

And first, with regard to actual observation of such a connection, the fact of the widespread belief in it which I have already noted as existing among the primitive tribes of the earth, and their founding of all sorts of customs on that belief, must count for something. Certainly the mere existence of a widespread belief among early and superstitious peoples—as, for instance, that an eclipse is caused by a dragon swallowing the sun—does not prove its truth; but in the case we are considering the matter is well within the range of ordinary observation, and the constant connection between the *choupan* and the *angakok*, the *ke'yev* and the *shamon*, the *berdache* and the witch doctor, the ganymede and the temple-priest, and their correspondences all over the world, the *basir* among the Dyaks, the boy priests in the temples of Peru, the same in the Buddhist temples of Ceylon, Burma and China—all these cases seem to point to some underlying fact, of the fitness or adaptation of the invert for priestly or divinatory functions. And though the tendency already alluded to, of a later religion to ascribe devilish potency to earlier cults, must certainly in many instances shed a sinister or sorcerous glamour over the invert, yet this exaggeration need not blind us to the existence of a residual fact behind it; and, anyhow, to a great many of the cases just mentioned it does not apply at all, since in them the question of one religion superseding another does not enter.

To come to more recent times, the frequency with which accusation of homosexuality has been launched against the religious orders and monks of the Catholic Church, the Knights Templars, and even the ordinary priests and clerics must give us pause. Nor need we overlook the fact that in Protestant Britain the curate and the parson quite often appear to belong to some "third sex" which is neither wholly masculine nor wholly feminine!

Granting, then, that the connection in question is to a certain degree indicated by the anthropological facts which we already possess—is there, we may ask, any rational ground for expecting this connection a priori and from psychological considerations? I think there is.

In the first place all science now compels us to admit the existence of the homosexual temperament as a fact of human nature, and an important fact; and not only so, but to perceive that it is widely spread among the various races of the earth and extends back to the earliest times of which we have anything like historical knowledge. We can no longer treat it as a mere local and negligible freak or put it in the category of a sinful and criminal disposition to be stamped out at all costs. We feel that it must have some real significance. The question is what that may be. The following is a suggestion that may cover part of the ground, though not, I think, the whole.

In the primitive societies the men (the quite normal men) are the warriors and the hunters. These are their exclusive occupations. The women (the normal women) attend to domestic work and agriculture, and their days are consumed in those labors. But in the evolution of society there are many more functions to be represented than those simple ones just mentioned. And we may almost think that if it had not been for the emergence of intermediate types—the more or less feminine man and similarly the more or less masculine woman—social life might never have advanced beyond the primitive phases. But when the man came along who did not *want* to fight—who perhaps was more inclined to run away—and who did not particularly care about hunting, he necessarily discovered some other interest and occupation: composing songs or observing the qualities of herbs or the processions of the stars. Similarly with the woman who did not care about housework and child-rearing. The nonwarlike men and the nondomestic women, in short, sought new outlets for their energies. They sought different occupations from those of the quite ordinary man and woman—as in fact they do today; and so they became the initiators of new activities. They became students of life and nature, inventors and teachers of arts and crafts, or wizards (as they would be considered) and sorcerers; they became diviners and seers or revealers of the gods and religion; they became medicine-men and healers, prophets and prophetesses; and so ultimately laid the foundation of the priesthood and of science, literature and art. Thus—on this view, and as might not unreasonably be expected—it was primarily a variation in the intimate sex-nature of the human being which led to these important differentiations in his social life and external activities.

In various ways we can see the likelihood of this thesis, and the probability of the intermediate man or woman becoming a forward force in human evolution. In the first place, as just mentioned, not wholly belonging to either of the two great progenitive branches of the human race, his nature would not find complete satisfaction in the activities of either branch, and he would necessarily create a new sphere of some kind for himself. Secondly, finding himself *different* from the great majority, sought after by some and despised by others, now an object of contumely and now an object of love and admiration, he would be forced to think. His mind turned inwards on himself would be forced to tackle the problem of his own nature and, afterwards, the problem of the world and of outer nature. He would become one of the first thinkers, dreamers, discoverers. Thirdly, some of the intermediates (though certainly not all) combining the emotionality of the feminine with the practicality of the masculine and many other qualities and powers of both sexes, as well as much of their experience, would undoubtedly be greatly superior in ability to the rest of their tribe and, making forward progress in the world of thought and imagination, would become inventors, teachers, musicians, medicine-men and priests; while their early science and art (for such it would be)—prediction of rain, determination of seasons, observation of stars, study of herbs, creation of chants and songs, rude drawings, and so forth—would be accounted quite magical and divinatory.

With regard to the early beginnings of poetry and music, we know that dancing had an important place; and there is an interesting passage in Leguevel de Lacome's *Voyage a Madagascar*, which indicates the connection of these arts, among the Tsecats of Madagascar, with sexual variation. "Dancers form a distinct class in Madagascar, though they are not very numerous. They have their own manners and customs and live apart; they do not marry, and even affect dislike for women— although they wear the dresses of the latter and imitate their voices, gestures and general habits. They wear large earrings of gold or silver; they carefully extract the hair of their beards; and in short play the part of women so well that one is often deceived. For the rest, these dancers have simple manners and are very sober in their habits; they are continually on the move and are well accepted wherever they go; sometimes, indeed, they receive considerable presents. I have seen chiefs who have been amused by them for some days make them a present, on their departure, of two or three slaves. They are the poets or the bards of the island, and they improvise rhapsodies in praise of those who are generous to them."

Very similar customs connecting the wandering life of dancers, actors, and singers with a certain amount of inversion of temperament are known to have existed among that strange and remarkable people, the Areoi of Polynesia: of whom William Ellis, the missionary already quoted [in the chapter "As Prophet or Priest"], says that they were honored as gods and were supposed to be inspired by the gods to become members of the Areoi society; also that their initiations began by a submission to service and to various ordeals and ended by a ceremonial in which the candidate snatched and appropriated the cloth worn by the chief woman present!

In all this—whether relating to primitive science or primitive art —there would, of course, really be nothing miraculous. It is easy to see that certain individuals, whose interests or abilities were turned in special or unusual directions, would seem to the general herd as having supernatural intuitions or powers. The "rain maker's" predictions in South Africa today may date from no more weatherlore than that of a British farmer; but to his tribe he appears a magician. Magic and early science have almost everywhere been interchangeable terms. The intermediate or Uranian man, from this point of view, would be simply an ordinary member of the tribe who from his double temperament would be rather more observant and acute an originative than the rest. There is, however, another point of view from which he might be credited with something distinctly additional in the way of faculty.

For, in the fourth place, I believe that at this stage an element of what might *really* be called divination would come in. I believe that the blending of the masculine and feminine temperaments would in some of these cases produce persons whose perceptions would be so subtle and complex and rapid as to come under the head of genius, persons of intuitive mind who would perceive things without knowing how, and follow far concatenations of causes and events without concerning themselves about the *why*—diviners and prophets in a very real sense. And these persons—whether they prophesied downfall or disaster, or whether they urged their people onward to conquest and victory, or whether by acute combinations of observation and experience they caught at the healing properties of herbs or determined the starry influences on the seasons and the crops—in almost all cases would acquire and did acquire a strange repuation for sanctity and divinity arising partly perhaps out of the homosexual taboo but also out of their real possession and command of a double-engine psychic power.

The double life and nature certainly, in many cases of inverts observed today, seems to give them an extraordinary humanity and sympathy, together with a remarkable power of dealing with human beings. It may possibly also point to a further degree of evolution than usually attained and a higher order of consciousness—very imperfectly realised, of course, but indicated. This interaction, in fact, between the masculine and the feminine; this mutual illumination of logic and intuition; this combination of action and meditation may not only raise and increase the power of each of these faculties, but it may give the mind a new quality and a new blending of subject and object in consciousness. It may possibly lead to the development of that third order of perception which has been called the cosmic consciousness, and which may also be termed divination. "He who knows the masculine," says Lao-tse, "and at the same time keeps the feminine, will be the whole world's channel. Eternal virtue will not depart from him, and he will return again to the state of an infant." To the state of an infant!—that is, he will become undifferentiated from nature, who is his mother, and who will lend him all her faculties.

It is not, of course, to be supposed that the witch-doctors and diviners of barbarian tribes have in general reached to the high order of development just described, yet it is noticeable, in the slow evolution of society, how often the late and high developments have been indicated in the germ in primitive stages; and it may be so in this case. Very interesting in this connection is the passage already quoted [in "As Prophet or Priest"] from Elie Reclus about the initiations of the Eskimo *angakok* and the appearance to him of his own genius or double from the world beyond, for almost exactly the same thing is supposed to take place in the initiation of the religious *yogi* in India—except that the god in this latter case appears to the pupil in the form of his teacher or guru. And how often in the history of the Christian saints has the divinity in the form of Jesus or Mary appeared to the strenuous devotee, apparently as the culminating result of his intense effort and aspiration, and of the opening out of the new plane of perception in his mind! It may be that with every great onward push of the growing soul and every great crisis in which, as it were, a sheath or a husk falls away from the expanding bud, something in the nature of a metamorphosis does really take place; and the new order, the new revelation, the new form of life, is seen for a moment as a vision in glorious state of a divine being within.

JIM KEPNER

I SHOULD HAVE BEEN LISTENING: A MEMORY OF GERALD HEARD

When Christopher Isherwood first met Gerald Heard in London in 1932, he described the young philosopher-writer as "witty, playful, flattering, talkative as a magpie, well informed as an encyclopedia and, at the same time, life-weary, meditative, deeply concerned, and in earnest." Gay activist and archivist Jim Kepner found the same enduring qualities at work twenty years later, when he encountered Heard in Los Angeles. Heard, who had made Southern California his home since 1937, was by then exerting considerable influence over a small group of writers and intellectuals, some who would later go on to lead the burgeoning gay rights movement in America.

Heard found his most popular voice regarding gay issues, however, through the pages of ONE magazine, the nation's first publicly sold, avowedly gay publication. It was published from January 1953 through 1968 (although four additional issues were produced in 1972 before the magazine finally ceased).

Heard contributed six articles to ONE and to the more academic ONE Institute Quarterly: Homophile Studies between 1953 and 1960, under the pen name of D. B. Vest. According to a longtime student of Heard, the pseudonym stood for double-breasted, referring to the duality of human nature and the principle of androgyny central to Heard's basic philosophy. Many of the magazine's four thousand readers at the time responded to Heard's theories and convoluted writing style with skepticism and anger. Here, Kepner elaborates on Heard's message and meanings. His memoir is followed by two short articles by Heard, written for ONE: "A Future for the Isophyl" (1955) and "What Is Religion?" (1954).

‎|‎ first met British philosopher Gerald Heard (tall, thin, elegant) in 1950 when he gave an exciting but nearly impenetrable talk to a science-fiction convention in Los Angeles. His thesis—that science is itself fiction—infuriated most of the listeners that day. They believed implicitly that science was on its way to solving all the problems of the world, so much so that A. E. Van Vogt, the visionary sci-fi writer who'd introduced him, apologized afterward to the audience for making the introduction! But I, in shock from the enormous effort to keep up with his talk, sensed a core message of special concern to me as a gay person. I had previously known of Heard as author of some fine mysteries and fantasies (*A Taste for Honey*, *The Great Fog* and a then-recent book about flying saucers that envisioned the evolutionary potential and limitations of a Martian insect society). I'd heard him called the Sage of Santa Monica and knew vaguely that he'd come to the United States in 1937 expecting to teach at Duke University—drawn by J. B. Rhine's experiments in extrasensory perception, which then promised to open up whole new areas of human potential.

Experimental Seminars

Shortly after I joined the early Mattachine Society (fountainhead of America's gay movement) in early 1953, I was invited to a series of small, informal seminars with Heard at the Echo Park home of *ONE* magazine's testy editor Dale Jennings. Two earlier series had been held the year before. Heard was a breathless, inspiring, gleefully clever and never doctrinaire speaker. His complex ideas came out effortlessly, but at machine-gun speed. I felt as frustrated as second-grade kid trying to follow lectures on trigonometry. No matter how intimate, reasonable and clear he was, only three times before had I ever tried to follow speakers as complex and challenging—a revered high-school mathematician, a missionary who'd departed enough from Christian superiority to learn from Gandhi and the Hindu mystics, and a Marxist who taught classes on dialectical materialism and political economy to the staff of New York's *Daily Worker*.

Heard attempted to lay down some general principles for the goals and strategies of the homophile movement (as we then called it). His elaborate and highly abstract presentation required at least four or five sessions with a perceptive and attentive audience to work through to the core ideas, moving onto metaphysical ground that I distrusted. But new people came each week, and their beginners' questions kept the discussion trapped at an introductory level. I think Heard wanted to progress beyond talk to some yogalike group exercises, but we were too uptight to be ready for that, too busy with the practicalities of the movement.

He repeated these seminars from time to time, holding a final seminar in his bungalow behind a mass of oleanders high above Santa Monica Canyon in mid-1965, while his longtime companion, Michael, lurked in the background, offering tea and crackers. Kaleidoscope manufacturer John Burnside and Mattachine founder Harry Hay (soon to be life partners), Dorr Legg and Don Slater (founders of *ONE*), two of Heard's gay UCLA disciples and I participated. His conversations were like diamond mines of interesting facts, and I at least was more interested in picking up the random bits of information he dropped constantly than the general direction of his thinking. Slater was cutely condescending, saying things like, "Oh, Geraldine, don't be so serious," while Hay and Burnside seemed argumentative. Heard terminated the third session suddenly and angrily when he realized how really unreceptive we were to his questing views. I was interested in what he had to say, but not interested enough to take the time to follow through, to lay aside for a while the day-to-day practical concerns of the growing gay movement.

That was sad. I think he'd already suffered a couple of heart attacks and seemed to feel that few of his disciples had understood enough of what he had to point to. But that very year, some of his long-rejected ideas began to see fruition on the Berkeley campus and in San Francisco's Haight-Ashbury—though not quite in the forms he'd conceived.

Henry Fitzgerald Heard, eighty-one, died in mid-1971 after five years in a virtual coma, and after an active life that took him from Cambridge to Oxford, to Duke University, and to the Society of Friends (Quakers) and the Vedanta Society (a Westernized version of liberal, universalist Hindu spirituality) in Hollywood.

He is less known for his own books (*Ascent of Humanity*; *Anatomy of Costume*; *Science in the Making*; *A History of the English-Speaking World, 1900–1930*; *Is God in History? Training for a Life of Growth; The Seven Stages of Man* and two books on Vedanta co-edited with Christopher Isherwood) than for his considerable influence on such intimates as Aldous and Julian Huxley, H. G. Wells, Bernard Shaw, Somerset Maugham, Wystan Auden, Rebecca West, Igor Stravinsky, Thane Walker of The Prosperos, Arnold Bennett, Swami Prabhavananda, Evelyn Hooker and Christopher Isherwood.

He was the model for Dr. Miller in Huxley's *Eyeless in Gaza* and for Augustus in Isherwood's *Down There on a Visit*, being dealt with more directly in the latter's *Christopher and His Kind* and *My Guru and His Disciple*, though I think perhaps that Isherwood, while deeply influenced by the man, made little attempt to grasp the main directions of his thought.

A philosopher of history, anthropologist, lecturer for BBC and, much later, for Los Angeles's KPFK-FM and on many campuses; a mystic and science fiction writer, he also repeatedly offered guidance to America's gay movement in its formative stages—though his advice was little heeded at the time, so locked in we were, each to our own views and pragmatic goals.

God in History

One of the last serious philosophers of history in an age when most historians say that history has no meaning, Heard pulled together information from the unswept corners of the sciences of human development. Combining theology and evolution, he argued that each part in man's ascent from "group consciousness, through individuality, to super-consciousness" had its own intrinsic worth. He was much influenced by Hindu philosophy. I don't know how much he explored Buddhism. He personally knew most major innovators in the sciences.

His thinking probed beneath the politicoeconomic preoccupations of the midcentury. The clash between capitalist individualism and communist statism was, he felt, beside the point. Neither system was fulfilling or really liberating. He called for a complete new way of life, with a concordant psychology and economy.

As a start, he proposed, somewhat as Gandhi had, neo-Brahmin societies—spiritual communes with cottage industries, economically as independent as possible (like hippie communes of the late 1960s), in balance with nature and involved in exercises for the raising and merging of consciousness. Consensual structuring of such communities would ensure that "the more you respect a personality, the better its chance of discovering that all personality is a prison."

Having evolved from the development of physique to technique, man must avoid degeneration and collapse, by a sudden, radical mutation, through the development of his psychic powers—not genetically nor technically, but through the expansion of consciousness beyond limits of individual ego—to an illuminated state of absorption in "the whole." Privately, he felt that gays were en route to becoming that mutation, but he didn't say that in his published writings.

Previewing ecology and gestalt, he insisted that the world process be viewed as an organic whole, neither in the simplistic view of the mechanists, who see merely an assemblage of accidental causes and effects, nor in the teleological conceit that counts only the end of an historic sequence as having significance. Our lives are justified by every moment we live, not by some ultimate purpose laid on us. To sacrifice our lives to someone else's long-term goals was, for Heard, the ultimate betrayal.

He viewed mankind not as a collection of individuals but as a single, living organism whose "cells," by bad habit, have forgotten to see their oneness. Most of his published books followed the view common to many mystics—that we must rise above the desires and commitments of the flesh. I felt that he had begun to go beyond the attitude that Isherwood found so attractive in his guru—that it doesn't matter what your carnal desires are, so long as you attempt to rise above them. Swami Prabhavananda granted that Isherwood might not be ready to give them up in this particular reincarnation. Heard, I think, had begun to see the essence of our gayness as something to be explored, developed to the full, and shared with others in physico-spiritual exercises, *not something to turn our backs on.*

The deeper implication of the playful-serious name Mattachine (not the trivial explanation given in its publications since 1954) and the metaphysical suggestion of the name *ONE* apparently led him to think that we homophile movement leaders had more in our heads at the time than many of us actually did. *ONE* to us was nothing more than the name cleverly chosen for a homosexual magazine we were putting out. Cosmic consciousness was the furthest thing from our minds.

God-oriented like the theological philosophers Teilhard de Chardin and Paul Tillich, Heard was not so much concerned with *whether* God existed as with the psychological, spiritual and social consequences of one's contemplation of godhead—that is, of seeking for directly intuited unity with the All.

He urged three forms of training to progress from physical control to control of impulses and feelings: diet, psychological retraining and respiratory control, and meditation to achieve self-awareness and non-attachment. In the retreat he built in Trabuco Canyon, later given to the Vedanta Society, he tried to focus spiritual energy much as cliff-dwelling native Americans had in their *kivas* or Wilhelm Reich with his orgone boxes.

An early proponent of "consciousness-expanding" techniques, he and Aldous Huxley (who'd come here together in 1937, becoming part of the colony of European intellectual refugees in Santa Monica Canyon) were alert to mescaline and LSD to "help the meditator stop the constant flow of associative thinking that prevents him from reaching the serene and silent regions of his mind." Things he wrote in 1930 sounded like forty-years-later reports on alpha-wave experiments.

A Future for the Isophyl

He was much concerned that the major words we use have the right meanings when broken down into their component parts—otherwise, those wrong meanings produce wrong habits. A minority group's proper self-image depends on what it chooses, or permits itself, to be called.

In place of *homosexual*, which he felt carried many layers of wrong meanings, Heard proposed that we call ourselves *isophyls*—lovers of the same—a good but not very contagious idea.

In his talks, in frequent visits and letters to *ONE*, and in articles he wrote under the pen name D. B. Vest for *ONE* magazine and *Homophile Studies* (some of which I butchered in the editing—his manuscripts always contained far too much that needed to be cleaned up and to be guessed at), he urged us to go beyond seeking fair treatment from the heterosexual majority (he especially felt it would be a disastrous tactic and bad karma to make the majority feel guilty for past or present injustices) to consciousness-raising within our own community. We must not be so lured by the hope of "acceptance" by a dreary, conformist, money-mad, prestige-mad society that we sally forth in hyper-male tweeds or leather to curry favor by putting down swishes and drags. He said gay men need to accept and act out their effeminate urges as well as their need for colorful male display.

Noting the therapeutic value—and just plain fun—of carnival costumes, he said clothes should be expressive and liberating, not status masks; also, that we should accept the natural odors of the body, intuiting the true character of those we meet by sniffing—rather than crippling our instinctual abilities with deodorants and various chemical salves.

Like Jung, he regarded "the great hermaphrodite" as the aim of human evolution. Dimorphism (radical physical dissimilarity in appearance and function of males and females), he said, tends to disappear in human evolution, and the once-functional contrast is now retrogressive—the mark of the caveman. He noted that species, such as the social insects, that develop specialization (individuals emerge from the egg already shaped to begin immediate service as workers of several possible specific types—infertile female soldiers or workers, male breeders, or queens) are an evolutionary dead end, despite their seeming efficiency.

He considered the mammalian prolongation of childhood as the driving wedge of evolution—and the isophyl as evolution's most successful type for prolonging the unspecialized condition of adolescent openness and creativity (though he felt that the destructive rowdiness and anarchism of adolescence could be dangerous). In the past it was all very well for most people to be born to the roles of their fathers: farmers, soldiers, tradesmen, priests or nobles. Society now needs accelerating flexibility and persons who remain open to new possibilities, who are not locked into the ways of the past but are more interested in keeping young, in keeping their options open, in exploring new paths, tending by their very flexibility to create evolution, socially rather than biologically. The more they abandon the traditional heterosexual ideal of "growing up," of being "responsible" or "stable," settling down for a lifetime of commitment to one mate, one job and one role as parent, the more they realize themselves and serve the needs of progress.

Such adaptability is best preserved by maintaining the habits of play, by feelings of communal kinship—tribalism—unlike the exclusive, selfish love that closes off the nuclear family from the community. But in order to realize their potential, isophyls or gays must break free from social conditioning that impels them to desperately imitate hetero marital patterns. (He was fascinated with the differences in the ways lesbians and gay men often escape the gender-role dichotomy.)

To sustain creativity throughout a rising curve of life, with the sort of outgoing warmth Heard noted in hippies as early as 1958, the *neotenic* person (one who retains certain so-called immature qualities) is to develop by Tantra-like exercises—a "co-charging of bodies by bringing the two electric fields into contact along their specific zones." This lining up of our hidden energy centers in such a way as to produce a synergistic burst of new energy was, he felt, what we were unconsciously attempting when we did what we called "having sex." He felt it was a dangerous misunderstanding to label such intimate play as *sexual*, a term he preferred to limit to action aimed at procreation. Somewhat like Whitman, he saw it as a physicospiritual sacrament, much in the manner of early Christian *agape*. Were he alive today, he might even suggest, gently, lovingly, and nonjudgmentally, that our susceptibility to AIDS may be a result of our misuse and misunderstanding of our unique energies—but here, perhaps, I presume too much.

While there was a puritanical current running through much of metaphysical thinking, I believe that Heard had begun to break away from this. He was not objecting to the activities we call sex play so much as to our misunderstanding of the purposes they serve *for us*. He envisioned an isophylic elite rising above the outmoded ideas of *sex*. He saw a new kind of creativity in the erotic interplay of two or more persons who were not committed to breeding—but were truly committed to exploring one another's potentialities, to enjoying and to charging up one another.

Heard was, as I also was, fascinated by the gnostic-colored newly discovered writings found in the deserts of Egypt, the Dead Sea and northern Syria in the later 1940s: the Dead Sea Scrolls, Nag Hamadi manuscripts and the Ras Shamra texts, with their many indications that spiritual growth involves the blending of "male" and "female" qualities. He would certainly have been equally excited by Dr. Morton Smith's report of the discovery of the fragment of a secret Gnostic Gospel of Mark in the library of the most ancient Mount Sinai monastery, which gave strong indication that Jesus engaged in physico-spiritual intercourse with his disciples, at least while initiating them.

The fragment, analyzed in *Clement of Alexandria and the Secret Gospel of Mark* (Harvard University Press, 1973) retells the Lazarus story in what Clement said was the original version: that the young man coming from the tomb looked at Jesus, loved him and begged to be with him; that Jesus insisted on certain preparations first, then met the youth, who had only a linen cloth over his nakedness, and remained with him that night and taught him the mysteries. Columbia history professor Smith relates this to several other secular and scriptural stories, including the transfiguration and the flight of the linen-draped Mark from the scene of Jesus's arrest.

If, in patching together notes and recollections of random things Heard said and wrote over many years, I have misrepresented, trivialized or distorted his views, the fault is mine. I haven't begun to deal with the encyclopedic range of his interests or with how he combined things that most linear thinkers regard as totally unrelated. I recommend a search of his writings—not easy to find. Writings published under H. F. Heard or Gerald Heard made no direct reference to gayness but a strong gay sensibility pervades them, and much can be read between the lines by those willing to work at it. (Knowing how to write and read between the lines is, unhappily, a talent we gays are losing in this day of public coming out.)

The news of his death and my study for the initial version of this essay in 1971 had a remarkable breakthrough effect on me. I got into the shower one evening in September before driving to a meeting of the new Gay Community Alliance, where we would consider bylaws, and several ideas that I'd been working through for some time suddenly burst together, accompanied by flashing lights somewhat like a moving, multidimensional Tantric mandala. (I'd never paid any attention to these; artistically they have seemed to me ugly.) As I stepped into the shower, I was thinking, almost concurrently, about the gnostic mythos as an analogy to how different sorts of gays begin their self-perception; about the distinction between "being gay" and engaging in homosexuality; about the crippling limitations of linear thinking; about how Pope John XXIII had revivified the Catholic Church when a somewhat similar Khrushchev had tried and failed to do the same with the Communist hierarchy; about our ability, materialist denials notwithstanding, to sometimes instinctively find our way in strange cities, to be able to sense that there's a gay bar just around the corner, or that that car coming down the street is Vice; about the counterculture and the magic of the play, *Hair*; about the parallel between gay love and real Christian love; about how differences in human character were at least partly reflected by the ideas of astrological signs; about my own realization that I was not Leo, as I had long supposed, but Aquarius, and my joy at that even if I thought the whole idea of reading character from the zodiac was nonsense; et cetera. Then, for about twenty minutes, I was enveloped in a shower of water and light as these random ideas rushed together into one idea that I tried to hold intact as I dried, dressed and drove from Torrance to the business meeting in West Hollywood.

I told friends there that if any of them had claimed to have had such an experience, I'd have thought them crazy. Within three days, I could only recall the component ideas that had led me to that experience—not how, specifically, they had come together. I took a lot of showers, tried running down those same idea paths, got a few pale bursts faintly resembling that one experience. I felt like Heinlein's stranger-in-a-strange-land trying to find his way back to the water-brotherhood in which he'd been conceived. I also felt sure that some of what Heard had been saying over the years had finally gotten through to me—and then slipped through my fingers, as I once more continued my "bad habit" of spending more time at endless business meetings than on the inner search.

When the Radical Fairie movement was just starting, I again began to explore these areas of experience, but those I associated with became involved in dreary forms of spiritual exercises (particular to an obscure Hindu cult) that did nothing whatever for my Western-bred spirit and which aimed at blotting out consciousness rather than opening it up. Besides, I was too busy then transforming my personal library into the public institution that is, now, the International Gay and Lesbian Archives in Los Angeles—an important, mundane job—but again, I feel that I should have been listening.

GERALD HEARD

A FUTURE FOR THE ISOPHYL AND WHAT IS RELIGION?

A Future for the Isophyl

The chief charge made against isophyls has been that they are "unnatural" (merely private jaded behavior). This is not true. Every known species of mammal produces intergrades. Further, with man, isophylia is commoner, because man's rapid advance has been due to his retaining unspecialized youthfulness longer than any other species.

With play, curiosity, wonder and creativity (largely lost by other adult animals), man retains psychosomatic generalization, that panaesthetic response, that need for caress and fondling, which is gay, exploratory and stimulant but purely erotic rather than specifically sexual, for it is preproductive.

Modern society faces two demands. The first is Malthus's Devil, brooding again over mankind: We must realize man breeds faster than he can produce food. When such societies as the Achaean Greeks—or the nomads on their failing grasslands—found population pressures threatening disaster, they seemed to alter their mores regarding isophylia and produced increasing proportions of those to whom this way of life was satisfying and inspiring.

When certain breeding changes are necessary to the race, biological modifications do seem to occur. After a war, male births increase, tending to readjust the male–female ratio. Thus, isophylia is nature's response to the population pressures on the food supply.

Never before have human societies approached such elaboration or changed at such unsettling speed. Taylor, pioneer in scientific management, discovered that the invention of a new machine requires a new type of machine mind. Western economy can only escape fission and collapse if served by experts who must be concerned with and feel loyalty to the entire accelerating process. They must retain the brave curiosity of the child.

All highly developed social creatures—bees, ants, termites—produce worker types, specific mutations to fit the elaborate socioeconomic structure. As human society grows complex and interlocked, man, too, produced a type to serve the need.

In advanced societies, the isophylic type, relieved of breeding, is produced and so specialized as to run the elaborate organizations. The increasingly complex social structure demands a type less restricted to the small pattern of the family than the heterosexual.

These are the two uses of the isophyl. One is outside his control—willy-nilly, he serves the biological purpose of nature. The other is more a promise than an assignation. Human society is still in a more rudimentary state than that of the more advanced creatures.

We have outgrown the family: The community educates the rising generation. Parenthood is increasingly confined to reproduction and parturition. But the community remains largely incoherent, a heterogeneous mixture of disputing creeds and conflicting social heredities. It will require much social planning before a scientifically designed society, its psychology balanced with its economy, will emerge.

This can only happen when society and the isophyl understand one another. Where other highly developed societies have created an apparently unchanging social structure, best served by specialized types (derived by atrophy of specific sex structure), human society is essentially mobile, progressive. This type, therefore, instead of atrophying retains youthful unspecialization into the stage of adult awareness and responsibility.

The isophyl is a further development of that human power to put off settling down—the resiliency that makes man civilizable. If our society is to progress (being mobile, it must progress, or crash) it must be manned by at least some members who, because they can keep young, have two essentials:

Emotionally, they retain the generalized response and outgoingness of children, which our loyalty-governed community must have to avoid moral bankruptcy. Intellectually, they keep that curiosity, also a quickly lost characteristic of youth, which our changing community also needs to use its new patterns creatively. An open mind is more important than a high IQ. By nature the isophyl is suited to develop emotionally and intellectually. He needs but realize that to equip himself for the services that will establish beyond doubt his value to this age.

When any species, under the struggle to survive, reproduces bisexually, the two sexes come to be excessively differentiated. The male gorilla may be twice the size of the female. Neanderthal woman was first mistaken as a different species from Neanderthal man, so great were the differences. As conditions became easier, the climate more genial, the sexes tend again to approximate.

The interpretive, administrative types (priest, prophet, artist) tend to rise among the intergrades. A balanced mixture of the "andric" and "gynic" factors seem to be the endocrine poise that best combines the exploratory urge with the compositional desire. Here such a type is most likely to arrive at profoundly new insights.

Analysis of the creative process has today become one of the great concerns of education. The open mind was never so necessary. All research into the mind shows that further evolution depends on retaining resilience. The isophyl has the mind—body makeup that makes possible the openness of heart and mind without which toleration disappears, progress is arrested and society declines into tyranny.

If mankind is to retain its liberties, rid itself of war and social violence and advance, two factors will establish themselves:

The andric—gynic blend will be established as the characteristic poise of the progressive type. Natural selection will favor this, as prejudice proves an increasingly high security risk. An atavistic mind endangers an accelerating community.

Our radical inventions call for minds of unusual openness. Our unprecedented awareness of other cultures, which we can no longer hope to deform to our prejudice, compel us to be anthropologically minded. The isophyl, retaining the child's uncrafty geniality and trusting friendliness, is most suited to negotiate with other social heredities. His future seems to be in the intellectual services he can render in exploring the further frontiers of the mind and in the diplomatic or anthropological services working toward the federalization of mankind.

What Is Religion?

"What is religion?" That's the first question. We must answer it before we can go on to the second: "What has religion to do with the isophyl?" Most people would say, "The last person religion wants to have anything to do with is the isophyl. Hasn't religion, whenever it caught sight of him, killed him?" That's all too true. (Torquemada, the horrible Grand Inquisitor of Spain, burned alive over ten thousand persons, a third of whom it is said were burned on the charge of homosexuality.) But this religion of hate and horror, blood and torture, is not the only religion. Indeed, it is a perversion of the original religion, the *true* religion, because that basic religion was and is exactly what the word *religion* means. *Religion means to re-bind.* (A *ligature* means a *binding*.) All religions begin—it is that which gives them their start—by being love religions. They have their first and great success because they show people how they may love one another. But then, instead of winning new members by *love*, they begin to try to make people submit by *force*. They also start having "party purges." Small, bitter, power-loving minorities turn themselves into heretic hunters. Those who won't submit to the threat are, when possible, tortured and killed.

No wonder rationalists and scientists are suspicious of religion and feel it should be opposed. The common fruits of the religious tree have for too long been cruelty and obscurantism, the refusal to show mercy or to respect truth. But the rationalists and scientists have been wrong when they said, "We don't need religion and can get along without it." *The real religion is necessary to man.* For as Pascal, the great mathematician, said, "The heart has reasons which the mind doesn't know." That means we have, beside our surface thinking mind, a deep mind that knows by feeling. Religion, this being together in a small group that feels unlimited liability for each member, is so necessary to our happiness and indeed to our sanity that people, in the hope of finding this, will join churches whose creeds they can't believe and whose intolerances they detest. For the core of religion (as was said by Royce, California's most famous philosopher) is "devotion to a beloved community."

Now this group of people devoted to one another demonstrates not only a *universal human need*, but the *particular* need of the isophyl. Many sociologists are puzzled by the fact that, while divorce increases, so does church attendance. This, however, is no real paradox. On the contrary, it is what we should expect. For as we are seeing the failure of the attempt to join two people together for life while denying them any other intimate adult tender companionship, we see them seeking a group that will understand them, a group in which love will be as intense, loyal and self-forgetful but also far richer in wisdom, resources and patience than any young couple, ignorant and infatuated, can be.

And today, besides this return to orthodox church membership (which return too often ends in disappointment), we see an even more significant symptom of the return to religion—that is, the rapid growth of a new type of religion. These new groupings have been called ad hoc churches. That is to say, they are made of groups of people who had found themselves in a terrible fix. Society rejected them and they were sinking. They came together to see whether they could help each other. No one else could, and very few even wished to try. Such groups (here called ad hoc churches, because each serves a special need of one particular problem type) are the Alcoholics Anonymous, the Narcotics Anonymous, and Recovery Incorporated for those in mental trouble. But, besides these recovery, self-salvage groups, there are groups that advance an already attained status. For instance, many people who have had psychoanalysis feel the need for companionship with others who have gone through this discipline and now want to go on to further self-integration, to further understanding and control of themselves. These people are not patients convalescing from an addiction (like alcohol or morphia) or from mental derangement. Successful psychoanalysis and psychotherapy do for the mind what a good gym does for the body—they make the still healthy still stronger.

Here, then, is what the isophyl can and should look for in religion: the group that understands him, in which he will find friendship and support and service, which will save him from discouragement and *bring out the best in him*. As Carl Jung has said, all men of good will are agreed now about four of the five natural moral laws: The rule of force should be "through persuasion, not by coercion"; the rule for wealth should be "to be creatively employed, not merely to be making money"; the rule of "the man of his word" is that he does not cheat; the rule of mental hygiene is, "Don't think one thing and do another."

So we find the answers to the four key questions: What is force, wealth, your word, your thought? But there is a *fifth* question, and it is causing most of our present confusion. Freud thought it was: "What is sex?" Modern psychology is increasingly convinced that that is to put it too narrowly. The real question is: *What is love?* And we are stalled trying to answer it, because those who believe in self-control don't believe in up-to-date psychophysical scientific knowledge, while those who hold by scientific knowledge often look on self-control as a hangover from the blind inhibitions of superstition. This, then, is the key question that confronts modern man. By setting himself to solve it by learning to work with a *devoted* group that believes control and love are two aspects of the same thing, the isophyl can not only aid himself and his fellows, he can forward religion and help mankind.

MARK THOMPSON

HARRY HAY: A VOICE FROM THE PAST, A VISION FOR THE FUTURE

Full of complex memories from an eventful life and, at seventy-five, quick to point out that he is still living it, Harry (Henry) Hay commands a unique place on the American scene. Generally acknowledged as the contemporary "father of gay liberation," Hay carries a vision as radical as it is simple. Using terms such as the gay window, subject–subject consciousness, *and* a separate people whose time has come, *Hay holds forth the ideas that gay people embody a form of consciousness as different from the mainstream's as their sexuality and that they have a special contribution to make to humanity. Although, he stresses, gay people must determine for themselves what this perspective might be.*

Hay's conception of the Mattachine Society in the early 1950s—the first successful attempt to organize homosexuals politically in America—is recounted at length in the following chapter. The society's rise, development and ultimate betrayal of Hay was to change profoundly not only the course of one man's life but the path taken by a major political and social movement as well. During the past thirty-five years, Hay has continued to live a life dedicated to social reform on many fronts, sharing much of that time with his life partner, John Burnside, whom he met in 1963. Still, the essential questions that first ignited Hay's imagination have been left largely unresolved, submerged by a movement's struggle for rights and power: "Who are we gay people?" "Where have we been throughout the ages?" "What might we be for?"

Hay and I first met in spring 1979. The pretext was to help spread the word about the Spiritual Conference for Radical Fairies, and the interview included here was the result of that meeting. Hay seemed larger than life at the time, history personified. Experience of his humor, his foibles, and his residing strength of character has made him more human to me since, making the depth of his convictions all the more real.

Knowledge of themselves and the world they inhabit has always seemed best passed on personally, one-to-one, among gay men. Hay excels in the role of gay storyteller, and one tale he tells about himself illustrates this point well. In January 1930, at the age of seventeen, Hay enticed a man fifteen years older than himself in Los Angeles's notorious Pershing Square. "The guy I seduced into picking me up and bringing me out into the gay world had himself been brought out by a guy who was a member of the Chicago Society for Human Rights." The society, says Hay, was basically a social group that had a short and abortive life in the Midwest city during the mid-1920s. "The idea of gay people getting together at all, in more than a daisy chain, was an eye-opener of an idea. Champ passed it on to me as if it were too dangerous; the failure of the Chicago group should be a direct warning to anybody trying to do anything like that again."

The germ of an idea was planted, nevertheless. It was a warning not heeded, and half a century later, the dream that gay people have a right to know who they are has effectively been passed on to yet another generation. It is a dream made all the more remarkable by the scope of Harry Hay's vision.

May Day, 1979

A minority has its own kind of aggression. It absolutely dares the majority to attack it. It hates the majority—not without cause, I grant you. It even hates the other minorities, because all minorities are in competition: Each one proclaims that its sufferings are the worst and its wrongs are the blackest. And the more they all hate, the more they all are persecuted, the nastier they become! Do you think it makes people nasty to be loved? You know it doesn't! Then why should it make them nice to be loathed? While you're being persecuted, you hate what's happening to you, you hate the people who are making it happen; you're in a world of hate. Why, you wouldn't recognize love if you met

it! You'd suspect love! You'd think there was something behind it—
some motive—some trick. . . .

—Christopher Isherwood
A Single Man

I set aside my copy of Isherwood's great novel and gaze at the clouds passing by the window. I'm on an early morning flight to Los Angeles, to meet a man who—without my knowing—will awaken a lifetime of dreams that, until now, have been elusive as the mist that floats just beyond reach.

Harry Hay is not a name recognized by most gay people. Yet, two decades before Stonewall thrust the need for gay civil liberties into national focus, Hay had already established the foundation from which these rights could be declared. Hay's pioneering efforts helped point the way to the thousands now coming out to families, in demonstrations and in the media across the country.

Hay announced his sexual orientation to friends at Stanford University in October 1931, at the age of nineteen. Even then, he realized that asserting oneself politically was not a full definition of gay liberation. Being a homosexual, he felt, meant more than just equal rights and privileges. It was a "gift" allowed to a certain percentage of humanity, offering a different set of biological, social and spiritual receptors through which the world could be perceived and interpreted. Whether this innate difference could be fully accepted and understood was another matter altogether, as Hay was later to discover.

Hay's vision has been informed by an amazing range of life experiences: He has been an actor, a Marxist organizer and teacher, an expert musicologist, a prolific writer, an Indian rights activist and an outspoken advocate for other progressive causes. Born in England on April 7, 1912, he moved shortly after the outbreak of World War I to the Chilean Andes, where his father managed Anaconda copper mines. His parents returned to their native America in 1916, however, bringing their children to Los Angeles, where Hay was to spend most of the rest of his life. Although he came from a privileged background,

Hay was exposed to liberal ideas and causes from an early age. As a teenager, he worked in the fields of western Nevada during the summer, where his Wobbly co-workers gave him International Workers of the World tracts to read at night, testing him on them by day. At home, he was tutored for a while by a Jesuit priest in the history of religion and philosophy toward the idea of recruiting him into the Jesuit order. He later studied in a Los Angeles lawyer's office for a year and by the end of 1930 was ready to continue his education at Stanford University, where he impressed the faculty with his precocious political insights.*

During the depression years, Hay worked in the theater, giving his first performance in 1932 at the Hollywood Playhouse. His imposing manner, both on and off the stage, earned him the title The Duchess. Within a year, Hay met fellow leftist actor Will Geer. Their two-year romance made an indelible impact on Hay, as Geer taught him street theater, exposed him to Hollywood's extensive gay subculture, and introduced him to the Communist party. Hay would maintain contact with the party for the next twenty years, earning a reputation as an effective teacher and organizer. In 1938, Hay married another party member and adopted two daughters. But his relationship to wife and party was increasingly strained as Hay became interested in organizing homosexuals. By the early 1950s, both commitments had come to an end—but were not forgotten. In July 1955, Hay was called before the House Un-American Activities Committee and successfully withstood questions about his earlier Communist associations.

Momentarily putting aside the facts of Hay's personal history, it is not at all unlikely that Southern California would give birth to the modern gay movement in America. Although there had been earlier attempts to organize homosexuals and there were known gay communities in the nation's major cities, particularly after World War II, the Mattachine Society was the first ongoing gay political organization in the United States. Los Angeles has always displayed a propensity for nurturing idealists and visionaries of many kinds. It is the West, after all, a social frontier less bound by convention, well tempered by

---

*Among others whom he impressed was fellow student James Broughton. Although the two men entertained a brief friendship, they would not meet again until fifty years later at a gathering for radical fairies in the Colorado mountains.

the special historic and natural elements that have formed its open character.

As reported in Jonathan Katz's landmark *Gay American History*, Hay used the word *androgynous* to describe the nation's gay minority when he first conceived the need for organization in 1948. The idea slowly grew during the months that followed, a time marked by escalating national paranoia. In July 1950, war broke out in Korea, and with Rudi Gernreich, Hay's first recruit, he collected five hundred signatures for the now-famous Stockholm Peace Petition on two strips of Santa Monica Bay known locally to gays as their beaches.

Hay and Gernreich also planted the idea for a gay organization, and while few committed themselves to action, some names and addresses were collected. This list later became the basis for the Mattachine Society's first discussion groups in December 1950 and January 1951.

A surviving report from one of these early meetings quotes Hay stating that "sexual energy not used by homosexuals for procreation, as it is by heterosexuals, should be channelized elsewhere where its ends can be creativity."

In fall 1951, Hay realized that organizing the Mattachine Society "was a call to me deeper than the innermost reaches of spirit, a vision-quest more important than life." In spring 1952, one of the original members was arrested by the Los Angeles vice squad on the charges of soliciting an officer to commit a homosexual act. The member denied the charge, and the society came to his defense. It was an important case. The jury deliberated forty hours and, with the exception of one member, voted straight acquittal. The case was dismissed, and for the first time in California history an admitted homosexual was freed on a lewd-vagrancy charge.

While a resounding precedent had been established for gay rights, the event also marked the beginning of the end of Hay's original vision for the society. The group attracted many new members and began to assert itself politically. Questionnaires were sent off to candidates for an upcoming Los Angeles city election asking, among other points, if they favored guidance programs for young people beginning to "manifest subconscious aspects of social variance."

The media began to report on this "strange new pressure group," and inevitably the Communist and liberal political leanings of some of the group's early founders and supporters started to become an issue. Hay explained that "we had been getting in this status quo crowd . . . they had to get control of that damn Mattachine Society, which was tarnishing their image, giving them a bad name. This is when the real dissension began between the founders and the middle-class crowd."

In April 1953 a convention was called in a Los Angeles church. Two hundred gay people attended, many of them delegates from other groups newly formed throughout the state. It was the first time in the history of the United States that such a congregation gathered. "You looked up, and all of a sudden the room became vast," said Hay.

He addressed the convention with a long speech designed to answer charges of Communist influence over the group and "to reiterate the foundation's aim to consider itself strictly nonpartisan and nonpolitical in its objective and in its operation." But Hay realized, even then, that the original dream was gone.

"The original society was based upon the feeling of idealism, a great transcendent dream of what being gay was all about. I had proposed from the very beginning that it would be Mattachine's job to find out who we gays were and, on such bases, to find ways to make our contributions to our parent hetero society."

The society after 1953 was also established in other cities around the country but primarily concerned itself with legal change, "with being seen as respectable—rather than self-respecting." The convention marked the end of Hay's principal involvement with the group. He set off alone—and later with Burnside and a few close friends—to continue to explore the significance of his original questioning.

I was one year old when Hay left the organization he conceived and founded. By the time I came out in the early 1970s, member-ship in the society had dwindled, its purpose having been subsumed into a larger context of events. Like most gay people of my gener-ation, I came to a full awareness of my sexuality during a time when political activism, feminist consciousness and freedom to explore alternative beliefs were established motifs in our culture. Yet the question asked by Hay over thirty years before—"Who are we?"—still remains relatively unexplored. It is a question still left unanswered within me.

Hay was waiting in a small apartment in West Hollywood. He and Burnside had recently arrived from New Mexico, where they have lived the past ten years, to help organize a spiritual conference for gay men in the Arizona desert. But future visions are built on acknowledgment of the past, and that is where Hay and I begin.

THOMPSON: *What were the early days of organizing like?*

HAY: When we first started the society, we were aware of the fact that we had no literature, nothing to go on. As we would learn several years later through chance visitors to one of our discussion groups, there were social groups in several countries in Europe who occasionally put out small magazines. But—until the U.S. Supreme Court's decision for ONE, Inc. in 1957, the U.S. post office refused to allow such materials to be mailed in this country. Such magazines as there were in the United States in 1950–52 would have been brought back by travelers. The original Mattachine founders and early society members were mainly left-wing political activists who didn't then number European vacationists among their acquaintances.

So, as I said, when the first five of us started to meet, we met five to six days a week after work, often until one o'clock in the morning. As far as we knew, we were the only people who had ever tried this. And because we didn't know any other group that had tried it before, there were no guideposts to go by. We felt we couldn't [afford to] make a mistake, because if we did, we might possibly deter the movement from developing for years to come. After all, we were facing McCarthyism and the Hollywood Ten*—all this was happening in 1950–51. So we operated by unanimity, which meant, among other things, the

---

*The Hollywood Ten was a group of writers and directors blacklisted within the motion-picture industry for their refusal to testify before the House Un-American Activities Committee.

meetings over weekends would often last sixteen to eighteen hours.

We set up the group on a cell basis because there were quite a lot of people who started coming to us who were security cases—working for the aircraft factories and all of that. We felt that the best way to protect everybody was to say that the people involved with one group would know only a single person from the other.

Then there was no real way of passing on common experience?

That we had had experiences in common that were sharable —even when we were under the illusion that we were the only one of our kind in the world—that all our lives we had been accumulating experiences to be shared, were the wonderful discussion group *revelations* we had not yet discovered. At this moment in 1979, it is difficult to project what our position in 1950 was like. Homosexuality was not only immoral but illegal—and therefore *criminal* doings of degenerate heterosexual *perverts* . . . we didn't have a protection to our name! So I had conceived our public face as being that of a philanthropic group that would be a nonprofit foundation fostering and hosting semipublic discussion groups based on the Kinsey report, which had been published two years before.* This was the Mattachine Foundation, composed of women of some standing in the community—business women, club women—and three men: a well-known labor lawyer, a practicing clinical psychologist, and a Unitarian-Universalist minister. But the real prime movers of the foundation's discussion groups were gay brothers in groups of ten in a closed society hidden behind the façade of the foundation. This group, consisting of what in the gay liberationist 1970s would be called a "consciousness-raising" collective, consisted of nine brother–sister members and a guide or counselor who would be their one contact and connection to the larger society. If you

---

*The Kinsey report was a ground-breaking, indepth study of sexual behavior among many thousands of American men and women which revealed a much higher percentage of homosexual behavior in the population than previously supposed.

came, for instance, to one of the foundation's discussion groups and showed interest by participating, we'd make a point of engaging you in conversation afterward. If we sensed you as a brother, we'd invite you a second time. If you warmed up and began to express feeling the second time, one of would make a date and take you to dinner and, in the course of the evening, share our "call" with you. If you responded favorably, you were invited to our next consciousness-raising meeting in the course of which our collective family circle suddenly opened to enfold you and welcome you home.

We were speaking of the dream of the marvelous brotherhood that gay people can be. I spoke of the feeling of love for one's own kind that is born in the hearts of each one of us—which we know is a beautiful thing, but everyone else thought bad. We were still being rather amorphous and indefinite because we didn't have a way to express it yet. We hoped that by being together, we would find a way. In the discussion groups, we faced the fact of what the gay lifestyle was like and what it could be.

What were the alternatives then? What were the bars like, for instance?

We didn't have many, and such bars as we had were generally miserable places—a dirty light bulb in the ceiling and sawdust on the floor. And always, total fear of being turned over anytime to the police. You couldn't show any sort of intimacy, like holding hands—and you'd never kiss or you'd get knocked over by plainclothesmen who were there all the time. So you lived in terror most of the time.

The first time we gave a dance, which I think must have been in 1951, we invited people openly and sent out a call in a great many places. It was a summer night, the doors were open, and people were coming in off the street. We had maybe fifty or sixty people in this house. I remember one young typist from my office who brought three or four rough street people who were used to picking up sailors—that was their life. They were standing in the doorway weeping and saying they'd never seen sixty men dancing together before in their lives . . . but thirty gay male couples dancing together *and being open and joyously themselves* was more than they were prepared for. We still danced in ballroom couples in those days. . . . I think that Rudi and I were doing a Viennese "showcase-type" waltz when Phil and his friends came in.

Did many gay people regard themselves as second-class citizens?

I don't think they even thought in those terms. We thought of ourselves as being illegal. The idea of self-respect didn't exist. We were talking about this for the first time. We were talking abut the *right* of self-respect and to appreciate that we are strong, not weak people—that a *sissy* means a stubborn person who's put up with an awful lot of stuff and comes through being exactly what he is. A lot of people were saying, "My God, I never thought of that."

Were role stereotypes very extreme?

We had our problem with this. I raised the question "Am I my brother's keeper?" I spoke of this to the street queens as well as the butches. An awful lot of people weren't ready for this. Maybe one of the reasons I got thrown out in 1953, in addition to being a "radical red" and giving us all a "bad name," was that I kept saying, "Let's hold out hands and work to hear and see each other." The conservative elements didn't like this at all.

The other thing they didn't like was my insisting that gay people were a social minority. I didn't even call it a subculture. I said, "We have our own culture, and we have to explore and find out about it. We've had a culture for hundreds of years, and it's high time we recognize our significant contributions." They fought the idea like cats and dogs.

So the concept that we are just like everybody else, except what we do in bed, was very strong?

Very strong, yes. The founders of the group were saying, among other things, that this was not true—that we are different in a variety of ways. The questions "Who are we?" "Where have we come from?" and "What are we here for?" were questions we began to ask ourselves in the discussion groups very, very early. A lot of people didn't want to look at that, because it meant that they were going to have to do a lot of thinking, a lot of reading. To do research at this time was almost impossible. We didn't yet know what to look for. I had been given a book by a lover, back in 1937 by the great Charlottenburg Institute authority Dr. Iwan Bloch, privately published by the Flastaff Press of New York.* I also had copies of studies by Westermarck and Carpenter, and Rudi gave me a copy of André Gide's *Corydon*. But none of these texts talked about contemporary social or political gay societies, or even study groups: They were concerned only to justify homosexual practice through detailed discussions of historical incidences or medical and missionary journals reporting anthropological observations around the globe. Pretty much "apples and fish" [non-related] material, to be sure—but we would have little else until Ford and Beach's *Patterns of Sexual Behavior*, whose appearance was still some years in the future.

We realized that we were going to have to go back to all the books on history ever written and read between the lines. We had to go back into mythology and suppose, interject, wonder, ask questions about—to get the sense that we were going to be finding ourselves between the lines. Certainly not in the front pages anywhere.

Earlier I had been part of a group called People's Songs—Pete Seeger, Lee Hays, Jenny Wells and Woody Guthrie on the East Coast, Earl Robinson, Billy Wolfe and me on the West Coast. We had collected a lot of books from various places, as well as songs and words. We were beginning to put them down in collections; but, more important, just after the war in 1945, 1946, 1947, there were a lot of problems that had to be worked

---

*Dr. Iwan Bloch was a turn-of-the-century sexologist whose works include *The Sexual Extremities of the World* and *The Sexual Life of Our Times in Its Relations to Modern Civilization*. His ground-breaking studies were followed by the work of anthropologist Edward Westermarck, who wrote early in this century about the varying forms of homosexuality in different cultures. His many publications include *Christianity and Morals*, *Ethical Relativity* and *The Goodness of Gods*. Although forgotten today, both men were among the leading writers on sexuality of their time, creating broad theoretical foundations for future understanding.

out. Labor was just beginning to become strong, and there were struggles against rent raisers and gougers everywhere. There were strikes and picket lines and evictions all over the place. So we said, "Here are all these wonderful tunes, and as far as we can see, folk tunes play their part." The words come in and the words come out as they are needed in political and social situations. Well, then a group called the People's Education Center in Hollywood began a number of courses in political science, economy and history. They asked if we'd like to teach a course in the history of people's music.

So these were the classes that were later used to describe you as a Marxist?

Yes, which is true, because I was teaching them on a Marxist basis. In the course of doing that, however, I came across a very interesting group in twelfth- and thirteenth-century music. They were a group in France known as *Les sociétés mattachines* and were men who dressed as women. Their leader was always known as Mother Pig. They were found in many places in France and Spain, and a particularly interesting thing is they were usually clerks and whenever they appeared in public they were masked. They were educated people in the cities who could read and write, yet who went out to the countryside dressed in costumes while performing songs and rituals for the peasantry. These were rituals that the peasants themselves were either too afraid to enact or forbidden to do so by the lords.

These people were lifelong celibates within the societies; they did not marry. They were former clerics now living and working as a secular group but also "religious" in that they took old magic rites from the Great Mother religions of the peasants to perform. I have always assumed they were gay people. You don't dress as a woman or take on the job of shaman lightly. Often they were wiped out by the lords of the manor, who felt their rituals were similar to a peasant uprising.

What I'm getting at is that members three, four and five came out of one of my classes. And when we were trying to figure out a name, they finally suggested that we take *mattachine* and make it into English. We liked the name because when we told gay people about its history, they would recognize themselves and each other in it. It's part of our history, but people would have to ask about its meaning. We thought this useful.

What happened to the original organizers when the group split in 1953?

A couple of us went through a couple of years of total trauma: A couple of us never related to the gay movement again in any way . . . Rudi Gernreich, for one—we'd been lovers during Mattachine's first years—who dropped away to begin his career as a world-famous designer. And the wonderful lesbian who had brought us all such loving and, at the same time, such critical support also dropped away from both Mattachine and the gay movement. She has gone on to become one of the great women photographers of the twentieth century, but she also never lent her name to the movement again.

The real heartbreak for the original organizers was not so much that the movement split but that our beloved *unanimity* had failed. We had never in a million years conceived that such a thing would happen. . . . the Magic carpet had fallen to earth. The middle-class faction was at the point where they believed they were not only exactly the same as everybody else except in bed but that gay people actually *had nothing in common* except their sexual inclinations—a position many of them continue to maintain to this very day. Well, the golden Mattachine dream was gone—vanished—and our sphere of influence of about five thousand people in California alone soon dropped to about five hundred. There wasn't any *call* anymore. There was nothing. . . . The loving cement that had held us all together had relapsed into mud.

One of the things we had done a year earlier was to bring back the Feast of Fools. We were trying to bring back rituals in one form or another. The Feast of Fools featured the Lord of Misrule. He who is not what he appears to be turns over in this period. The high-born and lowly traded places with one another—the bishop became the acolyte, and the acolyte the bishop, and all

other classifications were equally turned inside out in this fort-
night that immediately preceded the Feast of the Great Earth
Mother Oestara, or the vernal equinox. We had wanted this ritual
to help us all "turn ourselves inside out"—to, in effect, tear off
our workaday masks. We had hoped this could have been the
beginning of a cementing of what we dreamed to call the Guild-
Circle Family. But when the split occurred, the feeling of brotherhood totally disappeared and the so-called democratic
movement—the old hetero-imitating tyranny of the majority—
reappeared: Once again they were electing presidents and first
and second vice-presidents and all that jazz. But I myself was no
longer willing to retrogress back to that hetero-imitating,
subject–object, white-man, middle-class obsolescence. I never
joined any of the conventional hetero-imitating type of gay organizations again: I vowed that I would never have to submit the
golden treasure of my heart, my vision of gay consciousness, to
the ugly and distorting vicissitudes of *Roberts Rules of Order* . . .
ever again!

It wasn't until 1964, a year after I had met John, that we
revived the name Circle of Loving Companions and made it into
ever a channel through which those who wished to dissent could
be heard in the years between 1965 and 1969. The Circle of
Loving Companions was very active and quite vociferous in those
years. But we made it quite clear that we would walk with those
with whom we acquiesced, so long as we were both going in the
same direction—but only then! In keeping with some of these
concerted actions, John and I were not only on national radio
but also on national TV—as an openly gay couple expounding
positive values of our gay lifestyle.

When Stonewall broke in 1969, what effect did it have on you? All
of a sudden everyone was talking gay lib.

The idea of people coming together in a loving consensus—
these words, *loving, sharing consensus*, suggest we had much in
common—was exactly the opposite of the old middle-class groups
who would always assume we had nothing in common but our
sexual inclination. It was a whole other ball game. Over and over

again, we called for gay people who would stand together hand-in-hand. It was a family get-together.

Somewhere along in here, the word *gay* began to be used to describe us. Prior to that time we were homosexuals. Reporters began to feel pressure to deal with gay people, and the word *homosexual* was a headliner's nightmare. *Gay* gave us a name for ourselves around which we could put a sense of common nature and heritage.

I first used the term *gay window* in an address, subsequently published by the *Ladder* [a lesbian publication], to the Western Homophile Conference in February 1970. I had come across this concept the summer before and worked it out as a logical process. For instance, every woman knows that there is not a man living who understands what it means to be a self-loving, self-respecting woman. Every black knows the same about a white person. Every gay knows that no heterosexual man or woman knows what it means to be a self-loving, self-respecting gay brother or lesbian sister. Gays have a special window, our own way of seeing, our own vision.

We know how heterosexual men and women operate, because we had to learn in order to survive, to get through school. But we also know that what they do to each other is very different from what we feel about ourselves. Now remember, this was 1970. What was wonderful was just in saying that. All those faces in front of me began to glow—particularly, the young people's. After I got through speaking, they all came over to tell that they had been seeing through that gay window *all their lives.* All I did was help them see what they already knew, but now they could talk about it because they had a word for it. It worked as a trigger. I tried it again and again, and it always worked.

So you feel that gay people carry an innate, collective body of information about themselves?

I think we've carried it in our genes for a long time. We need these triggering mechanisms to awaken them. In a way, this is what happens to scientists when all of a sudden a new vision, a new idea comes. They have to invent new models, new words to describe what they've seen—a poetry or a mathematics. We have to find models to explain that body of information and knowledge we've been carrying for a long time, but which has no way to get out. We must be able to communicate this vision with each other and then to the world at large.

What is this vision? What are the characteristics of it?

All of us grew up knowing that we had a secret in ourselves that was different from other people. And regardless of what we heard—that it was dirty, it was bad, it was against God—we somehow knew that it was beautiful and good. We didn't know how to express it, but we had faith that someday we would. Then that wonderful day comes when you find that you're not alone, that there are others like you. You begin to fantasize that there is going to be that *one* who understands you and has gone through the same things. And the day will come when you'll take his or her hand and understand and share everything perfectly.

The thing was that, all the time, you were thinking about yourself, the subject. And when you start to think about *that other*, you're still thinking the same way as about yourself . . . you're thinking of him, of her, also as subject.

Humanity must expand its experience from people thinking objectively—thinking subject-to-*object*; that is, opportunistically, competitively and nearly always in terms of self-advantage— to thinking subject-to-*subject*, equal-to-equal, sharer-to-sharer, thinking in terms of loving-healing.

I say at this point now that we are the people with subject– subject vision. This is what we have to contribute. We must call to people to exercise the subject–subject relationship. And unless gay people begin to think this way and become conscious of it, we're not going to be able to apply it. We're going to have to reexamine all heterosexual-male thinking systems. We must recognize that there is a qualitative difference between heterosexual social consciousness and gay social consciousness. And our first responsibility must be to develop this gay consciousness to its deepest and most compassionately encompassing levels.

We are at a point now where we have to reinvent our movement in ways we never thought of before. In a sense, the earlier homophile movement and gay liberation movement were movements reactive to heterosexuals. For the first time, we have to create a movement that doesn't start with them, but within us. We can't keep going the way we are now. There has to be a breakthrough in consciousness. Gay people have a tremendous role to play there as healers, as teachers—things we already are.

Are we in danger of losing touch with this insight, especially as we become more accepted by society?

As I said, we pulled the ugly green frog skin of heterosexual conformity over us, and that's how we got through high school with a full set of teeth. We know how to live through their eyes. We can always play their games, but are we denying ourselves by doing this? If you're going to carry the skin of conformity over you, you are going to suppress the beautiful prince or princess within you.

The actual good of the marketplace—the ghetto in San Francisco, as an example—isn't worth it. I think that capitalism is a little bit closer to the end of the road than it used to be. And when a new way of living comes about, and if you've thrown off the frog skin and found out who you are as a gay person, you will be able to adapt to this new circumstance. We're saying that this whole marvelous thing of being gay, of being a fairy, is much more than just the beautiful part of our sexuality. There is more to be explored and discovered. We're calling on gay people to come out and fly. This is what we think the movement of the age is.

I think part of the confusion of running here and there and wanting one high after another is a lack of groundedness, a lack of knowing who we are. I hope in the 1980s we'll be coming together in different ways. This is one of the things we're trying to do over the weekend. It's the first time, to my knowledge, that a call has gone out like this on a national basis. It'll be a place to share, to see what's going on. And while we're doing that, we will also be touching and holding each other. We will be dancing together, and with luck we'll learn to levitate—as fairies should.

So when you ask what we have to contribute, we have nothing less than a whole new way of relating—which is the most ancient way of relating—subject-to-subject. We must rediscover and celebrate.

MARK THOMPSON
IN THE SERVICE
OF ECSTASY:
AN INTERVIEW WITH
JAMES BROUGHTON

Alan Watts, whose life pleasure was to illuminate Zen Buddhism for the modern Western mind, once described his friend James Broughton as "having the sense that the everyday world is not only marvelous but magical—that is, uncanny in a way that is not so much disquieting as holy and nonsensical." In the following interview, the poet and filmmaker talks about the magic of ordinary events within the cycle of living and dying—and the extraordinary perspective that gay people can bring to that process. In a long lifetime of work, he has continued to awaken audiences with a sense of surprise and delight, reminding us that there is no correctitude—political or otherwise—just particular frames of reference, at odd angles and thrusts, weaving an ever-changing consensus. Good gay poets, like James Broughton, keep wonder alive, and if there is a conscience, keep some of us honest with ourselves.

California—as a land and as a state of mind—has been shaped by the makers of myths. Dreamers and rarae aves of all types have prospered there, sending out seductive rhythms to other shores. James Broughton has stayed steady in the balance for nearly seventy years, yet "prays every night to wake up crazier."

Famous filmmaker, poet laureate and favored native son, Broughton epitomizes the experience of living creatively on the West Coast. A serious visionary who is the first to delight in his own absurdities, a subversive Buddhist who has traipsed through Western culture with glee, Broughton has a knack for putting elemental things together in his own way. He lives as a shaman, with many gods and an urgent muse or two, whose words and images have led many to new perceptions about the world that exists both within and out.

Widely known in the San Francisco Bay area as a poet and teacher, Broughton is the author of more than twenty books and as many independent films; *Mother's Day*, *The Pleasure Garden*, *The Bed* and *Dreamwood*, to name a few. He remains, in fact, the only established American poet consistently engaged in filmmaking. He helped launch the experimental film movement in the United States in the late 1940s, and many of his works—considered classics of poetic cinema—are housed in major film museums around the world. In 1954 he was presented a Cannes Film Festival award by Jean Cocteau; over twenty years later Broughton was cited as "the grand classic master of independent cinema" by a group of his peers.

Through the years his writing has flowed with similar fluency: His plays, prose works and volumes of poetry test the unmentionable, insist on the pleasurable, dig deeper into the realm of the imaginary. "I collapse upward," he says.

Broughton's message is a particularly urgent one for men. In his poem "Shaman Psalm," the poet proclaims: "Man must love man/or war is forever/Outnumber the hawks/Outdistance the angels/Love one another/or die." And in *The Androgyne Journal*, a remarkable chronicle of one summer's retreat, he writes:

> *I can address a lizard or a bull with respect for its essence. Why not a man as well? How do you look upon other men as astonishing organisms? Only by so regarding yourself.*
>
> *Love love love, with awe and delight, the facts and functions. As I become loving toward my bodily organs where formerly I fretted them, I begin to feel new hereness. My He and She shine brighter together.*
>
> *O to heal, to awaken, to redeem! To be a voice, not a literary*

*man. Yes. For I am in love with the eternities of things, I am in
love with the gods. I am in love with metamorphoses.*

When we spoke in November 1983—just a few days before his
seventieth birthday—Broughton had just completed two new works
that reflect a period of great introspection and change. The first, *Ecstasies*, is a collection of poetry addressing the power of love between
men. The volume concludes with a "Connubial Masque," a ceremony
written to commemorate Broughton's 1978 union with fellow filmmaker Joel Singer. They continue to flourish as lovers and artistic
collaborators, and one can imagine Hermes (the mythological figure
who plays an important role in *Ecstasies*) looking on with approval.
Devotions is a half-hour film that explores the seemingly unlimited ways
that men can come together. Using images of numerous couples, the
film makes an important statement at a time when many men are
probing traditional values and emotional vulnerability.

Obvious questions concerning career and biography were scrapped
that afternoon in favor of more essential issues: faith, trust and learning
to love, the real grist in Broughton's mill.

THOMPSON: *There is a definite resonance between* Ecstasies *and*
Devotions. *The messages inherent in both works seem particularly necessary in these confusing and intimidating times.*

BROUGHTON: Ecstasies and devotions are great human experiences more richly needed in the texture of all our lives. I
have been fortunate to experience ecstasy as a sustaining part of
my everyday life, not just as a momentary thrill. This gives a
giddy kind of harmonic effervescence to the body, whereby one
feels the ordinary world transformed. This is so wondrous a thing
that I wish every man in the world could share it.

This has been a long time coming for you, hasn't it?

A long time, yes. And I would assure every man that it is
never too late to be surprised by joy. The true love of my life
came to me when I was sixty-one, an age when I was beginning
to think it time to pull down the shades and fold up my fancies.
Then unexpectedly I was blessed with a psychic rebirth. Joel's

unequivocal devotion gave me a renewal of erotic energy at every level of my being. This gift has been such a glory that I have tried to share it in my *Ecstasies* book. I wish there were a sure-fire recipe to offer every lovelorn person.

The film Joel and I have made called *Devotions* was intended to indicate how much joy men can find in one another when they are motivated by a desire for affectionate sharing. The history of male lovers in recent centuries has usually emphasized their agonies and frustrations. I wanted to insist on the delights and the rewards and to suggest how innumerable are the ways of expressing devotion, from the playful to the profound. This same impulse motivates *Ecstasies*, for my life with Joel has revealed to me the variety of excitements in being devoted to one person.

You once said that promiscuity could be interpreted as the search for the divine in one's fellow creatures, that cruising should be called "the quest for the Holy Male." Because of AIDS, this search has now been denied many men. Obviously, when you use the word ecstasy, you're not meaning it to be understood in just a literal, physical way.

The Holy Male is potential in every one of us. Men should be shown how to reach and to cherish the divine in one another. A quest for the ecstatic goes beyond cruising for a congenial sex object. It is not enough to get it up, get it on, and get it over with. In the urgency of our present situation we should look toward connecting imaginatively with the souls of our brothers. How else will we become soul brothers? This does not mean denying sexuality. On the contrary, sexualized feeling as a creative force is the great drive for the flourishing of the spirit. We need lovingness in all our relationships. Love can take sexual drive on a glory ride to the soaring heavens.

Not too many years ago the gay movement seemed so alive and expressive. Silliness and sassiness and sissiness were all celebrated. The process of becoming gay seemed to offer a new way to look into other men's eyes.

It was inevitable that outrageousness exploded with the beginnings of gay liberation. Hooray for sassy risk and silly experiment and anarchic joy! After all, if you are going to call men gay, they need to take gaiety seriously and be as blithe as possible. This used to be known as brightening the corner where you are. Gaiety is a great moral good and a high spiritual value, as well as being a key to the universe.

God was certainly merry when he played around making giraffes and volcanoes and octopi and comets and toucans. The cosmos is full of *great* silliness. But it gets along with itself, it loves its games, it enjoys its mutations and upheavals. If it didn't like what it was doing it would fall apart. In human relationships the lack of love is destroying God's beautifully wacky world. Man's vandalism of the earth is similar to the way he treats his fellow creatures: bilking, raping, destroying, using living beings as objects of greed and exploitation. So much of human society is resentfully loveless, no wonder it is violent and guilt-ridden. All power seekers want to make slaves of other men; hence, they create abusive relationships.

For me the most beautiful thing in the cosmos is the human body. I have celebrated it in my works, most particularly in my films *The Golden Positions*, *Erogeny* and *Song of the Godbody*. I have campaigned for more respect and more love for the wonders of our flesh. Why are we taught to abuse and denigrate the temples of our souls?

While you've not always been "homosexual"—you were married for ten years and have two children—you've always exhibited a "gay" spirit. You said an angel came to visit when you were three years old, and apparently he has been touching in from time to time. How do you preserve gaiety in your life? What does gay mean to you?

I take *gay spirit* very literally. I believe that the universe is essentially a gay place and that we are lucky to have it as our playground. The cosmos could not operate if it was not cheerful and friendly with itself. It certainly doesn't take a dim view of all its worlds. It loves spinning its novas around; it loves entities that enjoy their own orbits.

When I speak of *gaiety* I mean recognizing that the dance of life is part of a transcendental amusement. In Tantric Buddhism the goal of enlightenment is participation in what is called the Great Delight. And that is the cosmic orgasm.

As far as my own life goes, I have always possessed what is termed a *gay* sensibility. I have cherished men passionately since I was a child. I have also enjoyed relationships with women who have helped me fill out the mandalas of existence, helped me to understand the dynamic of opposites so that I could come to unify the masculine and feminine forces in myself. This brings me to the image of the androgyne, which is a forceful symbol for the enlightened soul. An inward balance of yang and yin can bring vital serenity to the mind and heart. When the dark and the light move together, when the receptive and the assertive dwell hand in hand, there is an inner gaiety of liberation that puts one in lively touch with wholeness.

Do you think the mainstream gay movement needs to have a different agenda right now?

Most gay activists are concerned with what society will do for them. They want acceptance, they want to be absorbed into the social fabric of the heterosexual mainstream. I think this is ass-backwards. We should be considering what *we* can do for *them*, how we could free them from their misery and wrongheadedness. Who really wants to accept being accepted by straight society? Look what the heterosexual ethic has done to the earth with its shameless greed and its passion for war. We could show them how to love one another, we could teach them to trust comradeship, we could teach them the value of hilarity. Man is by nature a loving animal, but his nature has been perverted by bigoted, belligerent exploiters. It is essential that gay politics keep busy eroding homophobia, but the most exciting task that remains is how we can persuade the homophobes what a great gay life all men could be romping in.

There are little murders of the soul happening every day now. An entire generation of gay men—some of the brightest and fittest men in America today—are being overwhelmed by fantasies and realities of disease and death. How do we counterbalance this darkness?

AIDS is a disaster area in our lives, an intense challenge to our responsibilities toward one another. AIDS is comparable to a plague, an eruption, an avalanche. By the same token, it calls upon our full responsiveness to such emergencies. With gay liberation there was a great exhilaration, a crazy exuberance. Now we are confronted with the absolute opposite, the sorrows of mortality. Ultimately we all have to take responsibility for our lives, for our maturing, for our deaths. This is very difficult for golden boys to think about. We are the Peter Pans of the world, the irrepressible ones who believe in magic, folly, and romance. And, in a sense, we never do grow old. That's part of what being gay signifies: innocence of spirit, a perennial youthfulness of soul. The gay spirit is a young spirit. Which is why the world needs us. We refuse to become dowdy and dull, we refuse to dwindle into the doldrums, and we never die.

AIDS is an epidemic that threatens all of humankind. Its cause, I believe, derives from the obscene polluting of the earth that exploitive greed has practiced. The growth of cancer as a killing agent was the beginning of this poisoning. Now we have a second terrible result of our inhabiting a poisoned world that destroys our immunities. Gay men are in the vanguard of this tragedy, they are martyrs to the sickness of their destructive society. We all hope their suffering may help the finding of a cure that will save the rest of mankind. What would be most rewarding to their memories: if they effected a real change of heart in the body politic.

Theirs is not a situation of the purely accidental, any more than it is some vengeance of Jehovah visited upon sinners. In the largest sense, nothing is accidental. Forces ebb and flow, entities act and interact, the patterns of our sensitive chaos possess an underlying unity. Life is not a ruthless conspiracy arranged to make us unhappy, to punish us personally. Everything is connected; everything is part of the dance; and everything, alas, is part of the evil that men do. The victims of AIDS are the victims of their warlords and industrialists.

You have said that poets are priests in the service of the inexplicable. What do you mean, and how do you fortify yourself for work as a poet?

I have used a religious metaphor because I feel that the ability to express the inexpressible is a grace given to artists. Any poet worth his salt knows that his gift is not of his own making. His insights come out of nowhere (or out of everywhere), and he must be able to see the invisible and then to trust his vision. In my case I transcribe as accurately as I can what my particular guardians confide to me. And they caution me to be lucid and precise so that the message will be clearly heard.

I believe in wide-eyed innocence. I admire the wagging dog and the trusting child who approach strangers expecting the best from them. They are looking toward the soul in human creatures. I try to do the same. I like to *touch* people, in both senses of the verb. I want to savor their aliveness, I want to press their deeper buttons, I want to connect with their truths. I'm not interested in their armor nor the games of their egos. I am not fascinated with human unhappiness, I am not eager to make fun of or stab in the back. In return I want others to touch me, to trust me and share their soul-making. *Trust!* There's the beautiful key word. When shall all men take the risk of trusting one another?

But if you're a gay man living, for example, in a ghetto on the Lower East Side of Manhattan, you're going to find very little trust anywhere.

That's why we have to start a revolution. And soon! Not a revolution that waves banners and assassinates presidents. Ours will not be a revolution that marches in the streets or blows up public buildings. This is an inner uprising and overthrowing; this is the revolution in the souls of all of us. This is the realization of our oneness, our love, and our strength.

Obviously there's a lot of trust between you and Joel. You both have birthdays in November—Joel will be thirty-five when you become seventy.

To some onlookers this discrepancy may appear questionable. But Joel and I live beyond the jokes of generation gap. The inner experience is quite different from the outer appearance. In our souls we are truly equal. A really deep love between two people, where soul-mating has occurred, brings about a merging of identities that strengthens both individuals. Furthermore, it connects one deeply to all other lovers. This is a resonating kind of ecstasy: the sense that all other lovers are sharing in and supporting your own bed of rapture.

Does this connection also mean more sexual energy?

My sexual energy has been completely recharged. I feel younger than my children. By coming into my life when he did, Joel has actually extended my lifespan, since with him I have entered a new beginning. He was born in 1948, when my first film and my first book came out, signaling the birth of my creative life. The gods must have decided that I was doing something right and should be rewarded in due time. So they arranged Joel's incarnation.

There often seems to be a certain suspicion expressed on the East Coast about California and some of the values espoused here. Your work, for instance, has not always been taken seriously by the critical establishment in the East.

They consider we live in a lotus land and hence don't know how miserable life really is. In actuality, we just happen to be sensible about where we choose to live. I am happy on the western shore facing the Orient. I have no wish to live unhappily on the Atlantic just so I can be near its big-time noise. A both/and person like me falls between a lot of stools. I make films to waken people to wonder, I write poems to wake myself up, I don't know how to do things for money. I think being true to your own goofy nature is the only way to stay healthy. When I ran away to sea as a youth, the only book I had with me was Emerson's essays, and my motto then was the first sentence from "Self-Reliance": "Insist on yourself."

I think each of us is under an obligation to contribute our individual insights to the world, whatever they may be. This is one way of bringing luminosity into the dark of ourselves and our fellow beings. I try to brighten my corner even when I'm cornered in it, even when I'm ignored there. My love for my fellow men is the strongest determinant in my life. I think men are the most fascinating creatures in existence, and I want them to honor one another and respect themselves—not to misuse their bodies nor to twist their minds. I want to bless them all with ecstasies of devotion. This is a theme prevalent in all my recent poetry, and the following poem is an example.

Hermes Bringer of Heats

Promethean member of the divine order
    you are familiar with
    our fervid privacies
    You know the measure of
    our desperate needs
Restore the world to us as once it glowed
before our captivity in the chills of guilt

    Fuse us with genital genius
    Infuse us with anal sublimity
Rekindle the purity of original sin
    Bring us fresh heats from
    the testes of the gods
to rewake the fire in our natural affections

Men are not meant to dwell in disaster
    prisoners of shame
    servants of belligerence
Men are born to love   to love and be loved
Men are the disciples of heavenly fuckerie
    Hermes   Hermes
    relight our blithe birthright

MITCH WALKER
VISIONARY LOVE:
THE MAGICKAL GAY
SPIRIT-POWER

Mitch Walker tells a myth—"The awakening of gay spirit comes at a certain time in human evolution"—and an epic cycle of death and regeneration is evoked. Walker, a psychologist by training, has been relating gay experience to the archetypal realm for over a decade.

When his essay "Visionary Love" was published in the underground literary journal Gay Sunshine *during the winter of 1976, Walker had little idea that it would affect some gay men as deeply as it did. "When I started receiving long, enthusiastic letters, phone calls from around the country and even requests for visits from total strangers, I could hear a strong chord vibrating. Their responses were intense, personal, caring, often tinged with feelings of creative inspiration, as if the essay had reached down below their minds and stirred up pools of enspiriting juices. . . . The essay seemed to have a healing effect. I felt as if I had touched my readers, and some of them had touched me," he later explained. Walker's now seminal essay is included in the following chapter.*

Walker wrote a companion piece, "Becoming Gay Shamanism," later in 1977, the year Men Loving Men, *his highly regarded "gay sex guide and consciousness book," was published by Gay Sunshine Press. "Visionary Love" and its sequel were conceived as a pair, the author says, reflecting theory and practice, respectively. In 1980, he combined both essays with "Trans-mutational Faerie," a more poetic piece written while attending the first gathering of radical fairies in Arizona, and published all three as* Visionary Love, *a "spirit book of gay mythology."*

Walker's ongoing work has contributed important insights about the gay psyche, that interior world of images, instincts and feelings—of eros. There is a gay way to relate to the symbolic language of the unconscious, he says, and to the very task of finding out "whatever being a gay hero inside means."

W*e gay men are at a key time in the evolution of our gay consciousness. We've been struggling to reach a great vision buried in us, which we first sensed only in the vaguest ways. We have all felt this vision, lying inside, watching, showing itself in dreams, directing our acts and beliefs in unseen ways. In the modern gay liberation movement, the history of men's struggles has been the history of groping toward our vision, sensing it in the values of androgyny, in revolution, in free sexuality. It has led us to Stonewall, to genderfuck, to the birth of a new gay culture.

But during the past few years, it appeared that our movement ran out of steam; many militant groups faded, as did the brassy colorful rebels and our flagrant joyous celebrations. They seemed to be replaced by a new movement, the vocal gay Normals: fighting in the courts, the churches, the mental health professions; gaining advocate after advocate, victory after victory. It was as if the homophile movement for equal rights, taking new freedom from our radical flowering, thrust toward its goal of mainstream assimilation leading the mass of gays with it—deflowering our movement, the movement toward our vision.

The homophile movement for equality is a dead thing: dead to the gay vision, anti-magickal, counterrevolutionary. Its spokespeople and theorists shun the roots (the *radical*, source of nurturance and understanding) in favor of surface values: the social norm, success, integration, acceptance, assimilation. Its shallow reality suffocates the vision in us, co-opting gay people and vitiating the creativity and potential of the gay movement.

In response to the sterile domination of the assimilationists, many of us gay men have turned to a wholehearted embrace of a nongay theoretical perspective, Marxism. Our attraction to this tradition stems from our attraction to our gay vision, which is one of absolute freedom. Such freedom is universal and therefore must encompass all people, destroying every form of oppression. Since no current theoretical system within the gay movement can sustain and help actualize our sense of freedom, aware gay people have turned to that tradition that does promise radical freedom—Marxism.

But in this process we ally ourselves with another line of thought that doesn't develop our unique, peculiar gay potential. An economic analysis of gay oppression is absurd, like forming a composite animal by tacking the legs of a kangaroo onto a tuna: The resulting creature makes a big splash in the water, but doesn't go anywhere. The origin of antigayness is not to be found in economics. However, this doesn't deny the importance of people's liberation movements and our solidarity with them (or membership in them for those who are gay and Third World).

But some of us aren't satisfied with either of these dominant branches of the male gay liberation movement, whether assimilationist or Marxist. We want to seek out our vision, which we sense contains a unique and necessary contribution to the freedom of humanity, which contains the seed of a magickal healing transformation in consciousness, key to the evolution of humanity to a new stage of being.

We know we must bring our vision to birth, where its powers can act and grow in the world. We must develop it in a body of analysis and action, so it can take root in the soil of daily reality and generate a new liberation. For at the heart of our vision is a vital spirit-force, bringing a revolutionary change in how we see ourselves and other people and the goals toward which we strive.

In this essay we will explore this gay spirit-force, trying to uncover what it is and what it means. This exploration will not be easy, however, because the spirit-force is in many ways foreign to our Western-trained consciousness. In addition, it has been the special target of antigay oppression, forcing it into the unconscious, into hiding. All of this gives it a vague, elusive mistiness, making it difficult to grasp.

Because of this, an important first step is to provide the gay spirit-force with a conceptual handle for focusing our awareness, to give a semantic meeting place, a *name* by which we can evoke it. When I decided to write about the spirit-force, this was the first task I set myself.

I found the problem of naming to be quite perplexing. I puzzled over it and meditated on it for quite a while. Over a period of weeks, I became totally immersed in this quest, ignoring my other obligations and worries. I wrote to other gay people for suggestions and spent hours making up alternate words. However, nothing was satisfactory, and I sensed that the answer was beyond my intellectual grasp.

One evening I was contemplating a list of names for shamans in non-Western cultures. After a while, the room seemed to fade away from me, and I became lost in a growing feeling of joy or pleasure, much like being stoned on marijuana. Then the words on the page began to move about before my eyes. I felt a tingling in my body. I saw the words dancing on the page, and I started to play around with the letters, combining them in different ways.

I wrote the following words in a line: *yirka-laul*, which means "soft man" among the Siberian Chuckchee and refers to a male transvestite shaman; *brujo*, which means "sorcerer" among the Yaqui of northern Mexico; *boté*, which means "not-man, not-woman" among the Crow; and *enaree*, the word for a male transvestite shaman among the ancient Scythians, who lived north of the Black Sea in Eurasia.

I wrote these words in a line and began recombining the letters. I continued this in a haphazard way until something told me to stop, that I'd formed the right combination. This combination was *roika* (seemingly pronounced roy′kah).

I was somewhat awed by this whole event, and for several days thereafter I thought about this word, speaking it out loud and meditating on its sound. It seemed quite strange to me, somehow just what I was looking for. It seemed that this word truly named the spirit-force I had evoked. Because of the magick I felt in this word, I capitalized all the letters, and I offer it here as a name for the gay spirit-force: ROIKA.

Two other words had also come to me during my experience: *LOKA* and *YAN*. These, I later realized, were closely related to ROIKA and named other important aspects involved in this gay spirit-force. Their meanings are described later in this essay.

ROIKA is a name for the nonrational, nonlinear spirit-essence lying at the source of our gayness. The future potential of gay men lies in our uncovering and actualizing ROIKA. This is a complex, subtle process that must proceed on many levels and in many ways. In this essay, I'd like to suggest a method of analysis and provide a conceptual outline that may prove useful in this uncovering process.

I'd like to explore how this spirit-essence came into existence and how it is shaped through our gay experience. In this way we can uncover a doorway to it, seeing some of what it is and what it can mean for us.

But in order to get to this place, we must first take a look at several different factors influencing human life, basic factors underlying things people do and believe. Then we can see how these factors come together to generate the gay experience and its magickal vision.

Spirit-Forces

First, we must look at the notion of "spirits" and spirit energies. Our society exalts materialism, logic, and empiricism above all else, denying the part of reality that is nonmaterial, nonrational, nonlinear, and acausal. All other and earlier cultures recognized this part of reality, whose landscape is formed of spirit-beings, gods, goddesses, demons, sprites, nymphs, devils, ghosts and fairies. The major aspect of this spirit world is energy—dynamic numinous power beyond the concepts of time, space and cause–effect as we understand them.

This spirit world and its forces exist in the universe and also in each person at a deeply unconscious level. This mysterious place inside is the source of energies attached to the basic biological patterns of life, death, love, growth, decay and birth. All human societies attempted to organize and regulate the psychic powers connected to these natural patterns, through ideas called "myths." Through myths people could shape and channel spirit-forces into distinct beings, summon them or appease them, deny them or exalt them with the highest honors. We see this important human activity in the infinite variety of religions, cults, systems of spiritual knowledge and magick in the world around.

It would be unwise to suppose that such religions and magicks were mere delusions and fantasies. What was delusional about these institutions was their mythic ideas, but the powers they summoned were quite real. It's a delusion of modern society that such powers are nonexistent.

The thing that earlier peoples didn't see was that they themselves were the creators of the spirits they worshipped. This was impossible for them to understand, because the myths they used to summon the spirit-forces were also the structures that composed their ego identities; and since these myths originated from outside the individual—as past collective creations of the tribe—it was impossible to look within to find the true origin of spirits. Instead, all important forces were seen as originating beyond the realm of the person, in the sky, the earth, the wind, in the gifts and curses of the gods. This process of seeing a spirit- or god-force as "out there" when really it's "inside" is called *projection*. The Wise Women and Wise Men of a tribe projected the spirit-beings into plants, animals and other natural features, teaching that these objects were the sole source of power, inspiration and religious awe.

In modern society, our roots in the spirit world have been cut. We still have myths and the spirit energies still work in them, but in a feeble unrecognized way. This is a unique development in the history of peoples. Never has there been a society with so little rapport with the spirit world. Modern Western culture marks the death of an era in the meaning and life of humanity.

Social Falseself Systems

The religion of a society is one aspect of a larger institution that holds that society together. Every culture has its own way of seeing things, of seeing not only the spirits but also everyday life, society, and the people themselves—the things we call personality and identity. The way a society views and interprets human beings and the world around them forms an overall framework, a world view, a unique "reality." This "reality" is made up of imaginary concepts—myths—that are the rules, rituals, taboos and beliefs that form political, economic, religious and behavioral systems. These myths are created and maintained by the people of the society, who are the living embodiment of the myths they believe in (see Joseph Pearce, *The Crack in the Cosmic Egg*).

When people are born into such a society, it's already been determined who they'll be when they grow up. The myths form identity patterns that the growing child internalizes as personality structures. Everyone has to have an identity, because it's necessary for survival, organizing the chaos of infinite nature into meaningful forms. The internalized myths of a society, which coalesce into roles such as being a "man," a "woman," a "shaman," a "chief" and a "hunter," are the human equivalent to instincts, molding the patterns through which life can flow.

This is an important point to understand. Humans don't come into the world with an identity; this identity must be made. Adult humans have to have such an identity because this is the source of *ontological security*. *Ontological security* means "safety of being," and is that sense of groundedness, of firm substantiality, which upholds and binds psychic life. Without ontological security, the human mind/body has nothing to hold it together and collapses into confusion, death, madness and idiocy. Because of this, people are vitally (and usually unconsciously) interested in the creation and maintenance of ontological security, which they cling to passionately and, in times of threat, desperately (see R. D. Laing, *The Divided Self*).

The primal function of human societies is the creation of ontological security for its members. This is the psychic purpose of social myths, which are internalized as identity structures. These identity myths originate outside the individual and come in standardized forms like plastic molds. Because each individual is unique, such myths deny the true nature and potentials of that person. The contents of myths vary radically from culture to culture, but the process is always the same; a mythic identity is a prefabricated identity. If you are a "woman," for example, you must do certain things and not do other things; you have certain powers and you don't have others—regardless of who you are as an individual. Such an identity is false to the person's inner nature, and so I call it a *falseself*; and the collectivity of such selves is a *social falseself system*. All societies have always been social falseself systems, structuring the ontological security of personal identity in a web of myths unique to that society, in "a huge network of more or less successful attempts to protect mankind [sic] . . . the colossal efforts made by a baby who is afraid of being left alone in the dark" (Geza Roheim, *The Origin and Function of Culture*, page 131).

Our society is a falseself system. Simply look around you and you'll see the living myths that define the people; that are sex roles, work roles, sexual behavior roles; collective standards of moral belief, politics, religion and so on. Or go into any anthropology section at a library and read about any culture—the Arunta of Australia, the Chuckchee of Siberia, the Celts of Europe, the Hopi of the Southwest—each a unique falseself system with complex beliefs, taboos and social norms, each creating unique kinds of people.

The range of mythic possibilities allows for vast diversity in human expression. Some myths encourage a certain trait or behavior; other are discouraging. Middle Eastern society, for example, is open to same-sex sexuality; Christian society condemns it. The Siwans of Africa obliged every man to have homosexual affairs, while in the Mandan society of North America homosexual relations occurred between young men and the *berdache*, a transvestite shaman. Monogamy was the rule in Hindu India, while polygamy was normal in Moslem India. Certain West African tribes honored the birth of twins; the Aranda of Australia immediately killed them as evil devils. Celtic societies encouraged headhunting as a way to gain mystical power, whereas the thought never occurred to the Chuckchee shaman. In *Sex and Temperament in Three Primitive Societies*, Margaret Mead studied three cultures, in one of which both sex roles are by Western standards passive and nurturant, in another both are aggressive and hostile, and in a third the males are "feminine" while the females are "masculine."

The social falseself system is the psychic counterpart to the outward social forms of economic and political organization. The myth system is the mental institution paralleling the material institutions of family, clan, food supply, hierarchical structures and so on. Just as all societies contain hierarchies in which some people are more important, influential, and powerful than others, so too the falseself system legislates these hierarchical differences through identity myths, through which the meaning of some individuals is elevated and/or that of others devalued. Patriarchy, with its sexist myths creating strong "men" and weak "women," is a good example of the hierarchical structure inherent in social myth systems.

The falseself system as a human institution is itself the source of all hierarchies involving status and power. Since falseself mythology originates from outside the individual, a person must be taught their falseself identity; and for this to happen each person must submerge their autonomy, allowing themself to be led by others who "know." This gives rise to authority, to the individual(s) who will dispense the vitally necessary ontological security. Since a person needs this security, they will look to and believe in authorities. Thus emerge the two complementary falseself roles of leader and follower—the one with power and the one without it. This pattern is open to exploitation, to the self-aggrandizement of individuals and to the generation of oppressive social institutions perpetuating unjust power relations.

In large, complex societies like our own, the myth system is complex and relatively vague, but it's still the basis for identity, behavior and hierarchies. Because of this mythic vagueness, some people have turned to earlier eras or to other societies (such as matriarchal nature cultures) for a more secure sense of identity and belonging. However, it's a mistake to see the oppressiveness of modern society in terms of other cultures, because all are falseself systems that deny and destroy the inner center of the person. And it's this inner center that contains a potential for humanity never realized in any past culture.

LOKA

It's possible for a person to create an identity from within, to find their own truths and to build ontological security based on their own myths.

This is a trueself identity, as contrasted with falseself. There is a spirit-essence that underlies and guides the development of trueself, which I have named LOKA. One of the first acts perpetrated on growing children in a social falseself system is the merciless and brutal destruction of any allegiance to LOKA.

This LOKA is the golden magickal *starpoint*, the hub of the inner spirit world and all the kosmos as well, what the mystic Ramana Maharshi called "the very Core of one's being, the Center, without which there is nothing whatever." This starpoint contains the pattern for unfolding a person's spirit-being through self-realization of all their deepest aspects. Full identity with LOKA is the ultimate point in human evolution, in which the person is the godlike being formed of all human ideals and all the gods and devils of the spirit world—a supreme mystic, scientist, and erotic hedonist, identified with the totality of the universe. It's very difficult for me to imagine such a person, who seems to be a mass of fantasies and contradictions. Yet as Ramana Maharshi says, "the greatest power is at the command of the man [*sic*] who has penetrated to his inmost depth," and such a being is in harmony with all energies and wisdom.

The path of trueself toward LOKA involves the development of the kosmic forces that exist in oneself. In a social falseself system the spirit power of individuals is given by the social myths; in development of trueself a person seeks to become self-powerful, creating myths to shape and unfold their spirit energies. Thus those developing their trueself are characterized as people of power who function contrary to the social system and against falseself. Several esoteric spiritual traditions in the world have been concerned with the development of LOKA by a select few. One of these traditions is that of the Yaqui *brujo,* described by Carlos Castaneda in his books about the sorcerer Don Juan.

At the surface it might seem that LOKA is socially divisive and destructive, leading ultimately to a war of selfish Nietzschean super-people. But this is just another social myth to keep people in line. In following the path of trueself, a person must pass through the spirit doorway named YAN (the topic of the next section). This requires a transformation of identity, and results in the discovery of, and alliance with, a spirit-force called the *Androgyne*. The Androgyne, the union of masculine and feminine, personifies the harmony of opposites. It's the paradigm of *healing*, embodying all the diverse traits of masculinity and femininity together in oneness. When a person becomes the Androgyne, that person becomes a force for wholeness, for gentle balance, tapping into the endless nurturance of the primal Great Mother and the infinite energy power of the primal Sky Father (see below). Through the Androgyne a person seeking LOKA becomes an agent in the transformation of a conflicted, unbalanced humanity.

YAN

The basic myth in all societies is the one concerning sex roles: Social "reality" is divided in half, and one part is called *male*, the other *female*. In their religious or spiritual aspect, these roles are often expressed as the kosmic Primal Parents, the Great Mother and Sky Father, one or both of whom may become the dominant god in a culture. In terms of personality, this basic sex-role myth is expressed as the antithetical nature of men and women and the characteristics that distinguish them, such as strong/weak, active/passive and so on. This distinction according to sex role is the pattern through which all opposites are then formed: up/down, black/white, good/bad, life/death. Sex role is the root, because it's the Principle of Opposites internalized as personal identity, which in turn is the basis for all ego values and relationships.

In this mythic kosmic duality, the interface between male and female takes on special meaning. In almost all world religions, it is the union of the primal male and female principles that creates the earth or humanity. Thus, the way to reach the original wholeness of the kosmos is through the interface of male/female duality. I have named this interface YAN. YAN is the doorway of spiritual realization, of entering the worlds of power and infinity. In Chinese mysticism YAN is called the *Tao,* symbolized by yin and yang. In the Indian tradition of Tantra, the sacramental sexual union of a man and a woman evokes the YAN gateway. A Christian text describes it in this way: "For the Lord [Jesus] himself being asked by someone when his kingdom should come, said: 'When the two should be one, and the outside as the inside and the male with the female neither male or female.' "

All ancient cultures and all nature societies gave a central place to people who communed with spirits—shamans, sorcerers and priestesses. All these people entered the spirit realm through YAN—by obliterating opposites through trance, drugs and sex, and by appearing as both sexes simultaneously. In many societies shamans combined male and female attributes in order to personify YAN. They did this, in some cases, by taking on the traits of the "opposite" sex during rituals, such as a male shaman wearing painted-on breasts. In other cases the shaman would abandon the appropriate sex role, appearing and acting as a person of the other sex. Such shamans have been found in the tribal groups of all continents, and such cross-gender practice survives in Western culture as the skirt worn by Roman Catholic priests. Sometimes the sorcerer, in wishing to identify with the opposite sex completely, would take on the sexual love practices of the opposite sex, becoming the male "wife" of a man or the female "husband" of a woman. Thus, many sorcerers were homosexual, as this increased their contact with YAN. This was the case, for example, with the Chuckchee of Siberia, where "transformed" shamans of both sexes wielded the greatest power and respect.

The purpose of all such transformations was to attune the self to YAN, the Doorway to the kosmos. Within YAN, time, space, and cause–effect have no meaning; and it's possible to contact spirit-forces in order to effect various changes, such as healing sickness, effecting curses, increasing the tribal food supply and gaining spiritual wisdom.

However, YAN is merely a tool. Its uses depend on the mythology in which it's evoked, the values and goals seen as meaningful and important. In a social falseself system, YAN is subservient to the reality determined by social myths. In our Western culture, YAN is denied altogether and given no legitimate place in the mythology. In the service of trueself, YAN becomes the healing door to LOKA, leading to identification with the spirit-force of balance, the Androgyne.

The Primal Parents, the Double, the Competitor and Hermes

The myth of masculine/feminine splits the spirit world into two halves. In most religions these halves were personified as gods, the Primal Parents, often referred to as the Great Mother and the Sky Father. Their union was thought to have brought all things into existence. Usually the Great Mother was seen as the Earth, the source, who birthed the universe from her infinite womb, and also as the Moon, whose monthly cycle reflected the life patterns of nature. The Great Mother was the kosmic nurturing power, who raised and protected her children the animals, the trees and crops, and humankind. She was also Death, who took her children back into her womb at the end of life. In many cultures the Great Mother was seen as the principal god, and she was worshipped as the wielder of all powers and the arbiter of fate both good and bad. These societies where she ruled are called matriarchies, and in them women were seen as more meaningful and important than men.

The Sky Father in most religions was originally the wind or the clouds or some other aspect of the weather. His dynamic movement was seen as a life force that invigorated inanimate objects, giving them spirit power. In many matriarchal societies, he was a god of joyous vigor and growth celebrated in sexual orgies; his union with the Mother brought fertility to crops and herds. In many other cultures the Sky Father wielded the thunderbolt or the flaming sun, and he came to be seen as the dominant ruler of the universe. These societies are called patriarchies, and within them men were seen as more meaningful and important than women.

Within an individual person, the myth of masculine/feminine splits the unconscious psychic unity into two halves. Besides embodying the Primal Parents, these halves also form the basis for sex-role identity, for the roles of "man" and "woman." In this regard, that half which underlies a person's appropriate sex-role personality is called the *Double*, the source of masculinity in a man and femininity in a woman. That half which is left out of the person's identity is called the *Anim*, the source of femininity in a man and masculinity in a woman. The Double and the Anim contain many spirit-forces and kosmic values, depending on the mythology that has shaped them. In particular, Double and Anim contain both erotic and destructive forces in relation to other individuals.

The social myth system seeks to regulate and control these forces through their suppression or projection onto individuals. Mythic patterns are set up to channel what's often called love. *Love* is the projection of an erotic aspect of Double or Anim onto another person. When love occurs, the projecting person sees in the other the kosmic wonder, beauty and magick inherent in that spirit source. This is the cause of great happiness and sexual yearning and may lead to kosmic revelations seen in the sacred source of the projections.

When the Anims of a man and a woman are shared in this "love," there is a heterosexual union. Such unions have been told of in such stories as *Tristan and Iseult* or *Romeo and Juliet*. When the Doubles of two men or two women are shared in "love," there is a homosexual union. Relationships of this kind have been described in such tales as the Epic of Gilgamesh and Apollo and Hyacinthus.

These love and sex patterns are closely regulated by the social myth system. Who you can love and/or have sex with, how and when you can, are all controlled by myths, which manipulate these forces, encouraging some aspects and discouraging others. As can be seen, love and sex roles are very closely tied together.

All societies institutionalize Anim-love in some form such as marriage, concubinage or rape, since heterosexual union is necessary to the survival of the species. However, Double-love can be institutionalized or condemned in a myth system. Two examples are ancient Sparta and the Jews: In Sparta Double-love served the state in the education of the young men and the strengthening of warrior traits, while in Jewish mythology Double-love was taboo (although the story of David and Jonathan is a notable exception in the Bible).

When the social mythology shapes Anim and Double, it incorporates as part of the Double a spirit-energy called *Magickal Twinning*. When we see a pair of identical twins, we sense in their identicalness a common source or essence. This sense is a manifestation of Magickal Twinning, which is the numinous process that makes two things out of one or one thing out of two. The action of Magickal Twinning is a kind of duplication by which the spirit-essence of one object is infused into another, making spirit twins, yet the two duplicates are bound together through their common spirit-essence into a third object, an indivisible unity. The Greek tale of Narcissus, who fell in love with his reflection in a pool, is a story describing this Magickal Twinning force. Through the action of Magickal Twinning, a person's sex-role identity is formed as a vague reflection or twin of the unconscious Double. In this way sex-role identity gains solidity and substance through rootedness in the life-giving spirit world.

Because sex-role identity is based on the Double, when a person projects their Double onto another there's an unconscious sense of twinning or reflection of the ego, leading to the notion of identity or equality with that other person. In this way the Magickal Twinning force is evoked between two people. Thus Double-love is distinguished from Anim-love by uncanny feelings of unity, strength and reinforcement of personal identity. This can create an atmosphere between lovers of profound familiarity; a mysterious, joyful sharing of feelings and needs; a dynamic, intuitive strength and understanding. Confucius describes this in his commentary on fellowship in the *I Ching*:

> But when two people are at one in their innermost
>   hearts,
> They shatter even the strength of iron or bronze.
> And when two people understand each other in their
>   innermost hearts,
> Their words are sweet and strong, like the
>   fragrance of orchids.

This aspect of Double-love was exploited by many warrior societies such as the Dorians and the Japanese, since it increased the bravery, vigor and unity of soldiers.

Since Magickal Twinning inheres in the Double, Double projections involving others invoke the Twinning force between people. When this happens, there's a sense (usually unconscious) of being identical to the other person. If two things are identical, they must be perfectly equal. Since Double-love involves the most intense projections of Double, it gives rise to the clearest, strongest sense of Magickal Twinning. Because of this, Double-love is the source of ideals concerning equality. Double-love, for example, is the basis for that harmonious rapport between people sometimes called "brotherly love." It's also the source for the ideal of political equality referred to as "democracy." In the so-called birthplace of democracy, ancient Greece, pairs of lovers were often proclaimed as tyrant murderers and highly praised. Examples include Harmodius and Aristogiton, and Melanippus and Chariton.

Since all social myth systems have hierarchies, Double-love can become an equalizing force dangerous to a system that can't control it. This control is provided through myths condemning Double-love or by institutionalizing it as an acceptable aspect of sex-role identity. However, if Double-love can break free of social control, it gives rise to an insolent, vigorous opposition to mythic hierarchies. This equalizing force was celebrated by Walt Whitman in a poem:

> The prairie-grass dividing, its special odor breathing,
> I demand of it the spiritual corresponding,
> Demand the most copious and close companionship of
>   men . . .
> Those that go their own gait, erect, stepping with
>   freedom and command, leading not following,
> Those with a never-quell'd audacity, those with sweet
>   and lusty flesh clear of taint,
> Those that look carelessly in the faces of Presidents
>   and governors, as to say *Who are you?*
> Those of earth-born passion, simple, never constrain'd,
>   never obedient . . .

In addition to these characteristics, there's also a destructive aspect of the Double called the *Competitor*. The Competitor is a negative Magickal Twinning, Double-hatred, and it seeks to destroy a person's identity. When the Competitor is projected onto another person, that person is seen as a threat and an enemy to be destroyed. In ritualized form this is the basis for most "sports," such as boxing, football, tennis and so on. The Competitor has great potential in furthering the human activities of murder, war and genocide. It brings about the pattern of the "hero" and his "enemy," the two men or the two armies that struggle against each other for victory. Achilles and Hector in the *Iliad,* and the war described in that story, are a good example of this pattern. As Achilles says to Hector: "Lions and men make no truce, wolves and lambs have no friendship—they hate each other forever. So there can be no love between you and me; and there shall be no truce for us, until one of the two shall fall and glut Ares with his blood." Western culture has given an exalted place to the Competitor, who served the Western god in his ambitious plans (which are the subject of the next section).

The kosmic energy of Magickal Twinning, when not split up and projected as positive (love) and negative (hate) aspects of the Double, manifests in the spirit realm as a being whose energy is catalytic, who interpenetrates other spirit-forces and brings them together. This spirit-being resembles an ancient Greek god called Hermes, who was a god of sexuality, travel, and magickal energy. He was a merry trickster figure, who pulled clever pranks, and he was also the messenger of the other gods. His wand of two snakes or white ribbons twined about a rod—symbolic of the Magickal Twinning force—was the wand of the magician; his altar was the *herm,* a stone post with an erect cock (see Norman O. Brown, *Hermes the Thief*). Hermes was an important figure in medieval alchemy. His alchemical element was mercury (quicksilver), and his principal magick was the bringing together of the male and female elements to form the philosopher's stone, the supreme alchemical goal.

This Hermes being is not male or female but a catalytic force that can reunite the kosmic duality of masculine/feminine. In ancient Greek mythology, the union of Hermes and Aphrodite, goddess of love, produced Hermaphroditos, the Androgyne. Hermes's erect cock symbolizes her alive penetrating essence, sexual in origin. Her magickal silvery laughter melts barriers and carriers her far and fast through the spirit world. She unlocks spirit powers, and when she's summoned against a falseself system she leads the seeker to magickal forces that can transform that person into a healer and shaman of great beauty and strength.

The Myth of the Homosexual

Gay people are a modern Western phenomenon. There existed no such thing as a gay person or a "homosexual" before or outside of Western culture of the past few centuries. The people mistakenly called *homosexuals* by historians and anthropologists were never seen in this way by the people themselves: The shaman who practiced homosexuality did so to increase the contact with YAN; the husband or wife of such a person was considered a normal sex-roled individual; the effeminate young men of the Middle East and Greece were singled out by their contemporaries for their nonmanliness, not for their sexuality; the homosexuality common among Japanese samurai and Dorian warriors was a part of their warrior identity, which increased their courage, strength and discipline. In all these cases, facets of what we call gayness were seen in the context of the social myth systems in which they occurred and were interpreted according to the functions of those myths.

The "homosexual" is a myth of our culture. The word itself is only about a hundred years old. It arose as Western society attempted to define and control a new kind of person who threatened the Western myth system. This new kind of person was someone who saw through the gradually weakening myth system at its base in sex role, who saw through it in a vital sexual way, and who therefore passionately rejected social myth systems as oppressive.

The Myth of the Homosexual says that there exists a person defined by sexual attraction toward people of the same biological gender. This myth serves an essential function in the preservation of culture: It denies the reality, the legitimacy, of the culture-destroying vision of the so-called homosexual, and it does this by restricting that person's essence and meaningfulness to distinct sexual acts performed with other persons of the same sex. The purpose of this myth has been, and is, to rob gay people of the power inherent in them to destroy the established order and replace it according to their vision.

The Myth of the Homosexual arose from Christian morality, which condemned homosexual practices as part of the Christian myth system. This condemnation was then applied to the so-called homosexual in two pernicious ways: legally, in order to imprison and murder; and psychologically, as a self-destroying myth within the person themself. The Myth of the Homosexual rapidly became universal and was thus absorbed by potential "homosexuals" as they grew up, indoctrinating their thought and masking their vision. Thus, even from the start, gay people were forced to battle on society's terms, as to whether or not homosexuality was "bad" and, therefore, whether they won or lost this argument, they lost their vision.

Gay Personality Development in Modern Western Society

As soon as a child is born the social myth system, as personified in parents and other important individuals, sets to work shaping that child's identity through myths. The first thing parents teach is their power and authority and the necessity to be open to discipline (through toilet training and so on). The next thing parents and society teach, and which they go on teaching and reinforcing throughout life, is sex-role identity and the vast set of values, behavior patterns and morality that compose the sex-role myths. All other values and meanings are then built on those of sex role.

Children are born with the kosmic unity of masculine and feminine. At the center and deepest point of this unity is LOKA. The function of cultural myths is to break this primary unity and twist it out of recognition through bizarre and elaborate myths involving distinctions between masculine and feminine.

At some point in this sex-role building process, some children begin to fail. They awaken to qualities in themselves considered inappropriate in sex-role mythology or they have trouble internalizing the correct myths. For some, this may happen when they start going to school, where they're confronted by the vicious coercion of teachers and older students.

In most children, inappropriate sex-role qualities get forgotten through neglect or active self-repression. But for some others, inappropriate self-aspects remain in awareness. This leads to a vague sense of not belonging and seeing oneself as *norole*, as not sex-role identified, as connected to YAN. In this way, a part of identity remains loyal to LOKA, to the inner source.

However, all children need to belong, and there's no escape from socialization. Therefore the strange ones hide their strangeness and continue to participate in falseself socialization: "I first noticed that I was different from all the other little girls when I was five, and the horror and fear of not belonging led me even then to hide what I was actually feeling, thinking, and doing" (Karla Jay, *Out of the Closets*, page 276). Some of these children might rebel: They may identify with the "opposite" sex-role structures; but, regardless of this, any sex-role patterns they absorb and identify with, whether "correct" or "incorrect," are social myths and contribute to the formation of a falseself.

The result of this process is a young person with two psychological loyalties: one toward falseself identity and the other, feeble and undeveloped, toward trueself identity and LOKA. This condition is called a *norole-defended personality* and is the first stage in gay personality development.

Society, however, corrects most of these cultural maladapts during adolescence. This is the time when boys and girls become men and women and take on the responsibility of full participation in the myth system. The great biological energies unleashed during this time—sex and love—are shaped by the sex-role myths in order to cement the person's loyalty to falseself. Besides the need for ontological security, sex and "love" are the greatest source of energy upholding the mythology and can undermine earlier attachments to trueself.

During adolescence, special myths come into play regulating the powers of Anim and Double. These myths play up the sex/love projections of Anim and convert those of Double into "friendship" and, in our society, values involving distrust, suspicion, manipulation and competition (the Competitor).

However, for some adolescents with a loyalty to norole, sex/love projections involving the Double come to the fore. This tends to happen for several reasons, a major one being that sex/love involving the Anim has been co-opted entirely by the myth system, whereas sex/love involving the Double has been tabooed, leaving these aspects of Double free of the falseself system.

In norole-defended children, ontological security has come to be invested in two opposing identity systems, each driven by the urge for security to reinforce itself. Since Double-love is not controlled by the social myth system, its sex/love powers can help counteract the forces of acculturation. The trueself identity will resist Anim-love and encourage Double-love as the basis for channeling sex and touch/rapport needs. This gives trueself identity a much-needed boost to resist the fierce and otherwise overwhelming pressures of socialization.

When Double-love becomes constellated with norole in the struggle for ontological loyalty, the young person becomes acutely aware of internal conflict originating in the contradiction between falseself, with its loyalty to the myth system and sex roles, and trueself, with its Double-based urgings toward sex/love. Falseself can't be abandoned for two reasons: It forms an identity upholding ontological security and would bring on psychic chaos—madness—if it were lost; and this falseself provides the perfect, impenetrable disguise hiding the secret traits. Likewise, the inner being can't be expressed because the falseself system, both as persona identity and as society, is opposed to its existence. The result of this dilemma is a confused person in great pain, unable to reach out for love and help: the time of silent yearning and secret sorrow. This schizoid condition is called the *gay-defended personality* and is the second stage of gay personality development.

Eventually, the dual identity of a gay-defended person forces some sort of action to relieve the tension. Some people kill themselves. Others confess to a friend or see a therapist or start having sex with someone, and so on. These people begin to open up to others and express their inner reality in some way. This is the third stage of gay personality development, called *coming out*.

The process of coming out is a quest for ontological security through the resolution of conflicting self-identities. At this point, the Myth of the Homosexual comes into play. The myth is a way of interpreting the aberrant feelings from the point of view of the falseself system. Since it's the only available myth providing a way of understanding the gay-defended situation, the confused person (and everyone else) comes to see themself as "homosexual." The problem becomes "homosexuality," and the question becomes how to resolve it. A struggle ensues over whether or not to be a homosexual. As Dennis Altman said, "Most of us have struggled, for a time at least, against the realization of our gayness, and coming out is therefore a long and painful process. I fought my homosexuality for a long time" (*Homosexual: Oppression and Liberation*, page 19).

If the person has a relatively strong falseself identity and a relatively weak inner identity, they can—often with the help of a therapist or other authority—adapt to a normal falseself life and gradually forget about their other identity. Sometimes the person isn't entirely successful, becoming overtly "normal" with a family and perhaps an important occupational position while carrying on secret, furtive visits to tearooms or occasional gay lovers.

Others become so ontologically "stuck" that they can't make any kind of satisfying adaptation, remaining in an identity limbo. Such people are plagued by profound insecurity and hopelessness and fall into perpetual frustration and unhappiness, perhaps seesawing through homosexual and heterosexual attachments or sinking into alcoholism and despondency.

But many gay-defended people eventually discover that homosexual encounters are enjoyable and satisfying. They experience a liberating gust of sensations and emotions, and begin to see that it's good being a "homosexual." This encourages them to move away from the negative social morality and establish their own subcultures based on a positive Myth of the Homosexual. In doing this, they create a social myth system that expresses and maintains their falseselves, but in which they cancel the Double-taboo by instituting a myth that homosexuality is okay. These are the typical, traditional gay subcultures, and a person who reaches this stage of gay personality development is *homosexualidentified*. The Myth of the Homosexual becomes a psychic bridge, channeling Double-love from its trueself allegiance into falseself identity, decreasing the conflict over ontological security.

However, the identity dilemma hasn't been entirely resolved. A homosexual-identified person has become disloyal to their inner identity, which is opposed to falseself. This inner identity is a radical freedom from external myths, oriented instead through YAN, the time/space doorway to the kosmic starpoint LOKA. Its free space destroys sexist role mythology, emphasizing instead the loving warmth and idealistic powers of the Double—the absolute equality of all things—and evokes the silvery Hermes being, the magickal sexual spirit who unlocks wonderful energies and processes, leading to alliance with the Androgyne, the symbol of harmony and healing. This inner identity, its urgings and process of unfolding, I have named ROIKA.

ROIKA and the Myth of the Homosexual are in deadly enmity. The one points toward depth and vitality of being, personal power, and the kosmic center; the other points toward denial of being, personal impotence, and a shallow, mundane life. ROIKA moves toward the overthrow of falseself in oneself and everywhere and toward the evolution of humanity through androgyny. The Myth of the Homosexual moves toward the suffocation of basic change in self and society, toward reinforcement of power hierarchies, and aims at assimilation into the social myth system. ROIKA is the root and potential of being gay, while the Myth of the Homosexual is its premature stillbirth.

ROIKA is the force that makes gay subcultures unique, sustaining their integrity and distinctness in opposition to the dominant antigay society. In doing this, ROIKA asserts itself in several powerful but mainly unconscious ways. One of these is "promiscuity," a degree of joyful sensual flow and freedom not entirely controlled by falseself rules. Another is "camp," which is the humorous and satirical mockery of falseself patterns, especially sex-role myths, laughing at their absurdity and uselessness as personal identity.

However, since the gay subcultures are social myth systems, values originating in ROIKA can only be seen through the reality of falseself and therefore can only function in unconscious, unrecognizable ways. Thus, within a gay subculture, camp, for example, can only maintain a sense of ROIKA, not lead to its unfolding or the breakup of the myth system.

Because of this, it's impossible for a homosexual-identified person or subculture to actualize ROIKA, even though ROIKA contributes the audacious vitality of gay subcultures. This gap in awareness is experienced as emptiness, loss, sorrow and discontent. ROIKA contains the urge to unfold itself, and if this is denied through attachment to falseself, that falseself will feel incomplete, inadequate, unfulfilled. Almost all gay liberation writers have noted the sense of inadequacy within gay society.

There are only two solutions to this problem: to gain sufficient reinforcement for falseself reality to destroy ROIKA, or to open to ROIKA and destroy falseself.

ROIKA

The last stage of gay personality development is following the path of ROIKA. This path has several aspects that take on greater or lesser importance at different times. First of these is the vision: ROIKA-YAN. This is a set of images and feelings that reveal ROIKA and its unfolding through the YAN gateway. These are images of the abolition of all unjust hierarchies, and images of harmony—of fluid erotic joy, of nurturant empathy, of spirit-forces, of a society based on LOKA.

ROIKA-YAN is the source of our idealistic urgings. It becomes clearer and more powerful as we pay attention to it and, if seen with sufficient clarity, leads to militant action. It's the vision of ROIKA-YAN that makes gay people discontented, harnessing our anger against the source of our oppression. It pulls us to ally with the liberation forces of the world and to identify their causes as our own.

The gay liberation movement that flowered after 1969 was an attempt to actualize ROIKA-YAN. Tools were developed—genderfuck, zaps, support groups and so on—to bring forth our vision and undermine the authority of the myth system, both within gay people and as embodied in social institutions. The word *gay* itself symbolized the new consciousness, rejecting the Myth of the Homosexual and substituting the freedom of proud love, commencing "on the path toward human liberation" (Altman). However, without a key to unlock ROIKA, the movement soon foundered and splintered.

Since ROIKA and the Myth of the Homosexual, and their sources in LOKA and falseself, are diametrically opposed, gay people are bound to be confused and uncertain about who they are and what they should be doing. Gay people contain two identities, and their history becomes the struggle to resolve this contradiction. Movement toward one identity tends to be canceled by the counterpull of the other. Under these conditions, ROIKA-YAN can only be felt vaguely and at a distance. Without the creation of guiding myths, it's difficult if not impossible to find a way to it.

This uncertainty is ripe for exploitation. After the initial ROIKA-inspired upsurge of 1969–1970, the Myth of the Homosexual quickly regained (or never lost) the upper hand in some gay men and led to a co-optation of the Vision by their homosexual identities. These gay Normals created guideposts that many previously uncertain gay people are now following. Throughout the 1970s a spate of books and magazines, such as *The Front Runner, Consenting Adult, The Homosexual Matrix, Christopher Street, The Advocate,* and *After Dark* followed this trend.

For these people, the insights generated by ROIKA-YAN have led to the militant adoption of a positive Myth of the Homosexual. The vision is preempted by the myth system and expresses itself as a demand for socio-political rights for homosexual-identified people, for the absolute equality and mutually harmonious acceptance of homosexuals and heterosexuals. The spirit vision that has always been a part of homosexual-identified people is harnessed to legitimize that identity in society and to block further self-growth. As Ralph Blair, editor of the *Homosexual Counseling Journal,* said: "Men and women who are sexually attracted to members of their own sex have this attraction in common, but there is nothing else that is necessarily shared . . . [by] homosexuals. . . . *Homosexual* can be used simply to indicate sexual object-choice, just as *heterosexual* is used to indicate sexual object-choice" (vol. 2, no. 1, January 1975, page 48).

This movement for gay equality and assimilation is working to reverse the negative morality applied to homosexuality. Its basic argument is the *normal-excluded theory,* which says that gay people are just like straight people except for homosexuality, and the problem lies not in homosexuality but in straight people's condemnation of it. Because the social myth system is weak and rootless, there's a likely chance it'll yield to militant homosexuals in order to regain their loyalty. In a social falseself system, it's never particular myths that are oppressive but the system itself. The Western system will change myths in order to absorb opposition. This is how it survives.

Many of us gay men, however, haven't abandoned the quest for our gay vision. Through the cross-stimulation and criticism of gay (and feminist) theorists and writers, a few have been getting closer and closer to seeing and actualizing ROIKA. Ideas such as "gay is better than straight," gay shamanism, revolutionary feminism and genderfuck point toward our vision spirit. Harry Hay, who helped found the Mattachine Society, writes of a "gay window, our singular vision of love and beauty," and gay historian Arthur Evans has written about aspects of ROIKA with a new clarity. Arthur's idea, of an ideal harmonious society in which gay people play a prominent spiritual role, is a strong attempt to create a myth pointing toward ROIKA.

This uncovering work has been going slowly, and the reason for this is the psychological resistances to it. In addition to the lack of guideposts, there's a more active block against following the visionary spirit path. This is the fact that we gain ontological security from our falseself identities, and we're afraid their destruction by ROIKA will bring on madness. A person's identity is the bulwark against mean-ingless chaos, which is experienced as a painful and continuous death. Thus, at a certain point on the path of ROIKA, people must open themselves to psychic death, to their darkest fears and destructive forces, to the evil inside them. This is a time that vitally requires support and encouragement from others, and without it there can't be any progress.

This struggle with falseself is the second aspect of ROIKA, and is called the *Warrior*. The ROIKA Warrior moves toward utter destruc-tion of their mythic social identity and toward self-transformation into a new way of being. In this struggle the falseself resists any attempts to destroy its ontological power. The forceful breakdown of its mythic divisions of male/female, good/bad and light/dark unleash wild chaotic forces that can easily destroy a person. To counter this, the Warrior must develop ROIKA allies, spirit-daimons that give strength and guidance. The ROIKA Warrior moves through YAN into the numinous kosmic power realm, attempting to shape control of the awesome, terrifying energies there, to create and sustain a new personal identity. A good illustration of the process of the spirit warrior is Don Juan, the Yaqui sorcerer described by Carlos Castaneda.

If this struggle is successful, marvelous sources of wisdom and energy become available. This is the next aspect of ROIKA, the *Shaman*. The ROIKA Shaman is in league with a great spirit-ally who is Hermes, Eros (sexuality), and the Androgyne together. The person undergoes metamorphosis, emerging as a silvery luminous being of power and knowledge in the service of healing. This is beyond words and concerns a new stage of human existence.

A GROUP INTERVIEW
GAY SOUL MAKING:
COMING OUT INSIDE

In their retreat from oppression, gay people have often been labeled dreamers. Whether through fantasy or idealism, gay people have always been the possessors of dreams. In Los Angeles, a small group of gay men has transformed an abstraction—dreaming as metaphor—into actual practice. Gay liberation requires coming out inside as well as into the outer world, they say. Within you lies a universe as vast and real as the one without, and exploring and developing gay self inside gives a wholeness, depth and balance to the coming out process not otherwise attainable.

Established in 1981 by Don Kilhefner and Mitch Walker, Treeroots has approached the task of "gay soul making" through non-Western spiritual traditions, selected readings, and Jungian dream amplification techniques.* "We're not just a dream group organization," says Kilhefner. "We're a group that's exploring and reclaiming a gay-centered spiritual tradition." Kilhefner and the other facilitators in Treeroots see dreams as a powerful tool to further that investigation. Within five years this unique organization has helped several hundred gay men discover the reality behind their dreams, initiating a self-transformative process, "the underworld descent of the hero shaman."

In the following group interview, Treeroots dream workers talk about this exploration of gay spirit, beginning with their own religious and spiritual backgrounds. However, it's not the outer manifestations of spirit that count, they explain. "Gay spirit lives inside, and it's the ongoing process of coming out that generates gay soul."

---

*In *Archetypal Psychology: A Brief Account* (Dallas: Spring Publications, 1983), James Hillman describes soul-making as "imaging, that is, seeing or hearing by means of an imagining which sees through an event to its image. Imaging means releasing events from their literal understanding into a mythical appreciation. Soul-making, in this sense, is equated with de-literalizing—that psychological attitude which suspiciously disallows the naive and given level of events in order to search out their shadowy, metaphorical significance for soul."

KEN BARTMESS: My religious background is Episcopal, which I experienced as a very safe and socially oriented kind of nothing—Wonder Bread spirituality. I was involved with it as a child and teenager, but certainly not in my adult life. I came to Treeroots groups to explore what "gay" might be about, other than where I danced or what kind of clothes I wore. I was trying to find a *dimension* of my gayness that was something other than superficial or sexual.

CHRIS KILBOURNE: I was raised with no religion, although being in a Christian society I was definitely influenced by Christian values. I became involved in Treeroots as I was coming out, so for me being gay has a lot to do with certain desires to express myself to the fullest possible extent.

DON KILHEFNER: I spent the first seventeen years of my life in an Amish/Mennonite community in Pennsylvania and, since I left there, have spent a great deal of my time exploring Islamic, Buddhist, Hindu, American Indian, shamanic, gnostic and gay spiritual traditions and practices.

LUKE JOHNSON: I was raised as a fundamentalist, a Swedish Baptist to be exact. I left the church when I was about nineteen, just about the same time I was beginning to come out, and spent the next twenty-odd years being devoutedly areligious. And then, about the time my father died, I found myself going back to church, the Episcopal church this time. In ways that I'm still not clear about, my return to Christianity has been simultaneous with an interest in what it means to be gay and to be spiritual. At Treeroots, I'm trying to talk about that in ways that the church is not ready to deal with.

MITCH WALKER: I was raised Jewish, and I got an Orthodox bar mitzvah when I was thirteen. My father was the son of a Southern Baptist minister from Oklahoma, but I never really knew that spiritual tradition of my family upbringing. Since then, I've been through this and that.

MARK THOMPSON: I really didn't have much of a religious background. My parents sent their kids to an all-denominational Christian church on Sunday mornings so that they could have time alone. It didn't mean much. I'm doing this kind of work now because it feels very real and sustaining. Traditional religious training aside, what do we in Treeroots mean by "coming out inside"?

DON: I can say what it's meant for me. As a teenager, I knew I was gay. But there was something in me that was very mysterious and sacred about what was going on, and it was related to my gayness. I didn't know what it meant, but I certainly knew what I was being told "gayness," or "homosexuality" at that time, was all about certainly didn't fit me. Those definitions weren't about what I felt inside. In the early days of the gay liberation movement in Los Angeles—1969 and 1970—I had the good fortune to be in the company of an exceptional group of gay men—generally radicals, artists, shamans, heretics of one form or another. One man in particular, Llee Heflin [author of *The Island Dialogues*], got a hold of me and started to talk about being gay in a language that I had never heard any gay man talk before. It just *pulled* me on, in the sense of knowing that there was something else, some mystery there. When I started organizing the Gay and Lesbian Community Services Center in the early 1970s, again there was something *pulling* me, whispering in my ear: What does it mean to be gay? The kind of discussion that I heard around me on the subject seemed pretty one-dimensional and flat. I sensed that there was more to it. Is there some kind of gay spirit inside us that's different from being straight? What is "gay consciousness"? At the time, there was nobody around even interested in exploring those questions. The next big step for me happened in 1973, when I spent a night at San Juan Pueblo, New Mexico, and met Harry Hay. We stayed up the whole night talking. For the first time in my life, I came across somebody who saw the world much as I did, who was exploring some of the same questions. And again, it was part of that coming out *inside*, a much deeper, interior understanding or exploration of what gayness was all about.

That conversation led me to kind of dropping out for several years, going underground and doing a lot of interesting gay spiritual work. Organizing around the radical fairie stuff, which was more about "coming out inside," and then on to Treeroots. My dreams led me on.

KEN: For me it's a little different, because I come from a very conventional—if there is such a thing—gay experience. I came up in the 1950s, through the bar scene and social scene, and I've lived and worked in the gay ghetto in one way or another all my adult life. A byproduct of that scene was developing alcoholism and then having to deal with that. It was then that I had to begin to ask myself some questions. You know, "Isn't there more to this than sex, drugs and rock 'n' roll?" That eventually led me to the fact that there had been gay visionaries who tried to express ideas of gayness by finding a word for how we *love*. The idea that we could be defined by how we love rather than by what we do below the waist was eye-opening, or maybe I should say heart-opening. That, in some way, it was a matter of spirit rather than a matter of pathology was revolutionary. From there, coming out inside has been an ever-deepening process. I'm interested in dreams because they speak a truth that your waking life may deny. I mean, they just do it! They're down there expressing their gay selves, and you can't manipulate that while it's happening. Whereas we manipulate our social forms. We accommodate to society. We buy the right products. You can't mess around with your dreams. They tell it like it is, and what they reveal is, for gay men, *ultimately* gay, in some very special way.

CHRIS: I was raised in suburban Southern California. At around twenty years old, I became disgusted and angry at the unhealthy environment, so I moved to Berkeley and went to school. I soon realized that what I really wanted was to express myself, to contribute to the world's well-being, and to learn to live. So I dropped out of school. I couldn't keep my homosexual instincts at bay any longer, which I began to see was intimately connected with a desire to develop my creativity. I then met Mitch, who encouraged me to pay attention to my dreams. As I began to become aware of this inner world, my disorientation and confusion began to crystallize into a meaningful sense of reality. I believed that my gayness was like a vortex around which all issues seemed to revolve—for example, socially, I could live as a nonsexist man; politically, I could demonstrate that it is possible for men to love one another; and, psychologically, the doors to freedom opened through the melting of sex-role stereotypes. Coming out inside is a process of coming out to an inner world; becoming more aware of places, beings and potentialities within myself that just a few years ago I had no sense of.

MARK: Of course, this inner world is unique to you, but is this world also uniquely gay?

CHRIS: I really don't think that it would be possible to go into this inner world and let it grow without identifying myself as being gay. Because being gay allows me to be whatever I want, in a culture that is so riddled with roles.

LUKE: When I think about the phrase "coming out inside," it's largely a matter of what I pay attention to and what I value. When I was a child and growing up, I had what now seem to me deeply religious, deeply spiritual impulses. And the fundamentalist religion is one that focuses you in on the heart constantly. But I found it very difficult to look at my heart because there were all these uneasy things around sexuality and the church that I couldn't look at too closely. The vocabulary with which I had to look at those things didn't exist. To a certain degree, it took the coming of the AIDS crisis and the feeling that I was next in line for death in order for something in me to relax. It seems now there are whole worlds opening up that I can pay attention to.

MARK: I think the horror of AIDS has served as a trigger for a lot of gay men, signaling that something is obviously not right in their own society but also on the planet as well. You have a choice: You can ascribe meaning to something or not. I prefer the former. In whatever way possible, we have to connect with emptiness and then take responsibility for the fact that we create our own reality, including being gay. Outer reality tends to reflect the inner one. For instance, if in the past we have characterized gay life as being self-absorbed, superficial, victimized, then we must understand that this is a reflection on an inner state. For many people, AIDS hastened the awareness that perhaps gay culture—as popularly defined in the late 1970s—was headed for some kind of awful distress. I'm not being moralistic here, either. It's just that during the 1970s, when most of us were coming out, assuming a gay identity and moving to gay ghettos in major cities, we were somehow being artifically contained—like being put on a reservation. And, as I've heard it expressed, we were given "the booze and the pox."

One of the most insidious concepts used to develop our sub-culture has been that of *pride*. Because of the relentless nature of our oppression, gay people have had to seize upon the concept of pride in order to measure self-worth. Instilling a *sense* of pride is a justifiable component of any community, but a fixation on pride leads to isolation, inflation of individual egos and greed. Pride, in this case, may help to define the outer world but inhibits access to the inner, more compassionate one. So I see pride as being of no great spiritual value. It is our compassion, which helps others to see themselves, that is the gay gift to the world. This is why it is so important to continue to invent ourselves— not mindlessly consume somebody else's version of what we might be: that is, "come out inside."

MITCH: I first became aware of the idea of "coming out inside" at a time in my life when I was also getting into professional training as a psychologist. I was in a master's program, and I wanted to combine my work in psychology with my coming out as a gay person. I was exposed to the idea that there was such a thing as *psychological* man. That is, that one way to characterize people is by the fact that they have a psychological level of experience, a world that they experience. But it's not a world that's tangible, in the way that physical objects can be picked up and held, for example. How do you hold a thought? How do you contain a fantasy? The whole world of internal representations was something that I became aware of through this schooling.

The idea came together that you could be gay and explore that existence of being gay as "psychological man," as well as explore that existence of being gay the way people usually think of— you know, "I'm a gay accountant," "I'm the gay member of the Board of Regents of the University of California," or whatever. My feeling about that inner world is that it is indeed quite real and, as Jung would say, numinous, and exerts its own fascination, exerts its own attraction. It's a world of power. It's a secret world, it's a dark world, so it's the other side of this world of light and solid objects. It's everything that is *in*tangible; it's the opposite of Here. And it's possible to get into that. In fact, it'll almost pull you in of its own accord if you're just willing to listen to your unconscious.

MARK: For me, there's something very sensual, something very physical and real about working with dreams. In a certain sense, I believe there is a greater truth to one gay person's dream than all of the institutionalized gay culture we've built up to this time, as important as that has been. The inner world of images and instinct is the true well of our gay culture and consciousness, not some identity that has been formulated by others: If you *label* something, you control it. However, is there a certain quality about dreams that makes them a particularly rich experience for gay men?

MITCH: In the days of gay liberation the whole idea was, "Hey, you've got to realize that you're gay, you've got to accept that identity, and you're not really a healthy gay person until you come out as that identity." So there's already this model. It takes awareness that there's also another dark world that's the exact reflection of this outer world. It's the inner world, the inner reality. What else is there? If you're going to gain a real gay identity, you can't have just a gay identity in the outer world. That's what all the gay identity theorists talk of, homosexual identity formation—a constructed gay identity. When you're talking about forming a gay identity—coming out into the community and becoming a fulfilled, balanced gay-identified healthy individual—this is all in terms of the outer world, the world that the psychologists would call the world of projections. Not the original world at all, but the world of effects.

MARK: So many gay people are escaping from the dark of repression and discrimination, the dark of being rejected by their families. In terms of using the metaphor, the word *dark* is scary.

DON: I think there's a step before that. I take the position that none of us have come out yet; that coming out is something that will happen in the future but hasn't happened yet; that what we euphemistically call "coming out" really largely means accommodating ourselves to somebody else's definition of who we are. The concept of a "homosexual"—a person whose total identity is shaped and defined by a sex act—is a relatively recent formulation in the Western world. Yet it has been the only social myth available to us as gay people during the past century, as we searched for personal and collective identity and ontological security. Granted, there is a very powerful and mysterious eros connected with being gay; however, the myth of the homosexual represents a classic case of the tail wagging the dog. And today, with the AIDS crisis, we are reaping the tragic harvest of that mistake, just as an earlier generation was made to suffer as a result of erroneous concepts of psychopathology. We've been participating in a gigantic hoax. What *does* it really mean to "come out" as a gay person?

MARK: The whole concept of viewing gay men and lesbians as an autonomous people is an idea that's rejected even by most gays. A people would be defined by common myths or archetypes and symbols. Among the more prevalent ones today, of course, would be the image of the gay man as the sexual outlaw or as the effeminate sissy. For gay women, one image might be the bulldyke. Could there be such a thing as a gay archetype within the collective unconscious?

DON: You use the term "collective unconscious," and that's a term that comes directly out of the work of Carl Jung. I think Jung has certainly gone deeper into the psyche than any other explorer in the twentieth century and has mapped it out and written about it. Some of what he has discovered there has been very useful to gay people, and some of it is not. And certainly there's much more to be discovered. In a way, Jung discovered, to a large extent, a gay tradition. When Jung calls himself a gnostic, when he studied and talked about the Manichaeans, Bogomelians and Cathers, and when he writes about alchemy— he's talking in Western culture about an heretical tradition that I would say is basically a gay tradition.

CHRIS: When the individual starts to become more in touch with his inner world, the person begins to descend into what Jung would call the collective unconscious. And it seems to me that an appropriate myth for that process is the myth of the hero and his heroic journey through treacherous lands and unworldly experiences. It's a world where the journeyer begins to acquire knowledge and powers that he never knew existed.

MARK: The individuals in this group have worked with gay men's dreams for hundreds of hours. Have there been any common threads, experiences?

KEN: I have not done a lot of work with dreams of nongay people, but I'm convinced that there are very definite differences and that there are gay archetypes. I would suggest that a gay man's relationship to his internal female is quite different than a nongay man's. Certainly, the romantic allusions and sexual themes that occur within gay men's dreams are different.

I think that the image of the leather man is a gay archetypal figure, and he manifests himself in a kind of dark sexuality. By *dark*, I mean *shadow* in the most positive sense, things that are put behind one and not allowed but that may be very rich. Another gay archetype that has emerged for me is the diva, a strong dramatic woman. She might take the form of movie or opera star and has dual aspects—a powerful guide or the Queen of the Night, a bitch. She is an interesting figure to look for in both of her manifestations.

LUKE: I recently spent a week with my son, who is not gay and has suddenly, of his own accord, gotten into his dreams. He keeps a dream journal. Over that period he told me about ten to fifteen of his dreams, and we talked about them. I can't explain exactly what I felt, but it was clear to me that this was a straight man's dreams I was hearing. The major difference, it seemed to me, was the different location of eros in the dreams; that it was organized around women instead of around men, coming from a man. It just recolored everything, and though we're not a people defined by a sex act, there's something about the location of eros that changes everything in the dream world, as well as in the waking world. We were driving down the freeway in a blinding snowstorm, and suddenly this vision came; I could clearly see a fundamental difference.

DON: Within the past year I've been doing dream work with some straight men, so that I would have a chance to see if there's a difference. Where is the psychic energy, the erotic energy in the dream moving? How do the archetypal images in the dreams interact with each other? One image that I've done some fairly in-depth work on has been the archetype of the Queen of the South, the black queen that appears in many dreams and in different types of mythological forms. In gay men's dreams this figure appears as an ally, somehow or another. The intrapsychic material of gay men—particularly when it's compared to the intrapsychic material of straight men—does not support the idea that gay people are just like straight people except for what we do in bed. I would say basically our souls are gay, our vision is gay, and we move in the world in very different ways than straight men. This is what I talked about earlier when I said none of us had come out yet. What we're carrying inside of us is so profound that most of us haven't even begun to scratch the surface of what that's about.

MITCH: I would definitely agree with the position that's being described here; something's got to give. Now, previously, it's always been gayness that has given. In other words, we've been oppressed by Jungians just as by everyone else. Jung said that all men have this erotic, hypnotic anima fascination. Well, these gay men don't have that. They're experiencing something else. Jung's idea is that the soul, the anima, is going to be reunited with you, and that's symbolized through the work, the opus, of realizing yourself. That's what he called the *syzygy* of male and female. So how are we going to use this symbology for our gay experience of the Queen of the South? Is this what's going on? How do we understand this? These are the kind of questions that get us to this new world, this new way of understanding—which you reach by coming out inside. We're talking about re-owning, regaining our own *libido,* as Jung called it—the Freudian, electrical, energylike metaphor of eros.

The libido of gay men shapes itself in the dreams—we see it in the fantasies, the metaphors and the images—differently than it shapes itself for straight men. It's very obvious. So then there's the question, What is a gay *coniunctio?* That's the Latin alchemical term for the operation of bringing together, in sexual union, the male and the female: the anima and the adept, the adept and the *soror mystica.*

MARK: There seem to be profound implications inherent in this work for gay men.

MITCH: The idea of talking about the unconscious as being the shadow is not a bad one. The shadow is coming to us; we don't need to go out and chase after it. The shadow has already come to the gay community, death has come to the gay community in living color! No one can stop AIDS at this point, you see. But it can be related to and worked with, just like the unconscious! That's another way of talking about this "coming out inside." The idea of talking about the *other* side as the *shadow* side, the *dark* side, is not meant at all in the same sense as you get AIDS and die. It's just that it's a similar metaphor, one of death and rebirth—which is, of course, the basic shamanic metaphor of descent and rebirth. It would be healthy for gay men at this point in their development to discover and develop a real inner, gay world; or to articulate, or elaborate, with the collective unconscious, together, mutually. What Edward Edinger calls a creation of consciousness.

MARK: We've been treated as if we were a virus within the body politic of America itself, rather than an indispensable part

of its cultural fabric. I think gay people have to reinstate themselves as a kind of tribe, heal themselves deep within it, and then
proceed with the work we're obviously being called to do. What
did Jung, in particular, say about the role of gay men?

DON: Jung evolved his ideas on gayness from basically a Freudian psychoanalytic, caught-in-a-mother-complex tradition. He
remained relatively silent on the subject—which at least is to
our advantage. But late in his life he said things to the effect
that "homosexuality is always connected with or associated with
education." He didn't go any further, but that statement would
certainly relate to things that Edward Carpenter and Gerald Heard
said. Again, I don't think that Jung is the important thing, as
valuable as he's been. I think Jung has blazed a certain kind of
inner trail, and now there's a possibility of gay people exploring
the gay regions of the psyche.

I've been working with gay men around this material for the
past four years, and it's wonderful to see them come alive. They
know that there's something there. You can see it in their eyes.
They realize that they're connecting with something in their
interior world that has always been there. But no one, up until
this time, has asked them to look at it in ways that really are a
part of a gay psychospiritual lineage. While each one of these
journeys is individual, there is a collectivity to it also.

MARK: The concept of the hero's journey, or shaman's quest,
is implied here—a more profound understanding of oneself. What
does that mean for gay men?

DON: In going into themselves—in making a descent—people will discover many myths that they relate to. The myth of
the shaman is simply one myth. The Holy Grail is another one.
What's really important isn't taking a concept—call it shamanism or call it Marxism—it's much more, "What's your own
psyche saying? What's the journey like for you?" The idea of the
journey going down somewhere is common. It's in shamanism,
it's in the Greek spiritual tradition, it's in ancient Babylonian
texts, it happens in Los Angeles 1987. The myth that somebody

uses as a vehicle for going down isn't as important as the descent. That's the essential thing.

KEN: I don't like to use the word "shamanist" lightly—but my dream work with gay men feels more in that tradition, rather than in a priestly tradition. Because I feel like I'm taking the trip with the people that I work with. I'm going on that descent with them. Maybe I've gone down the trail some distance before, but nevertheless I feel that each journey is different, and I'm right there. There's a different dynamic at work here than the priestly function of saying, "I know and I will reveal all to you." I don't feel that I know and can reveal much of anything. The revelation is something that we discover among ourselves.

CHRIS: There are things going on in the world that are particular to our age, one of which is the assimilation or disintegration of hundreds of cultures throughout the world. It's also apparent that we live on the edge of nuclear disaster. So it has been extremely important to somehow fit myself into that image of what the world is right now. Part of the phenomenon of being alive today is the fact that gayness—as we know it—never really existed before a hundred years ago. Even thirty years ago, when Gerald Heard was writing, the gay movement was really unheard of. I think that gays must fit into the cosmic sphere of planetary evolution, if there is such a thing. Because, how is it that gayness and the women's liberation movement happened to be flowering at such a time? I pose this question not because I think there's an answer for it but because it might inspire new ideas or myths about how we can choose to live our lives. There must be some way that all these things fit together. As I come out inside myself, as I explore my dreams, these disparate things are coming together.

DON: Chris is touching on something very important when he says that he feels some kind of concern. And certainly there are lots of people concerned with nuclear and ecological disaster. But I would say that there's something about that concern that is uniquely gay and helps to define, perhaps, what gayness is about. I first began to pick up on that in the Peace Corps, back in the early 1960s, when I found out that most of the men who were in the Peace Corps were gay. There was something about the New Frontier idealism and what Kennedy was talking about that somehow appealed to us. I also noticed that in the mid- to late 1960s, with the antiwar movement, which I was actively involved in, that many of its leaders—those people who were really defining the struggle and moving out with it—were gay men, albeit largely in the closet. The War Resisters' League in New York City at times was like a gay liberation meeting. The 1986 pro-peace march from Los Angeles to Washington, D.C., was largely conceived and staffed by gay people. That's data! That information tells us something about ourselves. Yet today, when you use the words *spiritual* and *gay* together, people will say, "Well, that's a contradiction in terms, it's an impossibility." I think that's from a Newtonian point of view; from an Einsteinian world view it's almost as if that's the essence of what gayness is about. But there's no place in our culture, be it in the dominant culture or even in the gay community today, where we get any encouragement to explore and look at this. It's almost as if our own assimilationist leaders are leading us into a certain kind of psychic or spiritual genocide.

LUKE: It seems to me that what's happened is a question of vocabulary. We've suddenly got a new word that is a very useful word—*gay*—which collects a certain body of experience, iden-tifies it and separates it out. But we're just at the beginning of the vocabulary. There's an experience that happens to me a lot when I read about people in former cultures and different places. You get a glimmer of something. You say, "That feels real familiar." And it seems to me that in Western society, up until recently, we've not been able to talk about this glimmer. Part of our task now is to get the vocabulary so we can talk about it as clearly as possible.

MITCH: What's being talked about here is as revolutionary for gay liberation, for gay people and their ideas of themselves, as Einstein and his associates' innovations were in terms of where they took physicists—in terms of understanding the foundations, the bases of matter and energy and how they work. So we're talking about a gay physics here, so to speak. Everyone has mentioned the importance of actualizing this potential that's in us—the culture of gayness. Heretofore, there's been no elaboration of this sort, in a way that's going to bring about something that's absolutely vital in terms of continued survival of the planet. Jung talked about separating this old, dying age (that we're apparently part of) from some new age that was gradually forming in the distant future and that humanity was moving toward. Many of the gay authors in this book talk about this whole idea of Uranians, of gay people embodying a quality, an energy, or a meaning that somehow helps make the bridge from an old era, an old eon, to a new era. The new age is definitely more than relevant to gays and what they are. That's the numinousness, the thing that attracts you. That's the idea of the grail for you—you find it or, in hero myths, you might have to rescue it. Or you might be sick, and you might have to go get the answer—whatever the image is in terms of healing.

Now, that's why getting into the unconscious, into the shadow, making the descent, is something to do, why people get attracted to it. There is something that comes from inside to pull you in, because there's a treasure! It's within that inner crucible, through this work of coming out inside, that you find the inner treasure. The alchemists called it the "royal gold," or they used different metaphors entirely—the rebis, the hermaphrodite triumphant on the moon, for example; the philosopher's stone, the aqua permanente. So here we're talking about a science, then, of actualizing the treasure, the gay treasure, let's say, of the Uranian soul.

MARK: In regard to the relationship that gay men seem to have with particular archetypal images within, I think it is especially relevant to note how those images have been projected into certain cultural roles and forms of behavior. The role of the drag queen, for instance, is based on a particular form of realizing the internal feminine as ally (rather than a presence of opposition), not on any urge that compels some men "to become like women." Within many gay communities, cross-dressed men have served as mediators, nurturers and builders of community and political awareness, exemplifying the traditional role of the berdache—which is neither masculine or feminine, but something unique into itself; a third gender. Within the leather subculture, we see some men employing shamanic techniques of ecstasy, leading others into an "underworld" descent where powerful feelings and visions are encountered. The role of the mediator (berdache), and the role of the spirit guide (shaman), are ones amply played out in contemporary gay culture. I feel that these roles are primarily informed by images from within the psyche of individuals, rather than being shaped by specific political or social conditions, as some would suggest.

However marginal cross-dressing, ritualized sexuality and fairie gatherings may appear to mainstream gay society, I do think they have been, and continue to be, crucial experiences. The key word here is *experiential*; that is, the actual living out of unconscious impulses—literally grounding ourselves in a shared, created reality and not just an ideological or intellectual abstraction. It is by engaging dreams and fantasies that we liberate ourselves, concretize and give form to the business of our souls, arrive at some greater truths of who we might be. And rather than viewing this as separatism—leading us politically to a dead end—I see this as necessary work, which will ultimately reveal to us that our place in the human community is not at its edge, but often at its center. The exploration of differentness is not qualitatively about "better or worse," but about finding our authentic cultural roles.

DON: I'm thinking about people who are reading this book and saying, "Okay. All these ideas are fine, and at some level I connect with what you're all saying. But here I'm sitting in East Jesus, Iowa. What do I do, where do I go, how do I do this?" To which I say: "You have a treasure in your hands right now with this book. It's a sacred book. There are gay men talking about their inner lives. If there's one other gay person or a few of you, get together, form a study group and sit down and read this book together. And then talk about your own lives, how your own lives are seen through what's being said there. There isn't anything here about being right or wrong; it's about the journey, the exploration. Start a dream journal. That's how we do it at Treeroots. We sit down and we pay attention to our dreams, among other things, and we work with them. We see how they're reflecting what's going on in our lives today, and where our journey needs to go."

CHRIS: I would say that the treasure is not just inside of you, but it's here, now, with you now. That's what it's all about, creating ways of being for yourself that will encourage and develop and let that treasure in yourself grow and be.

DON: I'd like to address that issue by another road. There is a story told about a province in a faraway country in which there was a great drought. It had not rained for a long time, the plants and animals were dying, food could not be grown, there was famine and pestilence in the land, and the people were suffering greatly. They tried everything their leaders had told them to make it rain, the usual offerings and chants, and yet the drought continued. Finally, in great desperation, a delegation of villagers went to a far-distant province to bring back an old man—a shaman, perhaps—a man who had the reputation of *knowing* important things but of acting strangely. As soon as the old man entered the desolate province, he immediately stopped his journey toward the provincial capital and demanded that a small hut hurriedly be built for him out of branches and leaves. He disappeared into the hut without a word of explanation, not wanting to be disturbed. The villagers were puzzled and thought that maybe their leaders had been right when they laughed at their plan for bringing the old man to their province. The old man stayed inside the hut for three days, and on the fourth day it began to rain. The people, rejoicing, went to the old man. What did you do, they asked? The rain is falling and our province is coming alive again. What did you do? The old man explained that, as soon as he had set foot in their province, his body felt the chaos, confusion and lack of harmony in the land. He could not continue. So he had a simple hut built, went *inside*, and sat for three days to restore his own balance and wholeness. And then it rained.

I sense this old, old story is relevant to life in our gay village today, and to the historic challenge and sacred obligation of gay soul making.

Walt Whitman in 1841, at age 22.
(Photo courtesy Walt Whitman House,
Camden, New Jersey.)

Walt Whitman at 35. (Photo courtesy
Walt Whitman House, Camden, New Jersey.)

Walt Whitman and Peter Doyle, ca. 1865. (Photo courtesy Library of Congress.)

Walt Whitman in 1867, as photographed by Matthew Brady. (Photo courtesy National Archive.)

Edward Carpenter in 1905 at Millthorpe. (Photo by A. Mattison.)

Left: Gerald Heard in 1964, as drawn by Don Bachardy. (Image courtesy Don Bachardy.) Below: Gerald Heard in 1963. (Photo by George Kramer.)

Harry Hay, father of the modern gay movement. (Photo by Mark Thompson.)

John Burnside and Harry Hay in spring of 1979. (Photo by Mark Thompson.)

Members of the first Mattachine discussion group meet during Christmas of 1951 (left to right): Harry Hay (top), Dale Jennings, Rudi Gernreich, Stan Witt, Bob Hull, Chuck Rowland and Paul Bernard. (Photo courtesy of Harry Hay.)

Mud ritual during the first "Spiritual Gathering for Radical Fairies," held in the Arizona desert in the summer of 1979. (Photo by Mark Thompson.)

Ecstasy for everyone: John Burnside and fellow fairies at Arizona gathering in 1979. (Photo by Mark Thompson.)

Fairie ritual.
(Photo by Mark
Thompson.)

A shaman with an urgent muse or two, poet James Broughton. (Photo by Joel Singer.)

PART 3

A World of Our Making: Myth and Meaning

Definition of self, as a basic right and active pursuit, has only recently been seized by those people we now call gay. In America, where identity is not so much assumed as acquired, that definition has been shaped by a combustion of cultural motifs and gestures uniquely combined: "human potential" and civil disobedience, expanded mobility, media and concepts of morality, images of sexual outlaws in leather and denim, and new forms of pleasure, to name a few. Gay identity, as we currently understand it, has been created out of fragments of borrowed culture and has been fed back to the rest of the world as a kind of special vernacular. A familial language of known signals and signs is now shared by people throughout the gay global village, but it is a language increasingly tinged with the stigma of grief and future uncertainty.

A deadly virus that has undermined a community's sense of self, even one so newly formed, has also posited a spiritual crisis deep within it. Gay people had only just begun to sift through those qualities that somehow seemed intrinsic to them and less adapted from some other place—their parents' lives, perhaps, or the lives of other people who are not gay. In America, those qualities sprang from the images and icons of our native land, our youth, but even their transformation into a language of kinship often felt awkward and misbegotten. There was a need for something more expansive than what we had been handed and what we had managed to fashion from it. And now a new reality, with fear supplanting joy, has rendered us still further into a world peculiarly our own, one where the vocabulary must be even more keenly considered.

An intimacy engendered through loss, a dialogue created by displacement, now so widely felt, have always been subterranean currents in gay life. Throughout the evolution of gay identity in this country, and particularly in the 1970s, there have been gay men more self-aware than others about probing the shared language of their lives— the myths and meanings of what it is to be gay. *Understanding that the word itself need not imply a fixed destination, they used it as a device with which to burrow beneath personal and cultural surfaces: A truly gay life was one continually examined. Rejecting the acculturated, acceptable notions of gay identity, they pursued singular paths—ones marked by loss and displacement—and found different versions of that identity, some more authentically* queer. *These are identities forged from great pain and doubt, made from the remnants of many cultures and traditions, informed by questions left unresolved by a language not wholly adequate.*

The tragic dimension of gay life has not been anything innate to it but that it has been so determined by a reactive course; justifying itself against endless political and religious crusades and against the possibility of extermination. In its struggle to emerge, gay consciousness has seldom been able to choose cultural expression native to itself or to exert its own underlying potential. Not surprisingly, the opportunity to grasp such alternatives has largely been found on the West Coast, where the freedom to explore inner space has been less inhibited, partly because of a nationalistic imperative—that of Manifest Destiny—now finally realized on the Pacific shore, with no space left to go but into the psyche of individuals. As travelers without passport, gay people there have been more at ease to depart from the world of their fathers and into a world of their own making—forming an even newer language, one of origins as much of adaptation, and creating ever-renewed concepts of gay identity; in this case, of being fairies.

The following chapters explain a bit of that process. And while the writing reflects on history and ideas developed before a devastating health crisis irrevocably altered the context of gay life, the message is as relevant now as it was then. If anything, there has been an opening of the heart that could allow a body—collective and individual —to be more perceptive of signals that trickle up from deep within it, affirming its very life. The vision expressed in these concluding pages is an ingenuous one—yet when they experience it, most gay men say they've realized it all their lives. I think seed for future directions are planted there.

By liberating the language of self—whether it be as intermediate types, a separate gender, fairies or simply as enspirited queer men—we ensure our inclusion in the forming new view of a post-modern world. And by creating a multi-dimensional model of ourselves, we can only expect the continuous blossoming of our emotional and social capacities. What choice have we ever had but to seek out and engage the unknown?

AARON SHURIN

THE TRUTH COME OUT

Now we make the truth come out we find we have all kinds of ancestors—spiritual forebears—goddesses and gods as you will, stories to retell as they have been told thousands of years. We retell them in making our lives—the making that lies at the root of art, and as we "make love," at the root of our loving as well. This is our spiritual occasion: that we are a people who define our identities by the fact of love. In calling ourselves gay we say that love is central, and after the shame and guilt, and yes after the anger, love remains a word we can speak unabashed while others cringe at its too-telling power. We are the subjects of the power of love.

I say we "make" the truth and that is the other part of our occasion—we each face this definition that is at first a horror and then a joy. We do this sorcery: We stop the world, say "No, I am not that" (recoil)—look deep into ourselves—and "Yes, I am this" (expand). We make of our oppression a gift of direction. This we each do, must do, to find our route to love. That we are willing to face that unknown urge, fly in the face of that adversity to a home we only feel in our blood is waiting, is the measure of our courage. I say this "coming out" is a deep occasion of the spirit that will not be swayed, of a mind that must know itself through the body. Then at last we're on our way; then we *make* our way.

MARK THOMPSON

THIS GAY TRIBE:

A BRIEF HISTORY

OF FAIRIES

I'm not willing just to be tolerated. That wounds my love of love and of liberty.

—Jean Cocteau
The White Paper

One of the most remarkable offshoots of American gay liberation in recent years has been the emergence of "radical fairies," a nationwide, grass-roots movement of gay men seeking alternatives within their own subculture and society at large. Many fairie-identified men see little distinction between the two, arguing that as the gay middle-class assimilates into the cultural mainstream, deeper inquiries into the predominant structures of state and spirit are being left unanswered. This loosely organized faction of gay men, largely unknown (even within their own community), remains on the outer edges of both worlds.

In most instances, those who are aware of this underground movement discount its questions and values as naïve remnants of the 1960s. These critics invoke clichéd images of incense and vague Oriental philosophies, as if these things too should remain relics from another decade, trivializing history into sentiment and shameless nostalgia. But, in fact, the fairies are exploring the most personal and relevant of questions: What does it mean to be a gay man—alive, today? And rather than borrow answers from the East, they have gone to the very roots of Western spiritual mythology.

Although *fairie* has long been used as a hateful and self-effacing epithet, gay historian Arthur Evans was among the first to insist that the word—as applied to homosexual men—had an actual, living reality based in fact. We think of fairies today as being mythical creatures, stemming mostly from Northern European folklore, primarily Celtic in origin. The Celts, and the many indigenous tribes that preceded them, were nature-worshipping people with a strong matriarchal religious tradition. The many faces of the Great Mother were celebrated on special days throughout the seasons, often with sacred, sexual rites. Male sexuality, the world of the night, and the spirit of animals were embodied by a male deity known, in various guises, as the Horned One—a satyrlike figure referred to by the Celts as Cernunnos, and named Dionysus, Pan, Minotaur and Osiris in other pre-Christian cultures. The ancient tradition of nature worship persisted through Celtic, Roman and early Christian times, although it was increasingly suppressed by the corporate demands of the church. The archetypes of the Great Mother and her horned consort were eventually assimilated into Christian theology as the Virgin and the Devil.

In his ground-breaking work, *Witchcraft and the Gay Counterculture: A Radical View of Western Civilization and Some of the People It Has Tried to Destroy* (Fag Rag Books, 1978), Evans asserts, "Though outlawed, the worshippers of the matriarchal mix persisted underground and were known in folklore as fairies, named after the fateful goddesses whom they worshipped. Later in the medieval period, various remnants of the 'old religion' were to emerge again, only this time they were called heretics and witches. Their greatest 'crime' was that they experienced the highest manifestations of the divine in free practice of sexuality." Aspects of the Great Mother survived as the image of the three Fates, notes Evans, who were mythologized as fairies by the medieval Christian world (*fairy* coming from the Latin word *fata*, meaning fate).

Evans was a member of the Gay Liberation Front in New York City, which formed immediately after the Stonewall riots in 1969, and later helped found the outspoken Gay Activists Alliance, where he developed a form of militant, nonviolent protest that he called "zaps." Evans's world view of gay people as tribal-shamanic figures was central to his activism; later, when he moved to the West Coast in the mid-1970s, he began to publicly expand on this history. During the spring of 1976, Evans conducted a series of well-attended lectures in San Francisco, presenting a bold conceptualization of gay spirituality based on his research about "Faeries." More privately, he had already begun to give form to his ideas through the practice of ritual with a widening circle of other gay men in locations throughout the city. I remember one afternoon during this time at San Francisco State University, where one of the first gay academic conferences in the country was being held, when Evans and a dozen followers charged through the campus wearing robes, skins and scarves, clanging bells and waving boughs of leaves. A buried heritage was being announced that day, one far removed from the imaginations of those witnessing this pagan procession.

The need to create a new inner vision—and one not based on modern Western morality—was a vital issue for many gay people during this time. Drawing new historical conclusions from old myths was one approach, but others felt compelled to separate themselves physically from the dominant heterosexual culture and to seek alternatives for body, as well as soul, in isolated rural areas. A plan for one such refuge in 1970 touched a collective nerve in gay people across the country, even though the idea was later revealed as elaborate fiction. As a means to raise media awareness, a Los Angeles group also called the Gay Liberation Front (GLF) invented a story about gay people "taking over" remote Alpine County in Northern California. The story was interpreted as real, made national headlines and created controversy and outrage. It also gave hope to many that such a plan might be true. Wishful thinking aside, some gay men and lesbians did actually go on to establish small rural communities, such as in Golden, Oregon (1970); Elwha, on the Olympic Peninsula in Washington state (1973); in Wolf Creek, Oregon (1975); and a few years later (in the late 1970s), the Running Water and Short Mountain sanctuaries in North Carolina and Tennessee.

RFD, a magazine focusing on gay country living and radical fairie politics, was created at one such community—in a large, windy farmhouse, actually—outside Grinnell, Iowa, in October 1974. According to Stewart Scofield, the magazine's first editor, "The time was right for a publication for rural gay men. The idea or dream existed in the minds and hearts of many—activists, post-hippies, fairies, queers, hermits and just ordinary guys—from all parts of the country who hadn't yet connected with one another. That deisolating connection manifested itself quite magically as *RFD: A Country Journal for Gay Men Everywhere."*

Word about the new publication quickly spread, and a deluge of mail began to arrive at the Iowa farm. Two thousand copies of the third issue were distributed by the following spring equinox. Subscribers found packets of pansy seeds stapled to the back cover of their copies. "*RFD* was more than the newsprint, the words and pictures, more than those who were intimately involved," Scofield wrote in the magazine nearly a decade after its inception. "It was the lives of hundreds of early supporters who daily sent energy to it, who told their friends about it, who wrote poetry, who read it cover from cover, who waited by their mailboxes, who dreamed with lovers about that piece of land in the future, who gardened vegetables and flowers, who celebrated the solstice and danced by the light of the moon. The readers made love to *RFD,* and *RFD* responded in kind."

Although the magazine had obviously touched a collective need, Scofield also recalled critical mail from readers who "chided us for being hippie idealist pagan gay liberationists and for the lack of material of 'real' relevance to the thousands of 'ordinary' gay men living in the country in more traditional lifestyles." Harsh words were rare, however, as *RFD* was mainly shaped and written by its far-flung network of readers, many who found the journal an ideal forum in which to express their deepest and most personal concerns.

During the early 1970s, while complex gay business and social infrastructures were emerging in major urban areas, it was rural gays who were largely questioning internal needs and values—an exploration no doubt nurtured by their relative isolation, increased self-reliance and contact with raw nature. These gay men, on the fringes of a newly organized community, provided their movement with some of its most astute and visionary analysis. "*RFD* was the last gay liberation paper to begin," observed Scofield, that "advocated a separate gay culture, a we-are-different-from-straights attitude." It was a time when many gay people began to see rural life as a viable option to urban gay ghettos, and he further noted, "It seems to me no accident that not a small amount of energy in the early days of *RFD* came from gay lib 'heavies' who had either fled the urban madness or had returned to the country of their boyhoods."

Carl Wittman was one such man. He and his companion, Allan Troxler, had helped establish *RFD* from the West Coast and were among the cofounders of the Golden, Oregon, collective, in the area where the magazine was centered for a number of years after it moved from Iowa.*

Wittman, as writer and activist, was keenly interested in the potentialities of gay consciousness throughout his life (he died of AIDS in early 1986). His widely read "Gay Manifesto" was one of the most influential documents during the early years of post-Stonewall gay liberation. Written during the summer of 1969 in San Francisco, the manifesto offered a potent gay vision in which open acceptance of sexuality in all of its forms was an integral part. Later, in the mid-1970s, Wittman participated in several gatherings of gay men in the Northwest.

One of the most far-reaching of these gatherings was the Faggots and Class Struggle conference at Wolf Creek in September 1976, where the word *fairie* was asserted in a political context. But it was through work on *RFD* and his previous exposure to the visionary writings of Harry Hay that Wittman had begun to perceive the word as having a spiritual connotation as well.

Hay and his companion John Burnside were living among the Rio Grande Indian people at San Juan Pueblo (the traditional Tewa Indian

---

*The magazine, much like a movable feast, has been produced by various collectives of gay men around the country. It resides, at the time of this writing, with a collective in the Southeast and still remains a vital and lively reader-generated quarterly. Write: *RFD*, Route 1, Box 127-E, Bakersville, North Carolina 28705.

village of Oke-Oweenge) in rural northern New Mexico during this time. They had left Los Angeles in May 1970, bringing their small kaleidoscope manufacturing business with them. Six months earlier, the couple had helped found the Gay Liberation Front in Southern California with activists Morris Kight and Jim Kepner. Hay and Burnside had also hoped to carry their concerns about gay liberation to the Indian and Chicano pueblos when they moved to the Southwest. But it turned out not to be an idea whose time had come. According to Hay, northern New Mexico in the 1970s was a crossroads of many peoples, both indigenous and immigrant, "who were coming *from* something—a place, an attitude, an idea—rather that purposely going *to* anywhere." Nevertheless, the couple established their home as a spiritual nexus, named the Circle of Loving Companions, which for a number of years was the only openly gay listed address in the entire state. It was a place for "frightened, lonely people to develop as political gay persons, to be healed and reinspired."

During this period, Hay found himself realizing and deepening many of his ideas about gay spirituality. He began to create a multi-faceted approach to what he called "the lovely dream of being gay," an inquiry that required a more subtle and cross-cultural analysis than the politics of gay liberation had demanded up to that time. He had first used the word *faerie* to convey the idea of a separate gay consciousness in 1970, during a speech before the Western Regional Homophile Conference. "But, within this community, let the spirit be betrayed, let coercion or opportunism attempt to bind any of us against our will . . . and *presto*, like the faeries of folklore, suddenly we are no longer there. . . . Our faerie characteristic is our homosexual minority's central weakness . . . and paradoxically, also the keystone of our enduring strength."

Hay continued to expand on his concept of a *faerie* identity in public talks and published papers. It was an idea that many older gay men had difficulty accepting at the time but about which a younger generation was beginning to express curiosity.

Wittman met Hay in the summer of 1975. Hay and Burnside were returning to New Mexico from seminars they had been invited to attend in Seattle, when they stopped to visit Wolf Creek. The two men shared their views about a "circle of loving companions" with members of the Oregon collectives, and Hay asserted the need for a community land trust (a permanent rural site) where "faerie consciousness" could be explored to full potential by gay men. Wittman was especially moved by Hay's vision, and in the autumn of that year he wrote in *RFD* that "the notion of foundling, growing up a foreigner in family and culture, and returning to the larger whole—this notion I put on gently, like a new robe, wondering if it becomes me; afraid of vanity, but yearning for dignity, I find myself saying, yes, it fits. Ah, but politically, is it misleading? Where are my hard-won ideas about separatism, confrontation, group consciousness? Are we not members of a lost and dispersed tribe, rather than errant offspring? Isn't it a bit spiritual, ignoring the real needs to unite politically? I decide not. This vision . . . is a mantle to wear over whatever else is me, one which I feel will become my other attributes."

Wittman's debate echoed the feelings of many others—that the political and the spiritual need not be exclusive of one another. In fact, the synthesis of the two was a reality fully expressed in many gay lives during that time. According to Faygele benMiriam, a political activist since the early 1950s, "There was a time when fairies were the most politically directed of gays. We formed a nucleus of people who were trying to change patterns of dress and attitude and ways of treating each other. We were out there saying, 'We are different than others' —and giving that difference expression. Many fairies were looking at the next step."

BenMiriam was a resident of the Elwah community and then relocated to the Wolf Creek area, where he worked on *RFD* for several years. Later, he moved to North Carolina, and continued to work on the magazine, which had also traveled east. BenMiriam remembers gatherings of gay men in the early 1970s where questions about a unique gay identity were expressed. "We didn't call ourselves 'fairies' back then, but we were."

Groups of outrageously dressed gay men would travel between Boston, Ann Arbor, Seattle and San Francisco in cars painted with slogans proclaiming *Gay Power* or *Faggots Against Facism,* recalls benMiriam, who, in the spirit of the times, once went a year and a half without wearing men's clothing, including the time he was working for the federal government. "We were trying to keep some sort of gay spirit alive during a time of great attack and repression. Fairie-identified gay men refuse to be automatically ghettoized. We have long been on our communities' front lines and, in many cases, have formed its political basis."

The investigation of gay consciousness by small groups of gay men around the country; a growing inquiry by Carl Wittman and many others in the pages of *RFD* and elsewhere; the radical reevaluation of a gay heritage by Arthur Evans, whose work had appeared piecemeal in *Fag Rag* and *Out* magazines during the mid-1970s and then in book form; and the synchronistic reclaiming of a *faerie* identity by Harry Hay were all important foundation stones for the alternative movement soon to come.

The need to retreat and explore gay sensibilities in a protected environment remained a compelling issue within the subculture. But it was a minority opinion, a voice counter to the central thrust of a civil rights movement working hard to downplay the concept of difference. In 1979, Hay and Burnside and two other men decided to take the matter into their own hands and announced the first Spiritual Conference for Radical Fairies. Don Kilhefner, formerly of the GLF and one of the founders of the Los Angeles Gay and Lesbian Community Services Center, and Mitch Walker, a San Francisco writer and counselor, had also emphasized in their individual work the importance for gay men collectively to discover a way of being unique to themselves.

The site chosen to begin this exploration was a remote spot in the Arizona desert, and over two hundred gay men arrived that summer from throughout the United States and Canada. The gathering had a profound impact on many who attended, and despite personal and ideological conflicts that would split its founders a few years later, the fairie movement was born. During the next six years, over a hundred gatherings of "radical fairies" were held across the North American continent, from Key West beaches to Washington state forests, lofts in New York City to the mountains of Colorado, and up and down the coast of California, with anywhere from two dozen to three hundred men in attendance. And, at the time of this writing, there are ongoing gatherings being planned throughout the country.

The phenomenon has spread beyond national boundaries, with gatherings reported in Europe and Australia, and a new set of values, one with its own oral and written traditions differing from mainstream gay culture, has developed. (See Michael Rumaker's *My First Satyrnalia*, San Francisco: Grey Fox Press, 1981.) For several thousand gay men, fairie gatherings have provided a unique opportunity to examine and to reclaim a part of the self previously denied, an intense experience to be digested and then used in the context of everyday life. The fairies, as a kind of constantly rejuvenating tribe (there are no leaders; each gathering is locally organized), remain anarchical in spirit. And while their gatherings are frustrating and too unfocused for some, they remain essential for others.

On the surface, it would be possible to view the fairies as part of the growing popular interest in neopaganism and Wicca—the ancient word for *witchcraft,* meaning "to bend." (See Margot Adler's *Drawing Down the Moon*, Boston: Beacon Press, revised edition, 1986.) Or to regard their retreats as an idealistic leftover from the whole-earth, alternative-culture sentiment of the 1960s. Although the fairies have taken signals from both sources, the energy that propels their movement forward seems to come from a deep place within the gay psyche: a wounded and vulnerable place, but a place perhaps not unfamiliar to "fairies" of previous times. In so actively choosing to reinvent themselves, the radical fairies are dipping into a deep well of human myth and spiritual experience.

In saying this, I am reminded of a passage from Mircea Eliade's *The Sacred and the Profane:* "It is the specialists in ecstasy, the familiars of the fantastic universes, who nourish, increase, and elaborate the traditional mythological motifs. . . . In the last analysis, in the archaic societies as everywhere else, culture arises and is renewed through the creative experiences of a few individuals. But since archaic culture gravitates around myths, and these are constantly being studied and given new, more profound interpretations by the specialists in the sacred, it follows that society as a whole is led toward the values and meanings discovered and conveyed by these few individuals. It is in this way that myth helps man to transcend his own limitations and conditions and stimulates him to rise to 'where the greatest are.' "

I remember these lines by Walt Whitman: "In the need of songs, philosophy, and appropriate native grand opera, shipcraft, any craft, he or she is greatest who contributes the greatest original practical example." And, finally, his declaration, "Who need be afraid of the merge."

To outsiders, the fairies often appear politically naïve, however authentic the spirit that motivates their gatherings may be. Yet, for the men who respond to its call, the fairie movement is rooted in the firm belief that the only liberation movement worth having is one that first begins inside. Personal evolution is the true agent for change: Therefore, the personal *must* be linked with the political. Too many gay people have not really confronted their own homophobia, the internalization of society's stigma, that self-hate that pollutes the soul. It is a painful realization to face; and as a result, many have projected their own feelings of negative self-worth onto others.

Still, at its core, the message of gay liberation has been one primarily of love. And—on the surface, at least—the fairies have embodied this message well, taking to heart and expanding on the most radical impulses of the early gay movement. Their first gatherings appeared like a mirage, a *fata morgana,* on an otherwise arid landscape—an original and healing journey into the pathless lands of inner knowing.

A Recollection: In the Shadow of the Red Rock, The Radical Fairies Convene

A clipping from the *Farmers' Arizonan Gazette,* Wednesday, September 5, 1979:

> *Benson—A series of "strange doings" were reported by local sheriff, Waldo Pruitt, at a site about ten miles west of this small desert*

community. Pruitt first made his report Monday night, claiming that he had failed to locate a section of desert land after repeated investigation.

The land in question was the site of the Desert Sanctuary Foundation, also known as the Sri Ram Ashram. Locals in the area said they knew little about the activities of the sanctuary. Other sources reported yesterday, however, that a Spiritual Conference for Radical Fairies had been scheduled at the sanctuary over the Labor Day weekend. One organizer for the event was quoted as having said, "With luck we'll learn to levitate, as fairies should." No explanation was offered by the source overhearing the remark.

Pruitt first became aware of the event through reports about cattle displaying unusual behavior in the vicinity of the sanctuary. Informants also claimed that large groups of men there were engaging in orgiastic rituals.

"They said that all the animals in the area started to act real strange," the sheriff explained. "I guess I don't mind what you do as long as you don't do it in public. But when you start in on plants and animals, well, then you've gone too far."

Pruitt and three deputies drove out to the site to investigate the disturbances. He claimed that a flashing of colored lights could be seen from miles around. But when the men arrived, "The land out there had just got up and plumb disappeared. All that was left was an old Gunsmoke set a few miles down the road." Pruitt said he will continue his investigation of the incident.

I arrived at the sanctuary in the middle of the desert amid a great veil of dust. The taste of it lay choking in my mouth; fine rivulets of it slid across the hood of the car. Arizona was the final stop on a long journey that had also taken me across Europe, where I had been picking through the shards of gay heritage.

A castrated Dionysus in the Vatican, myths and legends perverted from original meanings, painters and writers censored by convention were among the relics. Only the men observed gathering night after night, usually at the site of the oldest ruins or wooded groves, offered tangible evidence of a culture that still might survive after centuries of patriarchal, heterosexual domination.

I was tired and wanted to go home. But the sensations before me of a garden in bloom, playful laughter and a beautiful man, flower in hair and hands reached out in welcome, quickened a hope that perhaps I needn't look further. As I stepped out of the dust, I stepped out of time, was hurtled out of gravity. The fairies, at last, had reconvened.

Harry Hay had a vision over thirty years ago when he put out a call for gay men to gather together and at last discover "Who are we?" "Where have we come from?" and "What are we here for?" These questions became the spiritual basis for the early Mattachine Society, a foundation stone for our present-day liberation movement.

Hay's vision was dimmed, however, when the group lost contact with its original purpose and its members "became more interested in being respectable than self-respecting. . . . They believed we were just like everyone else."

Hay left the group profoundly disappointed but eventually met his "other," John Burnside. Together they left for New Mexico where, during the past decade, they have been quietly rearticulating the need for a "circle of loving companions."

A century before, Walt Whitman wrote, "I dream'd in a dream I saw a city invincible to the attacks of the whole of the rest of the earth, I dream'd that was the new city of Friends. . . ."

Hay began to sense the need for reasserting this dream. And so, joining together with other men, the call was put out again. Much had changed in thirty years. Whitman's "new city of Friends" had now emerged as inner city ghettos. Like many of the men drawn to the conference, I had become weary of a "culture" defined by exploitive entrepreneurs, distrustful of religious leaders using spirituality in ways that did not move me, doubtful of a community unable to see beyond the pursuit of civil rights alone.

I remember the sting of a baseball driven hard into the palm of my hand as my father worked for hours trying to "make a man of me." I remember talking to trees and of the wonderful pictures left dream'd in a dream. I came to Arizona to accept and to reclaim, to shed the wounds of conformity as the snake drops its skin on the desert sand, to understand that variations in the human species extend past color and form and into modes of perception as well, to learn of the creative potentials still locked within my sexuality.

I came to shake the magic rattle, to roll in the dust, to take apart the pieces and reinvent myself, to be able to say finally, "I remember now what I want to become."

> Come forth, o children,
>   under the stars,
> And take your fill of love!
> I am above you and in you.
> My ecstasy is in yours.
> My joy is to see your joy.
> —*Aleister Crowley*,
> Quoted on the First "Call"

The tall man with the laugh in his voice slowly circled in the middle of the group. "Forget the linear associations you used to get here," he said. "Use fairie physics—turn everything inside out. Imagine, for instance, that the tops of the trees are really the roots." And then Mitch Walker sat down.

Gradually, other men stood up and presented their gifts. Actors, writers, teachers, priests, crop tillers and film directors. Gifts of movement and music, laughter and wit were all brought forth. The experience of age freely mixed with the exuberance of youth. Long-felt anxieties were exposed, tears unashamedly shed. Two hundred gay men forming an oasis in the middle of the desert, linking hands without competition and aggression, without the usual props of status and envy.

Hay had stood up the previous evening and unwrapped the gift of his insights. "We must recognize that there is a qualitative difference between hetero social consciousness and gay social consciousness," he said. "And our first responsibility must be to develop this gay consciousness to its deepest and most compassionately encompassing levels.

"Humanity must expand its experience from people thinking objectively—thinking subject-to-object; that is, in terms of opportunism, competitiveness and self-advantage—to thinking subject-to-subject, in terms of equal sharing, loving healing.

"Early on in human evolution, natural selection set into the evolving whirl a small percentage of beings who appeared to counterbalance the tendency of subject–object thinking characteristic of the emerging human conformity. Humanity would be wise to finally give consideration to these deviants in their ranks—gays—and to begin to grant us the peace and growing space we will need to display and further develop, in communicable words and actions, our gift. [It is] the gift of *analogue consciousness* by which we perceive the world through the gay window of subject-to-subject consciousness."

He continued, the night air carrying his words over the men sitting in front of him. "We must transform the experience of people viewing others as objects to be manipulated, mastered and consumed, to subjects like him/herself, to be respected and cherished.

"We must also remember that the social world we inherit, the total hetero male-oriented and -dominated world of tradition and daily environment—the sum total of our history, philosophy, psychology, culture, our very languages—are all totally subject–object in concept, definitions and evolution.

"To all of this we fairies should be essentially alien. The hetero male, incapable of conceiving the possibility of a window on the world other than his own, is equally incapable of perceiving that gay people might not fit in either of his man–woman categories, that we might turn out to be classified as something very else.

"If we, as people, will but grasp this, flesh it out and exercise this affirmatively, we will discover the lovely gay conscious 'not-man' shining underneath our disguises. We must begin gathering in circles to manifest the new dimensions of subject–subject relationships and to validate the contributions our consciousness is capable of developing within the world vision."

Hay's words for some men were comfortable and familiar; for others, new ideas full of turmoil and self-confrontation. Coming out is more than a prescription to a contained lifestyle; it is an ongoing experience of many dimensions. As the first morning progressed, and more and more men stood up to reveal old attitudes and assumptions, the many secure places left behind outside were, indeed, being turned "inside out."

Being integrated into a world conceived by sexist heterosexual males is not the full measure of equality. The men on the grass that morning, assembled from many points thousands of miles apart, knew that they still felt sad and alienated by the paradox of a culture reaping the benefits of civil liberation but still left spiritually impoverished. As gay men, we have been denied access to the watersheds of our culture and systematically suppressed for fulfilling the roles we once naturally assumed. At one time we embodied the creatures of change in myth and folklore: shamans and ritualmakers, conveyors of spirit, carriers of seed, tenders of the sun and moon; a people encoded with the function of empathizing with the elements.

How appropriate to reclaim the distinction of *fairie*; to return to a spot on the continent that had not felt such a gathering in centuries; to honor the full sum of ourselves and the spinning, biological entity once known as Gaia—the Great Mother of us all. As the hours of this first day passed, the cocoons of many former selves could be seen shriveling under the bright midday sun. New creatures, fairies of many different hues, were emerging.

I left the luxuriant grounds of the sanctuary late that afternoon feeling cynicism encroaching upon my exhilaration. I walked several miles, past groups of men making music, making love, making conversation, to a point where the desert plains begin their sweep up into the Rincon Mountains. I took off my clothes and jumped down to the sandy bottom of a dry riverbed. I cradled myself, rocking back and forth, some part of me wanting to disbelieve the events of the day, yet feeling the invisible currents of the water that had once been there, aware of the life under the desert floor coming up through the soles of my feet.

Now I was on the inside, somehow merged with the sand, the scrub trees, even the insect sounds around me. I felt I was seeing, hearing, consciously for the first time in my life. My "objectivity" had become unglued. Each man here was a companion to love and learn from; my ability and my need for trust was being renewed.

The cynicism sprang from my reluctance to accept yet another label, from my previous distrust of men in general. The term *fairie* seemed comforting, yet alien. I knew I often felt *fairylike*, but the word did not fully encompass the complexities of my thoughts and emotions as a *man-creature*. Still, it seemed the natural progression in the long derivation of words used to describe us: *Uranian, invert, homosexual, homophile, gay, queer, faggot* and, now, *fairie*. Each increment gets closer to the way I have always felt inside. *Fairie* is powerful and seems appropriate for these new ways of approaching ourselves and each other. It helps to define a state of inner awareness for me. *Gay* has always dealt with attitudes of lifestyle and politics.

I decided I was comfortable with the word for now, but I knew I could relinquish it as my evolution continued. If anything, fairies are flexible. Perhaps, someday, words will not be necessary.

Walking slowly back, I noticed an almost physical lightness in the air the closer I got. Entering the grounds, I saw the joy in each man's face as he connected with others and then drifted apart without pretense or stance. The day filled with music and dance.

That night, about seventy of us gathered by the edge of the large swimming pool. Murray Edelman, a group facilitator practicing in New York, arranged us in groups of six. Any clothes still remaining were dropped to the carpet of sleeping bags and blankets beneath us. Slowly, we began to explore each other's bodies—arms and feet, faces and backs. No one was too fat or thin, too perfect or old. Edelman had slipped out of view; the strong moonlight revealed a single body of men laying on hands and mouths to hardened cocks and shining bodies. We were calling forth Hermes, bringer of ecstasy; Luna, keeper of the moon.

The next morning another group of men arose early and went out to the desert, also leaving clothes behind. Buckets of water had been brought to a dry riverbed, and soon a great puddle of mud was produced. Cries for "more mud" rang across the cactus fields as each man anointed the other. Twigs and blades of dry grass were woven through hair, hands were linked and a large circle formed. Coming together, the group lifted one man above it, arms above shoulders, silently swaying in the morning sun.

In other areas of the sanctuary, groups of men were learning that loosening our laughter is as important as setting free our sexuality—that fairies can be silly, too. Elsewhere other discussions were in progress. A ritual was also being planned.

We spent the early part of the third evening carefully dressing ourselves and painting our faces and bodies with the brightest designs imaginable. A deep-toned bell rang and we gathered to take a silent walk through the desert. One by one, in a single line, we were led through the unfamiliar terrain.

Our path was lit by an occasional candle; we stumbled as our clothes caught on the hard branches and sharp thorns. Slowly, our resistance to the desert diminished. Our silence was no longer a nervous suppression but rather a contemplative awareness of our surroundings. The environment ceased to be an obstacle; we were learning to move through it, dance with it.

After twenty minutes we approached the site of the ritual, a large cleared area on the outskirts of the sanctuary. A ring of candles had been set in the middle; a band of musicians serenaded our arrival from the half-lit perimeters. We arranged ourselves in a circle. Nearly all of us were there. A great convocation of fairies!

The music dimmed and, quietly at first, came the evocation of familiar friends and guiding spirits. "I evoke Walt Whitman," said one man. "Marilyn Monroe," the next. "The shadow of my former self." "Peter Pan." "Kali, the creator and destroyer." Then a moanful wail, a collective sigh, arose out of the circle up to the starry sky above. We began to chant, letting each note linger deep in our throats.

The circle split itself in two, and facing each other, we greeted the man in front of us. Fond embraces, tender kisses for all as the two rings intertwined and moved forward with the reverberating sounds of "fairie spirit, fairie love."

Music was heard again. A basket was produced, and each man made an offering. A feather from Woolworth's, a stone from the bank of the Ganges river, some hair, a poem. We began to dance with the music, moving closer together, growing more excited. In the dark shadows surrounding the circle, the outline of a large, horned bull was spotted by some of the men. Normally shy, the animal was inexplicably drawn toward the center of the gathering. The hiss of a rocket being set off frightened him away. The fireworks illuminated the night with a splashy glow.

We left the ritual site and regrouped on the comfortable lawn near the sanctuary entrance. After being led in a Balinese folk dance, we passed around pitchers of clear desert water, each man inviting another to drink. The gathering drifted apart. Some men left together, others in groups; some men stayed to talk and laugh; others curled up and went to sleep, to dream. We all felt changed in ways we could scarcely begin to know.

The next morning was a time of good-byes. One man lying on the grass near his sleeping bag looked blankly up at the sky. "I feel that whole barriers inside me have crumbled," he said. Other men were expressing fears about leaving. Each one of us had come singly, but collectively we had built the nourishing, loving energy that enveloped us all now. There had been no plans beyond the first evening; there had been no messianic ego directing us along a prescribed path. Our experience of the weekend had arisen from a collective awareness, from particles released in the unconscious, from the intuitive, from dreams not remembered in the past.

Yet despite the emotional impact of the past three days, this illuminating conference hardly represented an end in itself. The event had provided a glorious experience for coming together in new ways, but few of us felt it to be an exclusive thing, or even that the word itself—*fairie*—should, or could, be taken so seriously. In a very real sense, our dance had included all other like-minded men, wherever they were, who also longed for a spiritually rooted connection. The conference was an important landmark on the path of our personal and collective unfolding, a lovely reminder of places we had all been, a touchstone for places we still hoped to arrive at.

I left wondering how I would keep my newfound awareness alive, wondering what circles I might find on my return to San Francisco.

Sitting in a car, a friend turned and looked out the rear-view mirror. The sanctuary was being erased from sight by the cloud of dust. "Just like *Brigadoon*," he laughed.

I remembered some words by Herman Hesse, who years ago had taken another *Journey to the East*: "Oh, which of us ever thought that the magic circle would break up so soon! That almost all of us—also I, even I—should again be lost in the soundless deserts of mapped-out reality. . . ."

HARRY HAY

A SEPARATE PEOPLE

WHOSE TIME

HAS COME

W_e have been a separate people, drifting together in parallel experience, not always conscious of each other . . . *yet recognizing one another by the eyelock when we did meet*, down the hundred thousand years of our hag and faerie history (*hags* being the proud and free women of the wildwood in the word's original meaning), here and there as outcasts, here and there as spirit people who mysteriously survived close contact with violent nature forces, in service to the Great Mother—acting as messengers and interceders, shamans of both genders, priestesses and priests, imagemakers and prophets, mimes and rhapsodes, poets and playwrights, healers and nurturers, teachers and preachers, tinkers and tinkerers, searchers and researchers. And always *almost all of them were visionaries*, almost all of them were described from time to time as speaking in tongues and in voices other than their own—possessed, as it were; always *almost all of them were rebels*, against the straitjackets of the hetero(sexual) conformities controlling and manipulating the given status quo—whatever the regimen and wherever the region. A separate people coming together—one by one—down the hundred thousand years of our journey, we began to discover slowly . . . hesitantly . . . painfully . . . commonalities we share from the heterogeneous bloodlines that had discarded us that:

· *It was not in our natures to be territorially aggressive, when the heteros around us would casually kill one another simply to become kings of the mountain.*

- *It was not in our natures to be competitive—we only yearned passionately to share with one another instead.*
- *It was not, and is not now, in our natures and never part of our dream, to want to conquer* nature . . . *we were always the shy kids who walked with clouds and talked to trees and butterflies.*
- *Whereas heteros believe that spirituality requires the fervent denial of carnality . . . for us gay folk the preprogrammed instinctual behaviors triggered by, and thus awakened by, our early sexual and sensual discoveries constitute for us the* gateway to the growth of spirit in heart and mind.

The above characteristics seem—even today—to signal the potential of new behavioral directions for the whole species. Appearing in us gay ones persistently, millennia after millennia, we propose that they have always carried the promise of adding sweep and scope to the capacity of the human species to adapt to changing evolutionary circumstance. Half a century ago, the biologist Julian Huxley pointed out that no negative trait (and, as we know, in biology a negative trait is one that does not reproduce itself) ever appears in a given species millennia after millennia unless it in some way serves the survival of that species. And now, perhaps, we are already discovering the no-longer-so-shadowy outlines of the DNA-related contributions we gay folk have been capable of all along . . . contributions we now must share in the service of that survival.

On our small planet, it is terrifyingly apparent that each hemisphere is riddled and wracked to its very foundation by spiritual contradictions. It must be glaringly clear that the traditional hetero male–dominated subject–object consciousness is bankrupt worldwide to the point of becoming lethal. A new consciousness must surface to replace it, and I propose that we gay folk, who Great Mother Nature has been assembling as a separate people in these last hundred thousand years, must now prepare to emerge from the shadows of history *because we are a species variant with a particular characteristic adaptation in consciousness whose time has come!*

Only in the last forty years have gay people in America begun thinking *collectively* of themselves as "we who have been different from the heteros around us all our lives." The process by which we began this reinvention and the self rediscoveries we have made along the way are curious and instructive. In the three years of the first Mattachine experience, from 1950 to 1953, we looked at ourselves as a particular community drawn from all races and classes—found ourselves good, forward-looking people with undercurrents of a collective point of view very different from that usually experienced in the above-ground communities around us. Chafing under the arrogant hetero stereotype that forbade our people to be seen *in any way other than as willful, perverse heteros performing unnatural, therefore criminal, acts*, we figured that, if we insisted on calling ourselves by a term they didn't understand, the media would have to ask us what it meant; and we—then—would be able to define and characterise ourselves, for a change. *It worked*— somewhat! By the persistent use of the term *homophile* (instead of the hetero designate gemixtepickle *homosexual*) we educated American public opinion to perceive us no longer as merely perverse performers of criminal acts but as *persons* of a distinct sociopolitical minority . . . albeit a psychologically sick minority until we finally got that cleared up in 1973, the year the American Psychiatric Association removed homosexuality from its list of mental disorders. Also, here in Los Angeles, in those incandescent first three years, 1950 to 1953, we did set before ourselves a series of questions:

• *Who are we gay people?*
• *Where do we come from, in history and in anthropology, and where have we been?*
• *What are we for?*

Because the basic perceptions in modern science, that made it possible for us to project this third question at all belong themselves to the mid-1950s, the pieces of the puzzle accumulated more slowly. First, we would have to survey *and re-survey* the whole ground, the chronicle of consciousness as it emerges into history from myth and legend and folk play, so that we could begin to sense our gay selves disentangling from the shadows *between the lines*. In San Francisco at the three-day retreat for gay activist men and women, as well ministers and scholars, in August 1966, I found myself inventing a gay concept of love as "the giving or granting to that other the total space wherein she/he may grow and soar into his own/her own freely selected fullest potential." The ministers as a group were quite unprepared to discover that, in contrast to their own experience within their own usual hetero constituencies, the gay community generally had little difficulty in accommodating the concept of "nonpossessive" love.

In late May 1969, while attempting to explain Whitman's poem "The Multitude,"

> Among the men and women the
>   multitude,
> I perceive one picking me out by
>   secret and divine signs . . .

I suddenly saw (as Whitman must have seen, even as he fashioned his poem) that he and I looked through a window on the scene quite different from that perceived as "being all there is" by the heteros hurrying on either side of him and, yesterday, on either side of me. And even as I said that, I realized with a sudden rush that I'd seen through that gay window all my life as, obviously, Whitman's poetry gave witness that he had seen through that window all *his* life. A year-and-a-half later, I would propose that what we saw through that gay window might be generalized as "gay consciousness."

Reinventing ourselves has been a combination of cautious tippy-toe stuff and dizzy leaps into scary insights, each leap and breakthrough being checked against the way it sounds—*the way it floats*—at a gut level; the way it harmoniously resounds at the diaphragm. If it feels right for dykes and faeries, we stand on it to see if areas of our vision before—usually in shadow, where not even totally obscured—may now be partially visible or observable. A lot of our insights have turned out to be sudden recognitions of things past that we could not have seen while we were still in them or still part of them. One day during a rap in 1974, I suddenly remembered that, when I was in the fourth grade, the boys at school would tell me I threw a ball like a girl, *but* wanted to appear, we probably *had* slipped out of the conformity. And when we grew up, many of us appear to have gone on being guided by that same mysterious inner vision to explore our freedom *to be*!

As adults—though similar to our hetero counterparts physiologically, we gay folk emotionally, temperamentally and intellectually, or, in a word that subsumes all three, *spiritually*—some of us may be a combination of both hetero masculine and hetero feminine, but mostly we are a *combination of neither*:

- *It is from this spiritual* neitherness, *evident in our capacity to fly free from historical conformities and prejudices, evident in our capacity to invent in the very teeth of nullifying rules and regulations, that our contributions come.*
- *It is from this spiritual* neitherness *that we draw our capacities as* mediators between the seen and the unseen, *as berdache priests and shaman seers; as artists and architects; as scientists, teachers, and as designers of the possible*—mediators between the make-believe and the real, *through theater and music and dance and poetry;* mediators between the spirit and the flesh, *as teachers and healers and counselors and therapists.*
- *It is from this spiritual* neitherness, *as the sissies and tomboys of the schoolyard, that the kids who grew up (each the only one of her/his kind he/she thought) on the outside of the chain-link fence looked in and observed both sides of the hetero social experiences of boy/girlhood, teenhood and adolescence they* had thrust us away from and then *had shut us out from.*
- *It is from this spiritual* neitherness *that we draw our capacities to see* them *as they can never see themselves, we draw our capacities to be to them as a nonjudgmental mirror, giving them back to themselves through theater, dance, music, poetry and*—above anything else—*through the affectionate mockery of* camp *that expresses itself in healing laughter.*

When we begin to truly love and respect Great Mother Nature's gift to us of gayness, we'll discover that the bondage of our childhood and adolescence in the trials and tribulations (dark forests to traverse with no one to guide us) of *neitherness* was actually an apprenticeship she had designed for teaching her children new cutting edges of con-

Maryellen Fermin and Helen Johnson said, "No, you don't
ball like a girl. You throw it like a sissy!"

In that 1974 rap, with my newly discovered gay window
flashes of insight, I was seeing that while these long-ago bo
saying that I was doing things in a nonmasculine *therefore)*
fashion—"After all, what else is there?"—the girls equally ha
saying, "No, you're not being feminine. You're being . . . *othe*
masculine—okay! agreed! But not feminine either. *Other!*" So, a
1974, looking back at that incident through the lenses of a fifty-
old memory, I realized how dazzling a witness it was to demons
just how radically different the hetero women's window on the w
could be from the traditional macho rant that never stops: "Everyb
knows that women—*when they're making any sense at all*—are think
exactly the same as men!" Yet even as the first enormous moment
generated by the 1970s, behind the ERA, faltered, gentle hetero m
began appearing for whom the macho credo was no longer acceptabl
I found myself defining them as nongays. Though it was clear in man
respects that our gay windows on the world continue to be as opaqu
to these nongays as the hetero male–derived windows *had always been*
opaque to us, faeries and hags alike; nevertheless, it was equally clear
that new dimensions in gender-related ways of seeing were being sought
after that were not yet materializing.

Four years earlier, when I was looking for a word to represent *neither*
masculine or feminine, I used the word the hetero bully boys had used
to describe *me* as they saw me all those years ago. "Fairy," they called
me, "not-masculine/not-feminine—fairy." Only now that I'm grown
up and have become a proper queer, I gussy up the spelling to make
it *f-a-e-r-i-e.* But when the little bully boys has used the word *fairy,*
they would spit it out venomously! Why was the *not*-masculine-but-
equally-*not*-feminine boy they saw through their hetero-male windows
so hateful in their eyes? I would suggest it was because he didn't fit
the conformity by which they knew themselves and each other, like
wolves in the pack or rats in the nest. If your tail bends wrong or you
don't smell right, you're driven out of the pack or you're shoved out
of the nest. Because many of us, even as little kids, assumed we were
free to follow our inner motivations to express ourselves the way we

sciousness and social change. In stunning paradox, our *neitherness* is our talisman, our faerie wand, our gift we bring to the hetero world to

> —*transform their pain to healings;*
> —*transform their tears to laughter;*
> —*transform their hand-me-downs to visions of loveliness.*

In 1975, my beloved companion John Burnside and I produced an essay—published in that summer's issue of *RFD*, a grass-roots publications for rural gay men,—to commemorate the silver anniversary, on July 10, 1950, of my finding my first recruit to what would become the first Mattachine Society. In it we said, "Homosexuality is a genetic means of high importance in preventing . . . disaster to the race, as we shall here endeavor to show, by acting to preserve variety and diversity in the range of traits inherited by each generation. . . . To produce such an effect, homosexuality must somehow produce a force in aid of human beings having quite different qualities than those favored and most rewarded by our society—the dominant, aggressive and manipulative men and women—in the competitive race for survival."

The giant leap in gay consciousness, the blinding flash through the gay window that would be a revelation of what that "force" might be, came—for me—in spring 1976. In a letter, I was explaining how— when we thought about ourselves as preteenagers during the bleak years when we thought we were the only ones of our kind in the whole world—we would naturally be thinking about ourselves *as subjects*. And then, suddenly, when we *somehow* discovered that there *might* be another just like ourselves *somewhere*, and we started to think about—and fantasize about—*him*, we would have been perceiving him in exactly the same way as we were perceiving ourselves. We would be perceiving him *as if* he were also subject.

In the letter I had gone on for about two more pages—when suddenly reality burst in my head like skyrockets. What had I just said? This was the link in the chain I had been trying to grab hold of for thirty years. Of course, I had perceived my fantasy love as subject—*in exactly the same way as I perceived myself as subject*, in exactly the same way I had always perceived my teddy bear *as subject, in exactly the same way as I had always perceived the talking trees and the handsome heroes in my picture-books as subjects*. Oh, I knew that all the other kids around me were thinking of girls as sex *objects*, to be manipulated—to be lied to in order to get them to "give in"—and to be otherwise treated with contempt (when the boys were together without them). And, strangely, the girls seemed to think of the boys as objects, too. But that was it! Writing the letter now, in 1976, I was remembering vividly how, in that long-ago fantasy, he whom I would reach out in love to was indeed projected as being another me—*and the one thing we would not be doing* was making objects of each other. Just as in my dream (which I would go on having for years), he'd be standing just before dawn on a golden velvet hillside . . . he'd hold out his hand for me to catch hold of, and then we would run away to the top of the hill to see the sunrise, and we would never have to come back again because we would now have each other. We would share everything, and we'd always understand each other completely and forever!

From that memory, which, once unleashed by that incandescent leap-into-speculation, continued seeming to validate itself ever the more strongly with each new adventure in the projection, came a new rush—a new "high," the sudden flooding from a second radiant memory. This would be the time when I actually *met* such an other, a boy I had been dreaming about for nearly a year. Between us at the instant of first eyelock, it was as if an invisible arc of lightning flashed between us, zapping into both our eagerly ready young bodies *total systems of knowledge*—instances of ethological "triggerings" such as the inheritable consciousness that Dr. Ralph Sperry of Cal Tech was, in 1979, rewarded for discovering. Suddenly we both were quivering with overpowering preprograms of knowledge and behaviors of which our gay flesh and brains had always been capable of but never, until that moment of imprinting, had actually contained. Now, through that flashing arc of love, we two young faeries knew the *triggered* tumult of gay consciousness in our vibrant young bodies—in ways that we in the moments before would never have imagined and now would never again forget, for so long as we lived. And this—*in ourselves and, simultaneously, in each other*—we also knew: subject-*to-subject*.

In the beloved fairy stories of our childhoods, the fairy godmothers—or, if we were lucky, the handsome fairy princes—would give the chosen subject of the story a "talisman": The talisman, in turn, unlocked secret treasures or gave the person holding it the power to fly, or made visions and wonderful dreams come true. New phrases such as *gay window on the world* or *gay consciousness* and new concepts such as *subject–subject consciousness* seem also to be talismans, because both faerie brothers and hag sisters, upon hearing such phrases and concepts for the first time, keep constantly finding themselves brimming with new visions and spiritual breakthroughs that they'd been bottling up inside themselves for years, maybe for a lifetime—because, until the moment of receiving the talisman, they'd had no shining words to contain the image, no metaphor for the ambient new idea, no frame of reference for a new multidimensional way of perceiving. Now—all at once seeing themselves as subject–subject people in a subject–object world—they, for the first time, began to comprehend the nature of their dilemma as well as the far-reaching widths and depths of their oppression. They found themselves appreciating, for instance, how the loving care with which one's mother and siblings pursued *total* conformity could be absolutely *lethal* for their faerie selves. So we, as subject–subject people, may also begin to wonder why in the world we continue to imitate hetero behavior *at all* when we very well know, with every breath we draw, that such behaviors suit us *not at all*: After all, we aren't heteros. And when we do imitate them, we usually do it badly—we either *overdo* or we *underdo*. Mostly, to be perfectly candid, we overdo.

The talisman of subject–subject consciousness immediately explains why faeries so often have had such constructively loving relationships with hetero women. It would not be because of the hetero-male stereotype that we are half-women ourselves and so are accustomed to seeing ourselves as objects, similarly to the way hetero women know themselves to have been traditionally perceived *and used* by their menfolk. It would be because we faeries see our women friends as subjects *in the same way as women perceive themselves as subjects*; and the women know this and luxuriate in the mutuality of sharing. Indeed, the women of the women's liberation movement are aching to learn how to develop some measure of subject-to-subject relationships with their men. And they wonder why we, who have known the jubilations of subject-to-subject visions and visitations *all our lives*, have neither shared nor even spoken.

Of course, we haven't as yet spoken because we haven't as yet begun to learn how to communicate subject–subject realities even to each other, using our traditionally inherited hetero male-derived and -developed subject–object language in our traditionally inherited hetero male subject–object world. The catalyst of spiritual crisis within the gay movement has brought many gay men face-to-face with the appalling dichotomy between, on the one hand, the nurturing sensitivity and concern for each other in a mutuality of sexual intimacy that we all profess to be seeking and, on the other, the desolation and alienation from self and from each other that more often takes place as we make sexual objects of ourselves and of each other in pursuit of the traditional and expected behavior in bars and baths. How might we apply subject–subject consciousness to gay sexual sharing? For starters, we might try *enjoying each other's enjoyment*. If you allow me to tune in, nonjudgmentally, on your enjoyment, whatever that might happen to be in your consciousness as we approach each other, as I hope you will, in similar fashion, tune into my enjoyment—it could follow that it wouldn't matter whether you were large or small, or fat or thin, or old or young, *or soft or hard*: We would be intimately tuned into sharing each other's enjoyment as subjects, each to the other, and each to himself as well. At this point it should become apparent that our previously unexamined habits of imitating heteros, not only in their sexual myths and taboos but in their possessive and objectifying sexual behaviors as well, are really for us not only unsuitable but quite irrelevant.

Through the interchanges of mutual pleasure into which subject–subject sexuality catapults us, we can discover one of the key characteristics that marks us gays as a separate people. In the best scientific thinking produced by the subject–object world of the traditional hetero male in the nineteenth century, hetero coupling parallels the still-valid scientific metaphor of electro-magnetism—*that of supreme complementarity*, wherein unlikes attract and likes repel. But in the world of our gay sensibilities, in the subject–subject consciousness by which we have perceived from as far back as any of us can remember, we have not sought *nor wanted to find* our complementary opposites—we sought instead others *like* ourselves. Subject–subject folk do not seek to possess or to manipulate; instead they seek to share, to slip off the impermeable separations of ego and meld collectively into the lover, or lovers, perceived as subject. We faeries and hags think of ourselves as subjects, as whole persons—self-reliant, independent, and whenever possible, free people: We seek others as whole and as self-reliant and as independent as ourselves. I do not seek someone who desires to lean on me: I seek someone who will face forward with me, shoulder-to-shoulder, who will circle with me, like two great soaring eagles dancing together at the edge of the sky—each capable of being quite total and complete in himself. *We seek supplementarity*: In the new world coming of subject–subject consciousness, in new dimensions of science where answers to many levels of new questions now being raised have not yet cohered into the eagerly sought but still elusive superseding metaphor, *likes attract and unlikes repel!*

A separate people, we must begin to wrench ourselves away from imitating the subject–object heteros in all ways possible, besides just the lovely and intimate ways of sharing ourselves with each other. Looking through the window of our gay consciousness at the gay marketplace, you see at once a whole host of hetero-imitative entrepreneurs—precisely because they conceive of themselves as in lifelong competition (each with the hetero he or she is imitating)—engaging themselves endlessly in tug-of-war games of domination and submission. The loftiest hetero ideal of governance—democracy—is, in the final analysis, the domination of minorities by a majority; a tyranny of the majority, if you will. If anyone knows the agonies inflicted, the lives misshapen and distorted *and* destroyed by the hate-filled oppressive majority, which a democracy usually is, it would be the black community, the women's community, the gay and lesbian community. In reality, all the hetero ideals of the democratic procedure, these jewels refined at terrible costs from the millenial bloody battlegrounds of relentless hetero competitions, must be exposed as conditions of sub-ject-*object* thinking: ideals such as fair-play, the Golden Rule, equality, political persuasion, the give-a-little-take-a-little of parliamentary reconciliation—and so democracy. In each case, a given person is the *object* of another person's perceptions, to be influenced, persuaded, cajoled, jaw-boned, manipulated and, therefore, in the last analysis, *controlled.* Subject-object consciousness, the epitome of the hetero-male competitive reality, has carried the human race successfully on a long and difficult ascent, to be sure. But perhaps the time is at hand for humanity to discover it ultimately obsolete.

In the forty years we have been engaged in reinventing ourselves as a separate people, we have learned many of the things we are going to need in relating collectively in subject–subject terms. For example, we seem to relate best in work groups of, say, fifteen to twenty-five; we've noticed that work groups flow best in circles where each partic-ipant is free to speak in turn through the employment of a talismanic object passing from hand to hand. Were we now to transform such circles so that each participant reaches out to relate to his/her neighbor, co-joined in the shared vision of that nonpossessive love we've glimpsed through our gay window, *we might develop for the first time in history a true working model of the loving, sharing consensus* of the whole society. In a community, or a community of communities, functioning through such consensus circles, *all authoritarianism—of course—would vanish*: For, in such circles, who would be head and who the foot? The par-ticipants would nourish, sustain, and instruct each other.

So let us begin. There is so much healing to be done, so much mending and so much tending; and time may be shorter than we know. Out of history we emerge

A separate people whose time is at hand.
Out of the mists of our long oppression,
We bring love for ourselves and for each other,
and love for the gifts we bear,
So heavy and so painful the fashioning of them,
So long the road given us to travel to bring them.

A separate people,
We bring a gift to celebrate each other;
'Tis a gift to be gay!
Feel the pride of it!

A separate people,
We bring the gift of our subject–subject consciousness
    to everyone,
That all together we may heal our planet!
Share the magic of it!

MARK THOMPSON
THE EVOLUTION
OF A FAIRIE:
NOTES TOWARD A
NEW DEFINITION OF
GAY

Solstice, 1981/Dance

We build a fire near the sweatlodge, in a field above the bubbling springs, and form a circle around it the night of the winter solstice. We evoke the elements, the four directions and then stand awkward for a while. Slowly, some men begin to sing or to join with others in a low rumbling chant. We draw instinctively closer as the sounds grow in intensity and men, young and old together, begin to move. Some break from the circle and dance to shaking rattles and the voice of automatic tongues.

Where do these cries come from, these primal sounds that pierce to the bone? Banshees in the night, red shadows prance in the surrounding meadow grass. Dim figures loom big, then small, then twist out of shape at the whim of the winter winds. But the central glow of the fire and my ache remain the same.

Later, I stumble away and leave with a friend, retreating to home down a dark country trail marked by old and craggy oaks. I can't contain the tears and turn to his arms for comfort. The glow of the fire is faint beyond the ridge. It is Will and I, the liquid night above, and a few whoops and cries still barely audible. I feel exhilarated. This was a dance of the fairies.

*   *   *

One morning, in downtown San Francisco I found scrawled on a wall the most telling epigram about the past fifteen years and its amazing confluence of trends, politics and attitudes: *Homosexuality Was the Hula-Hoop of the 1970s.* A satirist with a spray can had made a vital point: Gay men may have squandered their most profound opportunity for self-discovery during this century.

At the core of this statement are the observations that the majority of gay men continue to cling to the culturally endorsed concepts of masculinity and that they have not so much examined the Christian-patriarchal tenets that bind our culture as have tried to appease and buy into them.

Our differences have been subtly but swiftly incorporated into mainstream American culture—which means the marketplace—part of an experience that is economically mined and exploited. The social and political climate of the modern West has propelled us to come out, but in doing so we have limited ourselves to a shallow, consumerist perspective. We are the unexpected, nonrational curve in the heterosexuals' game plan, and it has made them terribly nervous. What to do with this odd tribe? Why, sell them things, of course!

Something got lost between earlier days, when some gay men and women began to vocalize how and why their lives were different, and now, when the substance of those words has ended up as the label on the affluent, glamorized package that purports to represent us. Too many of us have now been materially satisfied—which often works as a superficial inducement to shut up.

The price of integration thus far has been a mediocre, conditional type of acceptance into society, coupled with a lack of insight about the particular—sometimes even magical—perspective I believe gay men inherently have. In fact, we have yet to perceive that we are not the men of current cultural myth; that our emerging presence may have significance far beyond simple social and legal reform; that we are capable of a different way of seeing and of manifesting powers beyond our current imagining.

What follows are a few notes toward an evolving interpretation and understanding of what it might mean to be a gay man in the latter half of the twentieth century. (Lesbians, by necessity, have already begun this process of self-definition.) So, suspend your skepticism and—in a manner of a tradition very old—let me tell you a story.

Equinox/Mask

My father knew. He always did. At first it was nothing but pure instinct. He simply detected my different scent quite early. It wasn't a conscious awareness but more like a vague foreboding, one to be stored deep away and recalled later for use in the intimidation and remorse to come.

I became aware of this difference around the same time my father began to realize it for himself. We looked at each other, expressed our familiarity and then let the chasm grow. He had no words of advice, no training even from Dr. Benjamin Spock. He stood mute and, with increasing frustration and bitterness, watched me grow. He had one of *those*, a word for which could only be found on bathroom walls.

That different scent was my gayness asserting itself. Certainly it was not a matter of speech or movement, as behavior had yet to be codified. His realization dawned from signals much more simplified than that. It was a recognition beyond any point of reason—that ambiguous place where every animal senses the truth about its young. He could not detect any reflection of himself, because I was not the same kind of man.

But I was not the only one, and growing up, most of us learned the traits of our defense. Our natural spirits became enshrouded, hidden or warped by the absurd and dangerous polarities of our culture. We had no choice but to accept the scarcity of models and myths offered in our culture, and with a mixture of deadly earnestness and sometimes self-parody, we adopted them. We learned tenacity but also timidity, alacrity but also artifice. Our defense developed by layers until it seemed we were viewing the world through a dark tunnel.

Yet most of us continued to nourish the seeds of our gayness with interests in outer space and inner speculation, theater of the stage and of ritual. As the constraints of our daily lives increased, so did our fantasies. And everywhere, there was father, multiple-faced and manyexampled. But he couldn't keep a hard façade forever, and we began to notice the lines of fatigue beneath his sterile masks.

My father expected perpetuity, I anticipated only my survival. And around the same time I became aware that survival to some future point was, indeed, my chief concern, I also discovered the shaky foundations on which his expectations rested. Our nuclear family of six was experiencing meltdown, the radiation of failure seeping into every member.

We lived near the ocean, and it was a time right after dusk, soon after the sea had quieted a bit, when the air was filled with warm, saline smells. The moon was rising near full, and each star had a distinct glow. The hours before had been loud with bitter recriminations between my parents, and I had just stepped outside for fresh air when I came across a very strange sight. My father was committing suicide. He had rigged a hose from the exhaust pipe of his truck through an opening in the side window of the cab. He was just sitting inside. The motor was running. He didn't see me. I took the hose out and left.

Later that night I slipped out of my bedroom window, as had long been my habit, and walked a mile in the dark to a nearby river. Stripping off my clothes, I walked naked through the surrounding birch groves. My white skin and their pale trunks reflected the moonlight with equal intensity. Sitting in the shallow water with an erect cock, I felt less ashamed, less obscene than previous times. It felt natural to be there, justifiable in a way unknown from previous nights. The breeze from the sea stirred the birch trees into a humorous rustle. I answered back in a low, half-afraid voice, but one not heard before. My true voice, from somewhere beyond that dark tunnel, was finding its expression at last.

There was no point in assuaging my loneliness. I learned to contain it, even after moving to San Francisco many years later. Something vital, essential, as elemental as my dialogue with the trees had been forgotten in the massive rush of coming out in the 1970s.

In demanding our rights, we asked for equality under a heterosexist God without first building temples in which to honor gods of our own. Our militancy subdued to prodding insistence; we saw the progress of our assimilation everywhere. But could we truly say we had a center, that we understood who we are? Politics, after all, represents a popular consensus about a moral code specific to one point in time. And morality has always been the most efficient weapon against us. I needed to know: Is there a deeper meaning underlying our gayness? Why are we here? These questions are the most important questions facing our movement today.

There are some gay men who now understand the lack of comprehension reflected in their fathers' eyes. They have reconciled themselves with poets and forces of nature to understand that they are different kinds of men—men who have gone beyond the superficiality of sexual attraction into a deeper comprehension of the powers that sex may bring. Call them priests, shamans or medicine men; I call them *fairies* and they mark the beginning of a new wave in gay liberation—one that will be defined through *spirit.*

This different, third wave, will be in studied contrast to previous generations—the polite attitudes of the pre-Stonewall decades and the angry placards that followed after 1969. Its practitioners will bring an understanding of traditions more ancient than currently recognized, ready access to the cultural and informational circuitry now encompassing the globe, and an assured knowledge about their particular function. As a people, they will cut across all lines of race, culture or class background. In a sense, they are already here. For we are they. Our political awareness has brought us through that dark tunnel. If only now we will let intuitive knowing lead us to the next phase of our development—if we will but have the courage to honor and not to denigrate our differences.

Like ungainly weeds, we push up and crack through well-ordered landscapes—and thrive. We bring the seeds of the future; but, unwilling to conform to the limiting expectations of those in power, we are still wished as good as dead, or wished into death itself. So we have been put under a bell jar—the socially constructed myth of the homosexual—and given the name *gay*. It is sly poison, indeed, and it has begun to work.

On one very important level, the word *gay*—as it is currently defined and used—means little commitment to anything. Where the word was once charged with fervor and the promise of meaningful social redefinition, it has ebbed once again with the passions of the merely polite. We define ourselves always in terms of reacting to events, so seldom with creativity born from a culture of our own making. I have not, for some time, defined myself as gay. Who really needs another label? *Gay* to me always meant coming out—and out and out, a continuous process of self-realization.

Still, we stand among the best and brightest of our generation. The waste has more to do with ill-defined goals and means, rather than with the source of our humanity. We are lost, without realizing how or why. These are fighting words, of course, as well they must be. For in the very near future the fierce battle that is now being waged over *our* right to exist will assume planetary proportions: an epic rage of many against life-denying assumptions of a stagnant and dying culture. In the coming epoch we will align ourselves as human beings less by creed and ethnicity and more by a commonly held perception of how best to survive on a ravaged planet. There is growing awareness of a need for new human mythology, and we are its tails and horns.

Solstice/Shaking Secrets Loose

Our gayness has endowed us with a marvelous gift of insight; an intensely subjective vision we can bring to others and our environment, a way of seeing that must be affirmed and put to use. This vision of the world has enabled many of us to view a tree, a blade of grass, another animal with as much regard as we hold for ourselves; teaching us how to place each object and organism within a meaningful context; enabling us to empathize and to speculate on imagination and soul into other realms. Within some cultures, this has been the job of the shaman. And within some mythological traditions, this has been the role of the fairies: creatures of camouflage and change, of metamorphosis and mischief.

The job of a fairie shaman is also one of confrontation. Being on the edge of society, we are aware of its taboos and frequently experience them. Taboos, often mythologized as bogymen and demons, are usually meant to conceal liberating secrets, kept there deliberately by those who will benefit from their suppression. Cross-dressing and the fine tuning of power dynamics used in radical sexuality are two prevalent examples of gay men engaging in ritual exploration.

Part of the tragedy of our increasing assimilation is the denial of these explorations. Part of the oppression of our past is the clear lack of understanding about their magicmaking potentials. We have played the games of "who is or isn't," "who does or doesn't" too long to have any comprehensive awareness of our true heritage.

So what do I know of a "true" heritage? I have listened carefully to others but have mainly learned from my own experience, striving to understand the universality of my within.

One August, during a retreat to the mountains, I hiked several miles along the banks of a small, secluded stream. Eventually I found a desirable place, a natural bowl of white sand surrounded by fallen trees and boulders of various sizes. Creating a further circle of protection, I ingested a hallucinogenic plant brought with me and spent the rest of the day listening to the rhythms of the forest. I sat in silence and then sang, rolled in the sandy dirt until it completely covered me and then sat in the stream until washed clean. I felt I was living and dying throughout the day. By dusk I was spread out on the earth, holding it, caressing it, thrusting against it, aware that I was spinning with it. My initiation, begun so self-consciously ten years before, was being realized.

I returned to the stream early the next day. Small fish circled in the languid current and a large snake eased past me on the forest floor, finding its way to the water's edge. I remained sitting on a large flat rock, warming myself in the morning sun. Shadows ebbed as the sun continued its arc into the cloudless sky. Hours passed until I heard a distant rustle. Another man was standing there, just like myself; naked, tan in the midday sun, measuring each step in the shallow stream with care, searching. Our eyes met through a ragged veil of branch and leaf—a lingering, knowing reflection of the other. And then this image of myself faded away into a shady bower of stone, root and oak.

Gay ghettos, besides the cultural autonomy and psychic and physical protection they sometimes offer, have exposed a certain nagging suspicion: that gay people can be as banal, myopic and prejudiced as anyone else. Homosexuality does not *necessarily* imply a difference from the norm, and clearly this is what many of us would have the majority assume for "safety's" sake. Only when we interpret and use our homosexuality as a signal, a sign, a blessing will we understand it as the significant tool it can be—a sublime and wonderful instrument that propels most of us at least one step beyond prevailing social role patterns into an awkward self-awakening about difference. But what about *our* difference? No real purpose is served by idealizing nature; but nature, it should be remembered, commits no errors.

It is important to possess a symbolic representation, a mental image, of the world and one's relationship to it, just as some tribes have used various talismans to order and to direct their experience of life. One simple enough picture would be that of a tree, an ecostructure of many parts, all in perfect balance to one another. Each blossom contains the genetic codes necessary for the continuation of the species. Gay people could be regarded similarly as the blossoms of the human species— not in the sense of procreation but in the development of new ideas and modes of life that any species must use to evolve or die. Little did anyone know that someday we might figuratively reclaim our distinction as "fruits."

The word *fairie* trickles up from the basic roots of Western spiritual mythology, predating the ascension of the Christian church. The church fathers were aware of these earlier beliefs and appropriated "pagan" symbols, altering them to their advantage. All signs of ritualized earth worship were eradicated and, if not, assimilated.

Two examples of this are the Virgin Mary, a composite figure of the many fertile earth-mother deities honored throughout pre-Christian Europe, and the Devil, an adaptation of Pan, also known as the Puck and Robin Goodfellow (or Robin Hood) of folk myth. Mary was created to serve as a benign, sexless intercessor to a wrathful Jehovah, while playful, sensuous Pan of the quivering cock came to represent all that was demonic in man.

Such assimilation was a gross distortion of essences of the human spirit and marked a crucial stage in the development of Western consciousness. It moved people's spiritual center from within themselves to a station high above. With people thus directed to look outside of themselves for guidance, contact with immediate physical reality was displaced. Personal power was subjugated to the benefit of those in control. Gay people especially need to reclaim this displaced spirituality, to nurture it once more in our hearts.

A rigid, either/or way of thinking characterizes the limitations of our enemies, who believe that if something cannot be easily categorized, it is either nonexistent or is abhorrent. Western man has fortified himself with the powers of supreme logic and redoubtable reason. He has rationalized all things as being either above or below, of male or of female. And with these assumptions nurtured by an ever-spiraling base of technological righteousness, he pursued his dominance over the earth. And because of this, he may lack the clarity to understand (or perhaps does understand, but only in the blackness of his heart) the ambiguous nature of those who step beyond prescribed sexual or gender roles: that these aberrations, the strange blooms in his midst, spring from the very source he is systematically destroying.

It is no wonder, then, that—where not ignored or grudgingly incorporated into the political landscape—reawakened feminist and gay thought has been vehemently attacked as certain corrosions on society's benign foundations. But rather than being caustic elements, they point toward a more truthful and viable balance—positive signs of a new alchemy necessary for life on the planet. There now exists the possibility of constructing new metaphors; of bridging the political with the sexual and the spiritual; of building a circular—inclusive rather than exclusive—vision on a planet of diminishing returns. In effect, to heal it—this mother who is fighting for her time, too.

Equinox/Return

What Edward Carpenter, Gerald Heard and Harry Hay recognized was the "new city of Friends" described by Walt Whitman over a hundred years ago—a sustaining place where "robust love" might thrive, a deep source of empowerment. It has been a dream asserted by a few and glimpsed by others at crucial points in our development. The early

1950s and 1970s were times when our movement howled at the moon, briefly acknowledging that this dream could be a reality. That this rude awakening represented something instinctual, wildly alive, posed problems for our leaders. Here was nature, woolly and cloven-hoofed, taking on unexpected form. Here were luminous faces peering out on the edges of accepted reality. How strangely familiar, too, for others to suppress what they do not comprehend, to fear what they've been taught to distrust.

Power, status, the hierarchy of who's on top is the real currency of American culture, and so many of our leaders have been seduced by it all. These are the tactics of assimilation and they smell of panic. Thinking we have gained so much, we have been led to settle for less than we can be.

There is a tyranny implicit in any label, and certainly the label of *gay* has now been revealed as much for its limitations as for its liberations. Why not consider difference, whatever its reason, in terms of function? The concept of a fairie shaman is just one idea that indicates a purposeful role, beyond that of just political or sexual identity. In times past and in many cultures, we often assumed the tasks of the shamans—wise and creative ones—and were duly honored as such. If we can but take *gay* beyond society's definition—which we have internalized—and see ourselves as part of this function, our secret will be out.

I failed in my father's eyes, and he in mine, as, I suppose, it had been fated. More to the point, few gay men ever seem to find complete acceptance from their fathers. (And even tolerance, however honorable, cannot account for true knowing.) Gay men have even less hope of being accepted by the greater father, the world of our daily existence, which, despite tolerant inroads, remains disapproving to its core. But neither can an opposite reality—that is, the matriarchy—hold any more honest a place for us. Perhaps at one time, and according to current feminist myth, the dominant Great Mother societies of agrarian, pre-Judeo-Christian times accepted gay men as welcomed sons. But I suspect, more likely, as subservient sons, in contrast to the outlawed sons of our contemporary age.

So gay men remain suspended in a horrible dilemma. Both the matriarchy and patriarchy have, in effect, played themselves out; and the future, symbolized through an historic union of the two—the two in one—has yet to fully emerge. Gay male consciousness remains stymied, unable to come of age. This is why so much of recent gay-identified culture appears to lack deeper meaning; however fresh and guileless its messages, empowered as it is by ritual dance and sex and defiance against corrupt authority.

At what point do gay boys stop finding favor in their father's eyes? What stories are withheld, what rites of manhood lost in that uncomprehending gaze? Now, as gay men, we must begin by finding forgiveness in each other's eyes, seek favor in stories of our own telling—our own fairytales, the instructional fables we need to assume a mature and ever evolving gay adulthood. And for this we need to reinvest in wonder.

By learning more fully to evoke and to balance the powers of (what were once known as) the Earth Mother and Sky Father, we can set into motion our own whirling evolution as men beyond definition. We will no longer suffer from the constraints of living only a fraction of a life. We will evidence harmony as men who see clearly within and thus act cleanly without. We can learn to revel in our perspective, as much as our preference, and we don't need a name. Our freedom is our responsibility. We simply need to do our work.

But first, we must take the dark fantasies of our suppressed spirits out of their closets into the powerful light of reality. We can have a vision and, thus, a culture to affirm, until one day perhaps our fathers will knowingly proclaim: "I have one of those."

ABOUT THE CONTRIBUTORS

DENNIS ALTMAN is an Australian writer and political scientist. His books—*AIDS in the Mind of America* (1986), *The Homosexualization of America, The Americanization of the Homosexual* (1982), *Homosexual: Oppression and Liberation* (1973), *Coming Out in the Seventies* (1979) and *Rehearsals for Change* (1982)—have had a readership throughout the world, and his articles have appeared in a wide range of periodicals.

MALCOLM BOYD is a gay activist, author of twenty-three books and an Episcopal priest. He is the president of the Los Angeles Center of PEN (1984–1987) and serves on the Los Angeles AIDS Task Force. A guest fellow at Yale University and a writer-in-residence at Mishkenot Sha'ananim in Jerusalem, he has deposited his papers and writings in a permanent archive at Boston University Library. His best-known works include *Are You Running With Me, Jesus?* (1965), *Take Off the Masks* (1978), *Look Back in Joy: Celebration of Gay Lovers* (1981), *Half-Laughing/Half-Crying: Songs for Myself* (1986) and *Gay Priest: An Inner Journey* (1986). He is the director of the Institute of Gay Spirituality and Theology, based in Los Angeles.

MICHAEL BRONKSI is a gay activist and writer whose film, theater and literature criticism, as well as articles on sexuality, have appeared in periodicals and newspapers including *The Boston Globe, Fag Rag,* the *Boston Phoenix, The Advocate and Gay Community News.* He is the author of *Culture Clash: The Making of a Gay Sensibility* (1984), and has contributed articles to several anthologies.

WILLIAM S. BURROUGHS is the author of *Naked Lunch* and many other books. His most recent novel is *The Place of Dead Roads,* the second book in the *Red Night* trilogy; his early manuscript, *Queer,* was recently published after thirty years. He is currently working on *The Western Lands* and lives in Lawrence, Kansas, and New York. Burroughs is a member of the American Academy and Institute of Arts and Letters and a Commandeur de l'Ordre des Arts et des Lettres in France.

BOB GALLAGHER is studying for a Ph.D. in political theory at the University of Toronto; his thesis is titled "Theories of Power and Gender Identity." He teaches at Trent University. A longtime gay activist, Gallagher is the former chairperson of the Toronto Gay Community Council.

JUDY GRAHN has been active in the gay movement for the past twenty years as a poet, publisher and organizer. One of the foremost voices of lesbian/feminism, her works include *The Highest Apple* (1985), *Another Mother Tongue: Gay Words, Gay Worlds* (1984), *Queen of Wands* (1982), *True to Life Adventure Stories, Volumes 1 and 2* (1978, 1980), *Work of a Common Women* (1978) and *The Common Women Poems* (1969). She teaches gay and lesbian studies in San Francisco.

HENRY (HARRY) HAY was born in 1912 at Worthing, Sussex, England, but was raised by his American parents in Los Angeles. Hay later became a well-known Marxist teacher and activist (1933–1953), and conceived and was a principal figure in the founding of the first Mattachine Society (1948). During the 1960s, Hay and his life companion, John Burnside, were outspoken gay participants in the anti-Vietnam War and the traditional American Indian revival movements. During the 1970s they were cofounders and activists in the Gay Liberation Front of Los Angeles and of New Mexico, where, for several years, theirs was the only openly listed gay address in the entire state. In 1979, Hay and Burnside returned to Los Angeles to help organize the first conference for "radical fairies," a movement that has since become international in scope and in which they are still actively involved.

JIM KEPNER, self-educated historian and veteran gay activist, has struggled for liberation and gay concerns since 1943. The founder and curator of the International Gay and Lesbian Archives in Los Angeles, Kepner has worked with over 170 organizations and periodicals, written more than 1,400 gay articles, reviews and news reports (many for the early *Advocate*), and has taught gay studies since 1956, including courses at the UCLA Experimental College. Kepner's wide interests include science fiction, radical politics and gay spirituality.

DON KILHEFNER, Ph.D., is a pioneer gay liberationist and a founder of Los Angeles's Gay and Lesbian Community Services Center (the oldest and largest agency of its kind), the Van Ness Recovery House (the first residential treatment facility for gay alcoholics and addicts), the national fairie gatherings, and Treeroots. He is a Jungian psychotherapist in Los Angeles with a private practice for gay men and conducts research into gay archetypal psychology.

GEOFF MAINS combines a career in environmental-impact assessment with writing and community work. His book, *Urban Aboriginals: A Celebration of Leathersexuality*, completed in 1983, grew out of fascination with leather culture in a variety of North American cities, most notably on the West Coast. He completed his Ph.D. in biochemistry at the University of Toronto, helped found Vancouver's gay community services group, SEARCH, and worked with several major environmental and social planning organizations in Canada. Mains currently lives in San Francisco, where he is writing a novel.

WILLIAM MORITZ, Ph.D., was born in 1941 near the Grand Canyon and studied comparative literature at the University of Southern California. He has taught at such diverse schools as Occidental College, the University of Calcutta, California Institute of the Arts, and the University of California at Los Angeles. He has toured the world twice, reading his poetry and screening his experimental short films. His many one-man shows of films include a retrospective at the Stedlijk Museum of Modern Art in Amsterdam. He has worked as a guest curator for exhibitions at several museums, including the Los Angeles County Museum of Art. His poetry and critical articles about film, visual music and literature have been widely published in Europe and America, in periodicals including the special gay poetry issue of *Beyond Baroque* magazine and *The Advocate*. His Greek satyr play, *The Midas Well*, was premiered at the 1982 Fairie Gathering near San Diego. He is currently working on a volume of turn-of-the-century French lesbian poetry in translation (a collaboration with Margaret Porter) and on a biography of the experimental animator James Whitney.

WILL ROSCOE is a San Francisco–based writer, artist and community organizer. He has been active in the gay community since 1975, when he cofounded the first gay organization in Montana. Since his attendance at the 1979 Spiritual Conference for Radical Fairies, he has devoted his energies toward the synthesis of art, spirituality and politics in the form of gay consciousness and gay culture. In 1983, he began an in-depth research project into traditional gay roles in American Indian societies, which included trips to New Mexico in 1983 and 1984. In 1986, he began presenting the results of this research in a slide-lecture presentation, "The Zuni Man-Woman." In 1984, he helped secure funding for the history project of the gay American Indian organization in San Francisco, and he is currently serving as coordinator for the publication of *Living the Spirit: A Gay American Indian Anthology*.

TOBIAS SCHNEEBAUM, painter and writer, was born on the Lower East Side of Manhattan in 1922. He has lived on and off among preliterate peoples since his stay with the Lacandon Indians in Mexico in 1949. He has had seven one-man exhibitions in New York and has published two autobiographical works: *Keep the River on Your Right* (1969) and *Wild Man* (1979), in addition to two catalogues with lengthy essays: *Asmat: Life with the Ancestors* and *Asmat Images*. He has been the recipient of several awards and grants for both painting and writing—including a Fulbright fellowship to Peru, a CAPS grant, an Ingram Merrill Foundation grant, a Ludwig Vogelstein Foundation grant, two grants from the JDR Third Fund—and has been a fellow of the Rockefeller Foundation. He has also been at Yaddo, Ossabaw Island, and Ucross colonies. He is currently at work on the third volume of his autobiographical trilogy.

AARON SHURIN's books include *The Night Sun* (1976), *Giving Up the Ghost* (1980) and *The Graces* (1983). He teaches creative writing and gay and lesbian studies at New College of California and San Francisco Community College.

MARK THOMPSON (editor) is a journalist with a longtime involvement in the arts as a filmmaker, actor, writer and publisher. He helped found the Gay Students Coalition at San Francisco State University in 1973, and has worked for gay and feminist causes since that time. Thompson is the cultural associate editor of *The Advocate*, the national gay newsmagazine, and has contributed numerous feature articles, essays and interviews with prominent artists and writers for over a decade. He currently lives in Los Angeles, where he continues to expand his understanding of gay identity through the exploration of gay men's dreams and other cultural phenomena.

MITCH WALKER is author of *Men Loving Men: A Gay Sex Guide and Consciousness Book* (1977, and currently in its seventh printing), and *Visionary Love: A Spirit Book of Gay Mythology* (1980). He holds an M.A. in clinical psychology, is completing a Ph.D. in that field, and is a psychosocial counselor at the AIDS Prevention Clinic in Hollywood, California.

ALEXANDER WILSON is a Toronto journalist and horticulturist. He teaches courses in mass media and popular culture at Trent University. Wilson has written for *The Body Politic, Gay Community News, Social Text, Pink Ink* and *Vanguard,* and is an editor at the Toronto magazine *Borderlines*.

SELECTED READINGS

Altman, Dennis. *The Homosexualization of America, The Americanization of the Homosexual*. New York: St. Martin's Press, 1982.

Boswell, John. *Christianity, Social Tolerance, and Homosexuality*. Chicago: The University of Chicago Press, 1980.

Boyd, Malcolm. *Half Laughing/Half Crying*. New York: St. Martin's Press, 1986.

———. *Gay Priest: An Inner Journey*. New York: St. Martin's Press, 1986.

Bronski, Michael. *Culture Clash: The Making of Gay Sensibility*. Boston: South End Press, 1984.

Broughton, James. *Graffiti for the Johns of Heaven*. Mill Valley: Syzygy Press, 1982.

———. *Ecstasies: Poems 1975–1983*. Mill Valley: Syzygy Press, 1983.

Burroughs, William S. *Naked Lunch*. New York: Grove Press, 1959.

———. *Cities of the Red Night*. New York: Holt, Rinehart & Winston, 1981.

———. *Queer*. New York: Viking, 1985.

Carpenter, Edward. *Selected Writings*, vols. 1–3. London: GMP Publishers, 1984.

———. *Towards Democracy*. London: GMP Publishers, 1985.

Dass, Ram. *Grist for the Mill*. New York: Bantam Books, 1979.

D'Emilio, John. *Sexual Politics, Sexual Communities: The Making of a Homosexual Minority in the United States, 1940–1970*. Chicago: University of Chicago Press, 1983.

Eliade, Mircea. *Shamanism: Archaic Techniques of Ecstasy*. New Jersey: Princeton University Press (Bollingen Series), 1964.

Evans, Arthur. *The God of Ecstasy: Sex Roles and the Madness of Dionysus*. New York: St. Martin's Press, 1987.

———. *Witchcraft and the Gay Counterculture*. Boston: Fag Rag Books, 1978.

Fernbach, David. *The Spiral Path: A Gay Contribution to Human Survival*. London: Gay Men's Press, 1981.

Foucault, Michel. *The Foucault Reader*. New York: Pantheon Books, 1984.

Ginsberg, Allen. *Collected Poems: 1947–1980*. New York: Harper & Row, 1984.

Grahn, Judy. *Another Mother Tongue: Gay Words, Gay Worlds*. Boston: Beacon Press, 1984.

Halifax, Joan. *Shaman: The Wounded Healer*. New York: Crossroads, 1982.

Harner, Michael. *The Way of the Shaman: A Guide to Power and Healing*. San Francisco: Harper & Row, 1980.

Heflin, Llee. *The Island Dialogues*. San Francisco: Level Press, 1973.

Herdt, Gilbert H. *Ritualized Homosexuality in Melanesia*. Berkeley: University of California Press, 1984.

Isherwood, Christopher. *Christopher and His Kind*. New York: Farrar, Straus & Giroux, 1976.

———. *My Guru and His Disciple*. New York: Farrar, Straus & Giroux, 1980.

———. *October*. Los Angeles: Twelvetrees Press, 1981.

———. *A Single Man*. New York, Farrar, Straus & Giroux, 1986.

Johnson, Edwin Clark. *The Myth of the Great Secret: A Search for Spiritual Meaning in the Face of Emptiness*. New York: William Morrow, 1982.

Johnson, Robert A. *He: Understanding Masculine Psychology*. New York: Harper & Row, 1977.

————. *Inner Work: Using Dreams and Active Imagination for Personal Growth*. San Francisco: Harper & Row, 1986.

Jung, C. G. *Psychological Reflections*. Princeton, NJ: Princeton University Press, 1970.

Katz, Jonathan. *Gay American History: Lesbian and Gay Men in the U.S.A.* New York: Thomas Y. Crowell, 1976.

————. *Gay/Lesbian Almanac: A New Documentary*. New York: Harper & Row, 1983.

Larkin, Purusha. *The Divine Androgyne*. San Diego: Sanctuary Publications, 1981.

Leyland, Winston, ed. *Gay Sunshine Interviews*, vol. 1. San Francisco: Gay Sunshine Press, 1978.

————. *Gay Sunshine Interviews*, vol. 2. San Francisco: Gay Sunshine Press, 1982.

Licata, Salvatore J., and, Petersen, Robert P., eds. *The Gay Past: A Collection of Historical Essays*. New York: Harrington Park Press, 1985.

Mains, Geoff. *Urban Aboriginals: A Celebration of Leathersexuality*. San Francisco: Gay Sunshine Press, 1984.

Martin, Robert K. *The Homosexual Tradition in American Poetry*. Austin: University of Texas Press, 1979.

Norse, Harold. *The Love Poems: 1940–1985*. Santa Cruz: Crossing Press, 1986.

Plato. *The Symposium*. Walter Hamilton, trans. New York: Penguin Books, 1951.

Rumaker, Michael. *A Day and a Night at the Baths*. San Francisco: Grey Fox Press, 1979.

————. *My First Satyrnalia*. San Francisco: Grey Fox Press, 1981.

Saslow, James M. *Ganymede in the Renaissance: Homosexuality in Art and Society*. New Haven, CT: Yale University Press, 1986.

Schneebaum, Tobias. *Keep the River on Your Right*. New York: Grove Press, 1969.

————. *Wild Man*. New York: Viking Press, 1979.

Shively, Charley, ed. *Calamus Lovers: Walt Whitman's Working Class Camerados*. San Francisco: Gay Sunshine Press, 1987.

Starhawk. *The Spiral Dance*. San Francisco, Harper & Row, 1979.

————. *Dreaming the Dark: Magic, Sex and Politics*. Boston: Beacon Press, 1982.

Timmons, Stuart. *Harry Hay and the Birth of the American Gay Movement*. Boston: Alyson Press, 1988.

Walker, Mitch. *Men Loving Men: A Gay Sex and Consciousness Book*. San Francisco: Gay Sunshine Press, 1977.

————. *Visionary Love: A Spirit Book of Gay Mythology*. San Francisco: Treeroots Press, 1980.

Watts, Alan. *This Is It*. New York: Vintage Books, 1973.

Weeks, Jeffrey. *Coming Out: Homosexual Politics in Britain from the Nineteenth Century to the Present*. London: Quartet Books, 1977.

————. *Sexuality and Its Discontents: Meanings, Myths and Modern Sexualities*. London: Routledge and Kegan Paul, 1985.

Whitman, Walt. *The Portable Walt Whitman*. New York: Penguin Books, 1974.

Williams, Walter L. *The Spirit and the Flesh: Sexual Diversity in American Indian Culture*. Boston: Beacon Press, 1986.